Perceiving Truth and Ceasing Doubts

China has experienced tremendous developmental success since its reform and opening-up policy in 1978. What has contributed to China's high-speed economic growth? What lessons can be learned from China's successful case? What might be the challenges that China would face on its path to becoming a high-income country? These are some critical questions this book addresses.

Based on the facts and economic logic, this book briefly narrates the history of China's successful development in the past 40 years and explains why China's reform and opening-up has boosted the high-speed growth of its economy. Recognizing the change in the stage of economic development, the author reveals the emerging challenges facing China when transitioning from a middle-income country to a high-income country. He proposes that the country should transition from the demographic dividend to reform dividend to sustain the long-term development.

With its scholarly analysis and plain language, this book would not only attract scholars and students in economics and China studies but also readers interested in the development of the Chinese economy.

Cai Fang is Professor, Vice President and Party Group Member of the Chinese Academy of Social Sciences, Academician at the Chinese Academy of Social Sciences.

China Perspectives

The *China Perspectives* series focuses on translating and publishing works by leading Chinese scholars, writing about both global topics and China-related themes. It covers Humanities & Social Sciences, Education, Media and Psychology, as well as many interdisciplinary themes.

This is the first time any of these books have been published in English for international readers. The series aims to put forward a Chinese perspective, give insights into cutting-edge academic thinking in China, and inspire researchers globally.

Titles in economics partly include

The Chinese Path to Economic Dual Transformation
Li Yining

Hyperinflation
A World History
Liping He

Game Theory and Society
Weiying Zhang

China's Fiscal Policy
Theoretical and Situation Analysis
Gao Peiyong

Trade Openness and China's Economic Development
Miaojie YU

Perceiving Truth and Ceasing Doubts
What Can We Learn from 40 Years of China's Reform and Opening-Up?
Cai Fang

For more information, please visit www.routledge.com/series/CPH

Perceiving Truth and Ceasing Doubts

What Can We Learn from 40 Years of China's Reform and Opening-Up?

Cai Fang

This book is published with financial support from the Chinese Fund for the Humanities and Social Sciences.

First published 2020 by Routledge

2 Park Square, Milton Park, Abingdon, Oxon OX14 4RN

605 Third Avenue, New York, NY 10017

Routledge is an imprint of the Taylor & Francis Group, an informa business

First issued in paperback 2021

Publisher's Note

The publisher has gone to great lengths to ensure the quality of this reprint but points out that some imperfections in the original copies may be apparent.

English Version by permission of China Social Sciences Press.

British Library Cataloguing-in-Publication Data
A catalogue record for this book is available from the British Library

Library of Congress Cataloging-in-Publication Data
A catalog record for this book has been requested

ISBN: 978-0-367-85908-4 (hbk)
ISBN: 978-1-03-217569-0 (pbk)
DOI: 10.4324/9781003015727

Typeset in Times New Roman
by Apex CoVantage, LLC

Contents

Illustrations

Figures

Table

1 Changes of reform from 30 years to 40 years

Confucius said: "A kingdom must wait for 30 years to reach benevolent governance." The 11th generation of Confucius, who was also an authoritative scholar of the Confucius Classics in Western Han, Kong An'guo, interpreted this sentence as, "A generation may include thirty years, which is the period that a government must need to reach benevolent governance." That is to say, 30 years, which could be called a generation, is a time span that can preview effectiveness of benevolent governance. The reform of China, staring from the Third Plenary Session of the 11th Central Committee of the Chinese Communist Party in 1978, had been implemented for 30 years by 2008 and 40 years by 2018. During this period, China has undergone tremendous changes compared with the last several thousand years in the Chinese history, which is rather rare in the world economic history as well. Over the decade from 30 years to 40 years of reform, especially since the 18th CPC national congress, the changes are more prominent.

The most outstanding achievements in reform and opening-up are the general improvement of people's livelihood. To be specific, in the process of economic growth and overall improvement of income, the government has implemented a large-scale rural poverty reduction program to solve the "issues of agriculture, farmer and rural area"; while promoting the expansion of urban and rural employment, the government also tries to strengthen the labor market regulation and establish the initial social protection mechanisms to provide a basic safety net for the vulnerable groups in the labor market. These undisputed facts show that during the 40 years, China's economic and social development has been an inclusive style. However, the improvement speed of the living standards of urban and rural residents still varies; so does the degree of social protection improvement. They are shown in the income gap among residents and the widening inequality in accessing basic public services. These are the policy challenges that cannot be avoided.

1.1 The doubling of per capita income

Throughout the whole reform and opening-up period to date, namely 1978–2011, China's economic growth rate maintained an annual rate of nearly 9.9%. Not only just the total economy but its per capita income growth is also a miracle. During this period, the average annual growth rate of per capita GDP reached 8.8%

excluding inflation factor. According to the Thumb Rule in statistics, the average annual growth rate of 7% can achieve a doubling of per capita GDP in 10 years, while the average annual growth rate of 10% would do so in 7 years. So we can imagine what kind of effect may be achieved when these per capita GDP growth rates continue for 30 years or even 40 years.

Let's compare the time needed for doubling per capita income in different countries in a similar stage of development. Britain took 58 years in 1780–1838, the United States spent 47 years in 1839–1886, Japan spent 34 years in 1885–1919, and for South Korea it was 11 years in 1966–1977. China took only nine years in 1978–1987, and then in 1987–1995 and 1995–2004, using 8 years and 9 years respectively, it doubled twice, and in 2011, only 7 years after the last doubling, it did it once again. In the period from 2011 to 2016, GDP per capita in real terms was 6.9% per year, and doubling again is imminent.

Economic historians found that since the late 18th century, i.e., around the Industrial Revolution, the world has experienced the "Great Divergence" in the country's level of development, followed by the formation of the distinction of rich and poor countries. Since then, the pattern has been unchanged. Thus, the persisted passion and motivation of the economists engaging in research is to explore the way the developing countries can catch up with and even surpass the developed countries in terms of per capita income. The key lies in the ability to have a faster rate of economic growth and maintain it over a longer period of time. Those low-income countries, if they can maintain the high enough growth rate in the long term, they will undoubtedly create economic miracles.

In 1990, China's total GDP only ranked 10th in the world. In 1995, China surpassed Canada, Spain and Brazil, ranking 7th. In 2000, China surpassed Italy and was promoted to the 6th. Subsequently, in the first 10 years of this century, China has successively surpassed France, Britain, Germany and finally Japan in 2009 to become the world's second largest economy, ranked just after the United States. In 2016, China's total GDP was $11.2 trillion, equivalent to 60.3% of that of the US and 14.8% of the world. China, in the past four decades, has significantly reduced the gap between it and the developed economies in levels of development and quality of life. This experience has fully proved that as long as they choose the right direction, which is persisting in reform and opening-up policy and promoting economic development, the relatively backward countries can still catch up.

When the total GDP is created, the factors that determine the share level of economic growth are how to allocate the GDP between various factors of production, between the parties of the economy, e.g., distribution between capital owners and labor owners, or between laborers, operators and the state government. In other words, to judge whether the economic growth can really benefit people's livelihood, in addition to observing the growth rate of per capita GDP, we should also study the growth rate of urban and rural residents' income.

Data of urban and rural households by the National Bureau of Statistics shows that the real income of urban and rural residents is increasing at an alarming rate in 37 years from 1978 to 2015, during which the average annual growth rate of rural and urban residents' per capita income is 8.2% and 7.3% respectively after excluding price factor. Meanwhile, the proportion of rural population has fallen from 82% to 44%, which means a significant improvement in overall income level. From the trend of change, the per capita net income of rural residents increases faster than that of urban residents in the 1980s. After the 1990s, the increasing rate of rural residents' income had lagged behind that of urban residents, but after 2004 the income of rural residents once again increased gradually faster than that of urban residents.

In the analysis of income data of urban and rural residents, we can also see an often overlooked fact. The researchers used to fiercely criticize the income gap between urban and rural areas. But in fact, it is not generally that serious. The usual method of calculation is to set the rural residents' income as one, then calculate the ratio between the nominal annual income of urban and rural areas. According to this method, in 2015 the nominal income of urban residents was 24,565 Yuan, while that of rural residents was 7,917 Yuan, with the ratio standing at 3.1, which was no doubt higher than 1978's figure of 2.57, and was much higher than the smallest income ratio between urban and rural of all time in 1983 (1.82). However, due to the different cost of living and range of price changes in rural and urban areas, this method, which is based on urban-rural income ratio of nominal income but ignores the price factor, is unscientific.

After adjusting the method according to a different consumer price index in rural and urban areas, we have calculated the number of comparable urban and rural incomes and the urban-rural income ratio. The observation of the urban-rural income ratio suggests that, first, in 2012 the urban-rural income ratio was 2.18, and it was already lower than the level of 1978; second, the income gap is still much higher than the 1.52 in 1988, showing that the income gap has experienced a process of U-shaped change, i.e., it has significantly decreased after the reform and then expanded again; third, the income gap between urban and rural areas in 2012 was below the level of three years from 2009 to 2011, showing a shrinking trend. Finally, since 2013, the National Bureau of Statistics has adopted the expression of urban-rural integration, which has united pure income of farmers and disposable income in towns into per capita disposable income. According to the latest data, the income gap between urban and rural areas was reduced to 1.91 in 2015.

Moreover, the existing statistical system in the household survey has omitted the income of peasant workers. Therefore, the income gap between urban and rural areas shown in Figure 1.1 still contains ingredients overvalued for years. As the household survey in the official statistical system is conducted for urban and rural areas independently before 2013, the rural households that moved to cities and the family members of peasant workers are difficult to include in the sampling scope and are excluded from urban samples. Also, because of their long-term absence, they are no longer seen as rural residents and are excluded from the surveyed samples of rural households.

Some researchers have no doubt noticed the existing defect of urban and rural household income statistics. They try to dig out related evidence from the imperfect statistical system and give us a more truthful income gap between urban and rural areas. They chose a developed province, Zhejiang, and a Western province,

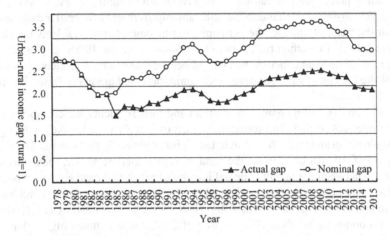

Figure 1.1 Falling in the Ups and Downs of Actual Income Gap between Urban and Rural Residents

Source: National Bureau of Statistics, China Statistical Yearbook, in relevant years

Shaanxi. With the accounts from the Statistics Bureau and the surveys of selected households, they revalued the income of migrant workers, which was previously omitted in both the urban and rural income sample scopes. Their conclusion was that only with the unscientific household survey sampling and definition, the average disposable income of urban residents was overvalued by 13.6%, the average net income of rural residents was undervalued by 13.3% and the average income gap between urban and rural areas was overrated by 31.2%.[1]

1.2   Worldwide poverty reduction examples

Since China adopted the reform and opening-up policy, it has not only achieved the world's most rapid economic growth and maximized the improvement of its people's living standards but also contributed to the largest poverty reduction in the world. In 1978, when the poverty line was determined according to Chinese government statistics as 100 Yuan per person per year, the number of poor people was 250 million, accounting for 30.7% of the total rural population. In 1984, the poverty line increased to 200 Yuan per person per year, the number of poor people went down to 128 million and the poverty incidence rate decreased to 15.1%. Furthermore, according to the 2010 statistics of poverty standard, i.e., 1,274 Yuan, the rural poor people reduced from 94.22 million in 2000 to 26.88 million in 2010, and accordingly, the poverty incidence rate declined from 10.2% to 2.8% (Figure 1.2).

In 2011, the central government significantly improved the national poverty line to 2,300 Yuan, on the basis of constant price in 2010, increasing by 92% compared to 2009. The introduction of this new standard enlarged the coverage of

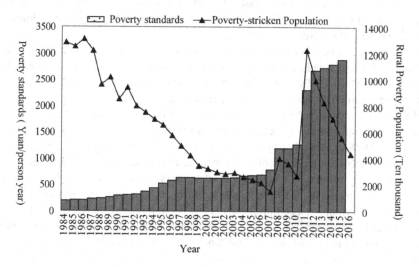

Figure 1.2 Improving the Poverty Standards while Reducing the Poverty Incidence Rate

Source: National Bureau of Statistics (2012), China Statistical Abstract 2012. China Statistics Press.

poor people from 26.88 million in 2010 to 128 million. In accordance with international comparable purchasing power, this new poverty standard was equivalent to US$1.8 per capita per day and surpassed the World Bank's international poverty standard of US$1.25 in 2008. As shown in Figure 1.2, according to this new standard, the number of rural people in poverty continued to decline substantially. Premier Li Keqiang pointed out in the "Report on the Work of the Government" at the National People's Congress in 2018 that, during the five-year period of 2012–2017, more than 68 million rural poor were lifted out of poverty, and the poverty rate calculated according to the new standard fell from 10.2% down to 3.1%.

China's achievements of poverty alleviation and its overall development of the Millennium Development Goals have been widely praised by the international community. The World Bank believes that China's achievements in poverty alleviation have profound impact on the international community. UNDP also believes that China's achievements in poverty reduction have provided a model for developing countries and even the whole world. The Asian Development Bank thinks that China has a lot of experience to offer in poverty alleviation, and it is worth learning for other countries. China's achievements in poverty reduction are top ones in Asia, and the Chinese government can be proud of them.

These international institutions admitted that during the last 30 years, among the achievements mankind made in poverty reduction, two-thirds should be attributed to China. Besides, during 1981–2013, the world's absolute poverty defined in accordance with the World Bank standard, the population making less than 1.9 dollars per day (constant price in 2011) decreased from 1.893 billion to 766 million; China has reduced from 878 million to 25.17 million in the same period. That is to say, China's contribution to global poverty alleviation is 75.7%. This is a great contribution China made to international poverty alleviation, as well as to human civilization and progress of mankind.

Recalling the years of development in rural China, the process of poverty alleviation can be divided into three stages. The first stage is the period from the early 1980s to the mid-1980s. Comprehensive reform of the rural economic system had become the main driving force in this period to promote the rapid development of the national economy. The overall income growth of rural residents has become a major factor in poverty reduction during this period.

From 1978, the farming system has undergone major changes. The household contract system replaced the collective management system of people's communes, which greatly aroused the enthusiasm of farmers. This, together with the rising agricultural prices, the accelerating agricultural restructuring and rural industrialization etc., promoted a comprehensive rural economic growth. Rural enterprises, on behalf of rural industrialization, began to develop during this period. These not only enhanced the vitality of the rural economy but also expanded the employment opportunities for a knowledgeable, skilled labor force in rural areas to achieve poverty alleviation. This round of economic growth was mainly achieved through institutional innovation of solving the problem of microscopic individual incentives. Therefore, the gains quickly passed on to the poor, and the rural poverty was significantly alleviated.

During 1978–1985, the national agricultural added value grew by 55.4%, the agricultural labor productivity increased by 40.3% and the agricultural comprehensive purchase price index increased by 66.8%. The estimated increase of farmers' income because of higher prices accounted for 15.5% during this period. In the same period, along with the rapid output growth of various agricultural products, rural per capita net income increased 2.6 times, and the farmers' per capita calorie intake increased from 1978's 2,300 kcal per person per day to 2,454 kcal in 1985. During this period, the rural population living below the absolute poverty line decreased from 250 million at the beginning of reform to 125 million in 1985 and dropped to 14.8% in the proportion of the rural population; the poverty reduction on average was 17.86 million per year. This is undoubtedly the world's largest and fastest poverty reduction process.

The mid-1980s to the late 20th century can be seen as the second phase of the implementation of poverty reduction. The Chinese government set up special poverty alleviation agencies, arranged a special fund in multi-channel, developed special preferential policies, radically reformed the traditional relief approach and identified the poverty development policy. By implementing special policies and measures, the government organized large-scale development-oriented poverty reduction. This stage can be seen as the government's poverty alleviation efforts for specific populations in rural areas with two special experiences.

First, after determining the overall idea of the regional development-oriented poverty reduction, in order to focus on the use of anti-poverty funds and effectively support the poor, the Chinese government formulated a national standard for poverty-stricken counties. In 1986, the Chinese government determined the national standard of poverty-stricken counties for the first time: the counties whose per capita net income of farmers was lower than 1,150 Yuan. Since then, because of the economic development, especially the improvement of economic conditions in poor areas, the standard must be adjusted accordingly. Back in 1986, 592 national poor counties were established, accounting for nearly one-fifth of the county-level administrative units in the whole country.

Second, in 1993, China formulated and issued the Seven-Year Priority Poverty Alleviation Program. The program strived to basically solve the problem of feeding and clothing the 80 million rural poor people in the last 7 years of the 20th century. This program tried to make efforts in a special way by the use of China's mobilization force and high level of consensus to achieve maximum effect in poverty reduction in a relatively short period of time. During three years, from 1997 to 1999, 8 million populations in poverty every year in China had enough food and clothing, the highest level since the 1990s.

By the end of 2000, the national Seven-Year Priority Poverty Alleviation Program was basically achieved. In those 7 years, China's rural poor population decreased by 50 million; the poverty incidence rate in rural areas was further reduced from 8.7% to 3.4%. This was a strong impetus to the second phase of the poverty reduction. From 1986 to 2000, the per capita net income of farmers in the state-supported poor counties increased from 206 Yuan to 1,338 Yuan and the national poverty population from 131 million to 32.09 million.

Alleviating rural poverty is not only reflected in the measurement of income and the decline in poverty incidence rate; it is also reflected in the development of human development and various social undertakings in poverty-stricken areas. During this period, the basic infrastructure in poor areas was significantly improved. Transportation, communications, electricity, schools etc. had reached an ownership rate close to the non-poor areas. With the government's poverty alleviation efforts, the overall distribution of rural poverty changed significantly with more obvious regional features. Poverty was more concentrated in some areas with harsh natural conditions in the Midwest.

With the basic completion of the Seven-Year Priority Poverty Alleviation Program, the Chinese government's poverty alleviation efforts entered the third stage. In 2011, China embraced a new stage of poverty alleviation and development. In the economically developed Eastern regions, the incidence of poverty has been significantly reduced. Accordingly, with the new feature that the poor were mainly concentrated in the Midwest but still distributed across the country, the government identified 592 key counties for national poverty alleviation and development in the Midwest. In 2002, the absolute poverty rate in the key counties accounted for 62.1% of the total national population, and the low-income population accounted for 52.8%.

Since 2000, the incidence of poverty in rural areas has basically remained at the same level. In the next 10 years, China achieved a total poverty reduction of 5.21 million. Taking into account the increasing national poverty alleviation funds invested annually, this means that the regional development plan no longer had a clear poverty reduction effect as before. The nature of rural poverty was mainly marginalized poverty. Poverty due to geography, climate and other natural conditions, as well as chronic poverty caused by personal ability, have become the main features of the marginalized poverty.

In this case, the means of combating poverty was also facing a relatively big adjustment. It had been difficult to benefit the poor through regional targeting to promote local economic development. Clearer and more direct measures would be the main means to solve rural poverty.

In 2001, the CPC and State Council formulated and promulgated the Outline of China's Rural Poverty Alleviation and Development (2001–2010). One of the notable features of the Outline was reaching down to the village, known as the "poverty reduction strategy in village level." Entering a new century, the nature of rural poverty began to change. Even within the poverty-stricken counties, the differentiation of the poor and non-poor has become increasingly evident. Whether the use of the poverty relief funds and the regional economic growth can truly benefit the poor has become an increasingly prominent problem.

Therefore, the pro-poor policies should narrow the scope to improve the efficiency in the use of funds so that resources can really benefit the poor. In this case, from 2011 the government identified a number of key poverty-stricken villages within the range of poverty-stricken counties, and it has identified 148,000 poor villages nationwide. With this more detailed screening, the efficiency of poverty alleviation was improved.

Through the implementation of the Outline, various social undertakings have made great progress in poverty-stricken areas. During this period, the whole village poverty alleviation effect was very significant. The household income growth rate in the key villages was significantly higher than its county and even higher than the national average. In poor villages, those with IVDP (Integrated Village Development Plan) enjoyed a higher revenue growth of 8–9% than those without. There were also significant improvements in productive infrastructure and social services facilities in poor villages, and the improvement speed was faster than the average rate of poor counties.

By the end of 2010, population in poverty declined further, and being the first to achieve the UN Millennium Development Goals of halving the poverty target, China began implementing the China Rural Poverty Alleviation and Development Program 2011–2020. It substantially increased the poverty standards and identified contiguous areas with special difficulties as the focus of poverty alleviation to provide stronger policy support and financial support for poverty alleviation work in these areas. Meanwhile, China increased the poverty line above the international standards. This not only showed that the government improved its own responsibility in resolving poverty by including more low-income rural population into the range of poverty and giving greater support to poor areas and poor people, but also that China's poverty alleviation strategy began to realize from the eradication of absolute poverty to addressing the relative poverty at the same time.

Since the 18th National Congress of CPC, China has intensified its efforts of alleviating poverty in a new battle stance. It has taken targeted and precise measures and shaken off poverty and supported poor population through different approaches, getting new achievement in poverty alleviation. Under the higher poverty standard, the rural poor population decreased from 122 million in 2011 to 43.35 million in 2016, with an average annual reduction of 15.81 million, breaking the rule of diminishing effect of marginal poverty alleviation. The 13th Five-Year Plan, which began in 2016, has established a more ambitious goal in accordance with the current standard of price adjusting of pulling farmers in poor areas with per capita disposable income of less than 4,000 Yuan all out of poverty and solving regional overall poverty by 2020.

1.3   China's featured policies of agriculture, farmer and rural area

At the same time as the Third Plenary Session of the 11th Central Committee of the Chinese Communist Party held in Beijing in the winter of 1978,[2] 18 farmers in the Village of Xiaogang in Fengyang County of Anhui faced a condition of how to deal with famine and hunger: to go out as previous years and become beggars, or to break through the institutional cage and contract the land to household operations. Eventually they chose to take political risk to be the first ones who engaged in a household responsibility system. The results were immediate: their problems of food and clothing were quickly solved. The effects spread like wildfire. Subsequently, with the gradual relaxation in the policy, the family contract system was rapidly adopted across the country. Early in 1980, only 1.1% of the production teams implemented the household contract responsibility system. By the end of that year, the number reached 20%. By the end of 1984, it reached 100%, and the households implementing the contract system reached 97.9%.

The implementation of the household contract system, i.e., farmers abandoning the allocation methods of the production team and choosing the household contracted form, is a fundamental change in the basic operating system of agriculture. At the same time, the state took initial step for the transition to marketing of agricultural products by raising the price of agricultural products and changing a series of agricultural acquisition systems from a state monopoly system to a contract ordering system; this also provided an effective incentive for agricultural production in aspect of price. Since this step of reform achieved good incentive effect, the agricultural production has been quickly restored. Farmers were benefited from this reform, while the non-agricultural sectors were enhanced, and the urban residents were also greatly assured. The potential of the household contract system to increase production efficiency seems to be released once and for all. Basically, working contracted to households was carried out nationwide, covering almost all production teams and farmers. Many scholars thought the deceleration of agricultural production increase that appeared after 1985 marked the conclusion of the first round of rural reform. However, there were a number of other factors that affected farmers' income increase and production efficiency, which continued in the late 1980s.

The most note-worthy point is that, due to improvement of labor enthusiasm and enhancement of micro efficiency, the use of labor in agriculture has been greatly reduced; surplus agricultural labor force has been manifested. Under the guidance of price signals after the reform of the agricultural product acquisition system, surplus agricultural labor has transferred from single grain cultivation to diversified development of farming, forestry, animal husbandry and fishery and has promoted the rapid growth of township enterprises. Therefore, this reform is the process of mining efficiency potential in rural areas by improving incentive mechanism and emancipating production factors. Large scale labor has migrated into a broader field of production successively, internal efficiency of rural economy has been improved comprehensively and the rural labor force has been more fully utilized, thus maintaining the increase of farmers' income and narrowing the income gap between urban and rural areas.

Overall, the rural reform in that period mainly focused on improving the incentive mechanisms in agriculture and the allocation efficiency in the rural economy and did not reach another pole of the urban-rural relations, i.e., the urban residents' vested interests. When the focus of reform shifted to state-owned enterprises of the urban economy, it was inevitable to use the results of the rural reform – i.e., an adequate supply of agricultural products and the stability of rural economy – but at the same time to try not to damage the established pattern of relations in the urban and rural interests. Thus, during the process of urban reform, the rural reform seemed to have been weakened, and farmers' income growth also slowed.

By reviewing the discussion then, we could see that there were a number of factors that led the agricultural production, farmers' income and rural development to have been constrained while the relationship between urban and rural areas had not undergone a fundamental change. For instance, in 1985, while the reform on the food purchase system had greatly lowered the price of extra food volume, it was not able to really free the grain market, which showed a negative sign for agricultural producers. In addition, this period also showed a trend of faster price increase of the agricultural production inputs than the agricultural products, as well as the government's reduction in agricultural inputs, etc. Throughout the 1990s, the proportion of state investment in agriculture in the total fiscal expenditure showed a wandering and slightly falling trend.

However, the process of obtaining the benefit of institutional change through reform itself has a spontaneous and irreversible effect. The Chinese farmers, who were still constrained by the system when the state's policies of agriculture, farmer, rural area and direct investments that were meant to adjust the urban-rural relations didn't reach a satisfactory degree, continued to look forward to economic opportunities to realize their productive potentials and increase their income. This has promoted the change of the traditional pattern of urban-rural relations at an alarming speed.

The main driving force was the large scale transfer of rural labor force and transregional flow, thus promoting the integration of urban and rural labor markets, and the reconfiguration of resources in a growing range has been significantly improved. Econometric analysis shows that during the period of 1978 to 1998, in the annual growth of gross domestic product (GDP) of up to 9%, the contribution rate of labor expansion is 24%, human resources is 24% and labor transfer from agriculture to non-agricultural industry is 21%.[3] However, the local governments, especially in areas of labor inflows, are often worried that the inflow of the rural labor force will result in the loss of social welfare from the local financial subsidies and that foreign labor will impact local employment. In this case, they would adjust their attitudes toward foreign labor according to changes in the employment situation and thus form instability in policy. However, labor mobility will eventually show a positive effect because of the cities' demand for labor in economic growth. Therefore, in most cases, urban governments are holding at least tolerant attitudes toward foreign labor inflow.

In addition, with the tendency to coordinate the development of urban and rural and regional development balance, the central government, in most years, regards the rural labor mobility as a positive phenomenon, makes gradual relaxation of labor mobility policy for peasant workers' residence and creates better policy environment for them. Throughout the 1990s, the central government and local governments introduced and tested a variety of reform measures, making efforts in favor of labor mobility.

Such policy changes to promote cross-regional flow of rural labor are the result of the interaction or game between several subjects. This interaction occurs between the labor outflow governments and the labor inflow governments, between local governments and central government, between mobile labor force and urban local labor force, as well as between the two categories of workers and the government. Overall, the policy adjustment process is also residing in the reform into economic development and observing the principle of "Pareto Improvement."

Because of the unlimited supply of labor and the household registration system, migrant workers, despite some discrimination in wages and benefits, with the expansion of the scale of labor mobility, obtained constantly expanding income from their urban works. For example, there is no real growth in 1997–2004 of migrant workers' wages, because the labor migration scale increased from fewer than 40 million people to more than 100 million, the total wages achieved an average annual growth rate of 14.9%, and, even under undervalued situations, the proportion of farmers' net income also increased from 24.6% to 34.0%.[4] On the other hand, migrant workers also fill the gap of urban employment. They have made an important contribution to the local economic and social development and thus to the overall development of China's economy. Urban residents and local and central government undoubtedly benefit greatly.

However, the transfer of rural labor to urban areas is eventually subject to the constraints of the traditional pattern of rural and urban relations. In the Planned Economy period, the employment of urban workers was arranged by the city plan. Whether skills and posts are commensurate or not, no matter whether the attitude is good or bad, and regardless of business conditions, the urban workers were not in danger of being fired. Social security welfare of the workers and a considerable portion of welfare coverage were provided through their working units. The basic education was provided in accordance with the household registration by the urban community. Urban infrastructure and a series of public services all included government subsidies.

All these aspects have severely restricted the thoroughness of the transfer of rural labor to urban areas and thus delayed the reform of the household registration system. As a result, rural labor flows like migratory birds, so that the growing group becomes marginalized people in cities, known as the floating population. At this stage of the reform, unequal resource flows and unequal public services are still maintained and in some ways even expanded.

Scholars have estimated the free transfer of rural resources to the cities in various forms throughout the period of Planned Economy, and the figure sums up about 600 billion to 800 billion Yuan.[5] Even for a long time after reform, this one way flow situation of agriculture resources flowing to non-agricultural sectors has not been reversed. Other scholars estimated that during 1980 to 2000, with a set constant price as in 2000, it has drawn 1.29 trillion Yuan surplus from agriculture to various channels for industrial development. If viewed from the urban-rural relations, about 2.3 trillion Yuan capital flew from rural to urban sectors.[6]

Meanwhile, official statistics show that in 2000 the ratio of primary industry in GDP fell to 15.1%, and the primary industry labor force in the proportion of the labor force dropped to 50.0%. From the perspective of research, the proportion of agricultural labor in this year is likely to fall to 28.9%. According to the experience of Korea and China's Taiwan, the Chinese mainland has reached the stage of implementing the policies of "cities supporting rural areas, industry nurturing agriculture."[7] In the 21st century, especially since the 16th CPC Congress held in 2002, along with in-depth implementation of the "people-oriented" concept of scientific development and the practice of building a harmonious socialist society, China has entered a phase of comprehensive reform of urban-rural relations. In this stage, the content of rural reform was very rich and constantly expanded.

The greatly strengthened national finance is the important material security to implement the "giving more, taking less" policy in agriculture, rural areas and farmers, as well as the key to completely change the pattern of urban-rural relations. The reform, aiming to resolve these long-standing rural issues, was initially based on the implementation of "cities supporting rural areas, industry nurturing agriculture" policy. Then, it was implemented in the specific form of "building new socialist rural areas." After proposing the aims of "production development, affluent life, village civilization, clean and tidy environment and democratic management," the connotations of rural reform were further focused on more infrastructure and public finance to rural areas, as well as coordinating urban and rural employment and social security.

So far, this round of adjustment of urban-rural relations has made great achievements, such as creating a favorable policy environment for migrant workers to live and work in cities; the abolition of the agricultural tax that has been implemented up to 2,600 years in Chinese history; direct subsidies for grain in various forms; the implementation of free compulsory education in rural areas, the rural minimum living security system, the new rural cooperative medical care system and the new rural social pension insurance system etc. Since the 18th Party's Congress, the people-centered development thought taking integration of urban and rural as the core has led to urban-rural relationship adjustment and realized a series of landmark achievements.

1.4   Social protection that develops from nothing

In many cases, people's happiness is not proportional to the degree of affluence. In other words, higher incomes may also lead to lower happiness. Although researchers of related disciplines have not given a satisfactory explanation to date, it is no doubt that the sense of security determined by the social protection mechanism will have a huge impact on the degree of happiness. The so-called social protection usually refers to the ability of raising income and living standards and reducing economic risk and employment impact with the government and society as a main body and by nurturing an efficient labor market, thus reducing the poverty and vulnerability.

Obviously, the social protection-related institutional arrangements should mainly aim at the employment policy and labor market system designed to protect workers' rights and job security; the social security system that protects residents from unemployment, disaster, disease, disability and old age; as well as the social assistance and welfares for the special difficulties and vulnerable populations, such as children, the elderly and residents from special areas.

In the planned economy era, much social welfare is provided by enterprises or units, forming the opposite situation under the market economy, that is, the state exceeds its duties to make various production decisions, while the unit takes over the socialization to provide services in a small range, lifetime employment ("iron bowl") and replaces social unemployment insurance; companies undertake public health care and workers' subsidies; and the state funds provide pension for enterprise employees, allocate houses, send their children to kindergarten or even run compulsory education etc. It can be said that a low level of cradle-to-grave protection is implemented.

Along with the reform of the economic system, the related social services have been gradually stripped from the enterprises especially in order to reduce the social burden and responsibility of the state-owned enterprises and to clarify the operating losses and policy losses and thus invigorate the state economy. However, getting the enterprises out of social responsibility does not mean that the government should fully take over the relevant social responsibility in way of public services, resulting in inadequate social protection and an institutional gap in a certain period. The gap is caused by the interface between both systems and also the certain stage of related development. Because in this period local governments focus their resources on economic development, the resources for social development are very limited. Moreover, due to the huge legacy cost left from the planned economy, the government's financial capacity is rather insufficient.

Prior to the 1994 tax distribution reform, fiscal responsibility and fiscal decentralization reform had strengthened the local government's financial incentives to mobilize the enthusiasm of local economic development. At the same time, the central government's capabilities of transfer payment were greatly reduced, thus resulting in a corresponding lack of macroeconomic coordination. Along with the increase of differences in economic development, there have been strong calls for narrowing the gap between the financial districts and increasing the amount of transfer payment.

Tax distribution reform responds to such a request and strengthens the capacity of the central government to solve the corresponding problems. For a long time, the central government's transfer payment had increased the level of equalization of public services, made up for the lack of local government social protection gap and, through the implementation of the regional development strategy, improved the level of balance between regional economic and social development. We can say that during this period, with economic growth as the main objective of the government, this financial system, in a large sense, provided necessary regional coordination, protected public services and provided social protection. Its overall effect was positive.

However, both the government's focusing on economic development and continuing to leverage corporate social responsibility are undoubtedly a rational political economy in line with the characteristics of the development stage. Chinese leaders, at the beginning of the reform, had unswervingly taken economic development as the most widely supported premise of the reform, benefiting the masses by making bigger pies. In addition, taking responsibility for social protection through redistribution and stratification to maintain social stability was also the key to getting support from the masses and ensuring smooth advancement of reform and development.

Thus, during the process of labor market development, the reform mode of deregulation is equal to the formulation of labor market regulation. On one hand, the secure jobs disappear gradually and the competitiveness of the labor market is enhanced. On the other hand, enterprises, especially state-owned enterprises, are allowed to offer social protection for workers to continue undertaking social responsibility. Such government responsibilities include: obliging the unions to fulfill the functions of rescuing workers in difficulty, persuading companies encountering operating difficulties not to lay off workers, trying to keep the original workers from the labor market competition and both maintaining the level of institutional wages and protecting jobs to the maximum. The most typical example in this regard is during the late 1990s when employment suffered; the responsibility was borne by the state-owned enterprises. At that time there had been mass unemployment that had never happened in the planned economy era. As the unemployment insurance system was not perfect then and the unemployment insurance fund accumulated was not enough for use, the central government called for the establishment of laid-off workers re-employment service centers at enterprises and proposed that the government, society (the accumulated unemployment insurance then) and enterprises, with the ratio of 1/3, share the burden of the living allowances for laid-off workers. Although actually the direct costs borne by enterprises did not reach the level of 1/3 (in 2002 it was 17.2%), the enterprises still bore the responsibilities of the continuation of social insurance for laid-off workers, providing job training, job information and helping re-employment.

Meanwhile, in the process of coping with employment impact, the central government has implemented a proactive employment policy, providing public services for employment and re-employment and established a social security system basically covering urban residents as a safety net. Since the 21st century, under the concept of equal public services policy, public services extend rapidly to rural areas, with social security and social protection as the core.

First, the legislation is more focused on the protection of workers. The first "Labor Law" after the reform and opening-up was enacted in 1994. Since back at that time China was still in the stage of unlimited supply of labor, surplus labor transferring from the agricultural sector to non-agricultural employment was urgent for both the employers and employees. Therefore, the law did not perform well, and the expected losses with the law enforcement did not happen. This flexibility in the labor market surpasses the characteristics of adequacy of social protection and is even seen by other developing countries as a positive experience that is conducive to enhancing the competitiveness of industries, products and employment.

With needs to enhance the protection of workers in the new stage of development, in 2008 there were three employment-related laws in implementation: "Labor Contract Law," "Employment Promotion Law" and "Labor Dispute Mediation and Arbitration Law." They set up rules and norms for signing labor contracts, joining the social security, prohibiting discrimination in employment and building harmonious labor relations respectively. Although, after the introduction of these laws, China's real economy suffered the impact of the global financial crisis, and the local governments made appropriate relaxation on the enforcement of some of the laws, they still regulated the employment practices of enterprises and improved the level of institutionalization of the labor market.

Many observers cite the recent labor dispute cases after 2008, especially the substantial increase in labor dispute cases concerning migrant workers, to suggest the deterioration of labor relations. In fact, the increase of records and reports of such labor disputes is somewhat endogenous, that is, compared with the previous times, there are several factors that encourage workers to bring labor lawsuits.

There are many factors affecting the workers to bring labor litigation; since the promulgation and publicity of three labor laws and regulations in 2008, workers feel they have more legal basis. In the case of changes of labor supply and demand and the degree of government concern for social harmony, good results may be expected from labor litigation. The cases of labor dispute arbitration and adjudication are significantly biased in favor of the workers' party, giving good results in the labor litigation. In addition, a minor but not insignificant factor is that Labor Dispute Mediation and Arbitration Law provides for a "free of charge labor dispute arbitration," which greatly reduces the cost of litigation. All these changes enable ordinary workers, especially migrant workers, to stand up and take labor dispute proceedings.

Second, the role of labor market institutions strengthens. In fact, the changes mentioned above are also the result of policy orientation of government after the Lewis turning point, characterized by labor shortage and wage rise. Many studies have shown that, at different stages of development, the extent and scope of labor market institutions are not the same. With the arrival of the Lewis turning point, wages and other benefits, employment conditions and thus labor relations, are not determined by the spontaneous labor supply and demand of the market but by the labor market institutions.

A representative similar change is the variation tendency of minimum wage adjustment frequency and amplitude. In the initial implementation of the system, i.e., in the 1990s, it was characterized by a lower standard with very few adjustments and was usually not applied to migrant workers. With the widespread shortage of migrant workers since 2004 in China, meaning that labor shortage had become a regular phenomenon, in 2004, the central government asked the local governments to make adjustment at least once every two years and make it widely applicable to migrant workers. Each city government felt the pressure of labor shortage and competed to raise the minimum wage level.

Overall, since this century, the number of cities that have adjusted minimum wage after 2004 has increased significantly, and the range of adjustment also increased. In the face of the global financial crisis in 2009, the minimum wage was not adjusted in various cities. However, with strong macroeconomic recovery and the return of the labor market activity, compensatory adjustment began around the year 2010, in which almost all cities raised the minimum wage, with an actual average increase rate of 20.8%. Since then, there is a big adjustment in the minimum wage adjustment every year.

Third, the social security system became more inclusive. From the late 1990s to the early 2000s, social security and social protection coverage was greatly improved, including full coverage of the urban minimum living security system, the basic old-age insurance system for basic coverage of retired workers, gradual increase of workers on the job, the coverage of urban workers' and urban residents' medical insurance system as well as unemployment insurance and other social insurance systems.

Since 2004, the focus of the work of constructing the social security system has been extended to rural areas. The projects that have been achieved provide full coverage, including the rural minimum living security system, the new rural cooperative medical care system and the new rural pension insurance system. In order to implement the labor contract law and social insurance law to encourage the migrant workers to participate in the social pension insurance initiative, the government implemented the urban basic pension insurance relationship continue and transfer approach including migrant workers in 2010. Take the coverage of basic pension insurance as an example. In 2016, 887.77 million people participated in urban and rural areas; this wide expansion is mainly due to the implementation of the basic old-age insurance for those not based on units (Figure 1.3).

The initiative of local governments in providing better social security and social protection is mobilized. In some areas of labor shortage, local governments utilize looser requirements of the central government during financial crisis that allow for postponing or paying less social insurance in financial crisis to consciously reduce payment level of migrant workers' joining social insurance, as well as expanding

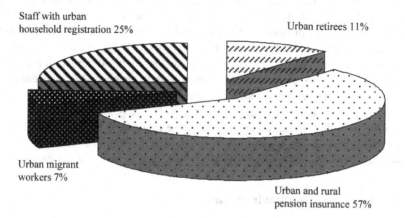

Figure 1.3 Significant Increase in the Coverage of Basic Pension Insurance

Source: Ministry of Human Resources and Social Security "Statistical Bulletin for the Development of Human Resources and Social Security in 2016," released on May 31, 2017 and downloaded on October 1, 2017.

the coverage. The compulsory education of migrant workers' children has been obviously improved, although the central government has a clear requirement, yet the expenditure responsibility of compulsory education lies in local governments; this problem can be finally solved mainly due to the initiative of local governments where labor immigrates. The role of local governments in helping migrant workers' recovery of unpaid wages, arbitration of labor disputes and equal treatment as urban registered workers has been enhanced greatly, and the orientation has changed significantly.

Finally, the reform of the household registration system is getting faster. Many researchers believe that the reform of the household registration system has not embraced as much as hope because they just observed the changed surface, that most people who work in cities have not yet obtained urban registration but neglect the household registration system as well as the function of unequal social security and social protection as an obstacle to prevent labor migration and population transfer. If viewed from the latter point of view, progress made in the reform of the household registration system should not be denied.

Indeed, it is true that the urbanization of China can be understood from the two concepts in a broad and narrow sense. First, the urbanization rate according to a permanent population of more than six months was 57.4%, an annual increase of 3% based on 17.9% in 1978 and 29.0% in 1995, the fastest urbanization rate in the history of world economy. However, the rate includes migrant workers who have been working in the city for a long time but do not have urban household registration. Second, according to the index of urbanization rate, this index with Chinese characteristics reached 41.2% in 2016 and 23.8% in 1995, increasing at an average annual rate of 2.6%.

There are two factors that promote the increased urbanization rate of the household population. First of all, there is no doubt that the government reduces settlement conditions for migrant workers due to the pressure of labor shortage, that is, local governments have promoted migrant workers obtaining urban residence. Second, to a large extent, it is also driven by changes in the administrative division of county upgraded to city (district), countryside to township and village into community. Compared with international countries, experience drawing from that is 33% of this level, and the average annual rate in the range is between 0.7%–1.8%. It can be seen that, if annual average increase rate of the population with non-agricultural household registration is considered as the urbanization rate with Chinese characteristics, it is much faster than world average level in the past period.

1.5   Development of inclusiveness

The fundamental purpose of economic development is to make residents enjoy higher quality of life, happiness and security, which can be measured to a large extent by per capita income. However because people's happiness and security depend on basic services and public services provided by governments, manifested as increasing level of social development and equalization, so it is often separated from the improvement of overall income level due to lack of inclusiveness and unequal distribution.

The unprecedented miracle of China's economic growth achieved in the last 40 years is accompanied throughout by the unparalleled increase of the living standard and enhancement of social security. However, many researchers also believe that China's experience so far has not been as extraordinary as economic growth in terms of economic development simultaneously benefiting all urban and rural residents. In fact, if it is not cognitive prejudice or observational alienation, it is at least the result of different observation angles.

The general inclusiveness and sharing of economic development is well manifested in that the labor market development promotes more employment of both urban and rural residents and favorable conditions are created for all residents to share the fruits of economic development. Meanwhile, the effectiveness of the labor market, the efforts of governmental poverty relief and the construction of social protection mechanisms substantially decrease poverty incidences and increase social protection coverage.

Of course, because of the imbalances and incongruity of China's economic development itself, as well as the role of government in social development, the regional development gap still exists especially among Eastern, middle and West China; the expansion of income gaps between the urban and rural residents in a period of time, employment and payment discrimination are common in the labor market, and the household registration system and other institutional obstacles hinder the full coverage of social protection and the equal enjoyment of basic public services.

The developmental effects of economic society should be finally judged by common residents. Looking at public concern on hot social issues, we can see problems exist in inclusiveness and sharing of economic development. For example, according to surveys by socialists in 2006, 2008 and 2011, many problems such as rising prices, difficulties and high costs of getting medical services, wide income gap, polarization of wealth and even corruption are highly concerning.[8] Whether scholars abroad and at home or Chinese leaders give recognition to social development achievements as performance results of economic development and also notice the comparative backwardness of social development, there are many issues and relevant social risks[9] in that circle. Many studies describe the unbalanced development issues from different aspects.

Since the 18th Party's Congress, the Central Committee of the CPC with Xi Jinping as the core has further defined the people centered development thought, advocated the concept of shared development and made a series of policies to benefit the people's livelihood by unprecedented efforts. Not only are urban and rural employment more adequate and the income gap narrowing, but new progress has also been made in the basic public demand for education, employment, medical and old-age care and housing. According to the experience of a large number of countries regarding the relationship between economic growth and income distribution, previous development economists summed up two models. The first is the mode of "first growth and post distribution," that is, to tolerate expansion of the income gap in an early stage of economic development until total income reaches a certain level (such as Kuznets turning point) so that the government begins to solve the problem of excessive income gap. The second is the mode of "marginal growth and marginal distribution," that is to say, economic growth, maintaining a low-income gap through policy design and system construction.

Generally scholars favor and suggest the second mode. Scholars and policymakers later bring social protection into this mode and measure by income level, income equilibrium, happiness, security and finally develop the so-called inclusive development mode or sharing development mode.

Here, we can summarize the development of China since the reform and opening-up as a kind of "imbalanced and inclusive development." Then it transfers to more inclusive development, which can help us to understand causes of problems, drawing lessons from this development mode according to characteristics and stages of China's economic development so as to find out the way to solve problems, grasp future trends of change and explore more inclusive development.

Actually, from the increasing rate of residents' income, improvement of quality of life and expansion of social protection coverage, the development of China over the past 40 years can be equated with developed countries' achievements for hundreds of years. From a dynamic point of view, it is more and more in line with standards of the inclusive development model. The reason dissatisfaction exists is the gap between expectation and reality. People's expectation of life quality improvement, happiness and security does not just come from its own before-after comparison but also from the comparison between social development progress and economic growth rate. The faster the economy grows, the higher the expectation of social advancement, the easier to arrive at the conclusion that economic development and social development are not synchronous and the more obvious the social issues will be.

The fast rate of China's economic growth is quite rare in the world's economic history. When the economy accelerates, the social development is relatively backward and unbalanced and unfair sharing exists, so people are quite unsatisfied. Thus, some believe the over high expectation of the masses is attributed to the plentitude of social conflicts and even think the policies to meet the over high expectation are features of populism. However, if the common people yearning for and expecting beautiful life is adaptive to the economic growth rate and level, it's reasonable and should be satisfied, and lowering expectations to relieve social conflicts is a dead-end.

Compared with economic growth, social development needs longer and more complicated institutional construction. Thus, when economic growth is kept beyond a normal speed, social development will inevitably fall behind the economic growth. However, it cannot be an excuse to tolerate the backward social development. The social development level and the relevant institutional environment are especially essentially indispensable conditions for sustainable economic growth.

According to the per capita GDP, China has entered the rank of middle-income countries defined by the World Bank. On one hand, from the stage of economic development, disharmony between social development and economic development is more and more obvious; on the other hand, the future economic growth has higher demands on social cohesion. The degree of sharing is the purpose and result of making the economic cake bigger and also the social and institutional guarantee of cakes to continue to be bigger.

Notes

1 Gao Wenshu, Zhao Wen, and Cheng Jie. (2011). The Impact of Rural Labor Mobility on the Income Gap between Urban and Rural Residents. In Cai Fang (Ed.), *China's Population and Labor Report No.2: Challenges of the 12th Five-Year: Population, Employment and Income Distribution* (pp. 228–242). Beijing: Social Sciences Academic Press.
2 The meeting re-established CPC's ideological line of emancipating the mind and coming down to earth. It is considered to be an important milestone that marked the start of economic reforms.
3 Cai Fang and Wang Dewen. (1999). China's Economic Growth Sustainability and Labor Contributions. *Economic Research, 10.*
4 Cai Fang, Du Yang, Gao Wenshu, and Wang Meiyan. (2009). *Labor Economics: Theory and Reality of China* (p. 220). Beijing: Beijing Normal University Press.
5 See Cai Fang, Justin Lin Yifu, and Cao Yong. (2009). *The Chinese Economy: Reform and Development* (p. 193). Singapore, Boston and others: McGraw Hill Education.
6 Jikun Huang, Keijiro Otsuka, and Scott Rozelle. (2004, November 5–7). The Role of Agriculture in China's Development, Presented at the Workshop "China's Economic Transition: Origins, Mechanisms, and Consequences." Pittsburgh.
7 In Korea and China's Taiwan, this change has taken the form of agricultural protection in the 1970s, when the proportion of the agricultural output and labor proportion dropped down to 1/4 and 1/2. See Kim Anderson and Yujiro Hayami. (1996). *The Political Economy of Agricultural Protection* (Chapters I and II). Tianjin: Tianjin People's Publishing House.

8 "Chinese Social Survey" Research Group of the Chinese Academy of Social Sciences. (2012). 2011 Survey Report on Chinese People's Livelihood and Urbanization. In Ru Xin, Lu Xueyi, and Li Peilin (Eds.), *2012 Analysis and Forecast of China's Social Situation* (p. 120). Beijing: Social Sciences Academic Press.

9 Assar Lindbeck. (2008). Economic-Social Interaction in China. *Economics of Transition, 16*(1), 113–139; Wen Jiabao. (2010). Some Issues on Social Program Development and People's Livelihood Improvement. *Qiushi, 7.*

2 Development is an unyielding principle

Most politicians in developing countries happen to coincide with the promise that people's lives would be substantially improved, which is what the people expect earnestly. But if there is no substantial economic growth, the improvement of people's livelihood is just like water without a source or a meal without rice, in the end the promise won't be fulfilled. During the reform and opening-up in the past 40 years, the Chinese people's lives have been significantly improved; after all, it's the achievement of effective economic development. Deng Xiaoping's "development is an unyielding principle" is best the best illustration. Furthermore, China's successful practice has also given new implications to the term "development." It can contribute to China's wisdom and provide Chinese solutions in solving human problems.

2.1 "The scenery here is exceptionally beautiful"

In the early spring of 1992, Deng Xiaoping visited a township enterprise on his Southern tour in history. When he heard that this small 7 that was originally unknown increased its output by 16 times in seven years, ranked first in the country and exported to some Southeast Asian countries, he delightedly said that "our country has to develop, otherwise we'll be bullied. Development is an unyielding principle." The last sentence is repeatedly quoted and still popular so far. This "unyielding principle" has also met with some people's doubts, but today, over twenty years later, no matter from the perspectives of Chinese people's real feelings of life or the objective statistics, this unyielding principle has been repeatedly revealed and verified.

Gross Domestic Product (GDP), a metric index of economic growth, is criticized by a wide range of international scholars. Although economists and statisticians have made various efforts, so far, no index has been found that is more comprehensive than GDP itself to better reflect the performance of economic development. Therefore, when we observe the economic growth after China's reform and opening-up, the index of GDP growth rate has been used to make both horizontal and vertical comparisons.

According to the statistics of the World Bank's annual growth rate of GDP for each country during 1978–2016, we compare China's economic growth performance during this period with a group of countries with different types of

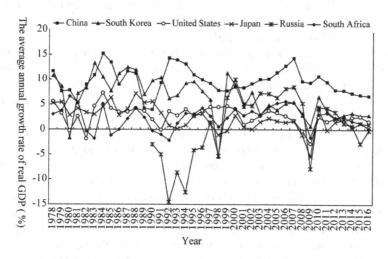

Figure 2.1 China's Economic Growth in International Comparison

Source: World Bank Database: https://data.worldbank.org.cn/indicator/NY.GDP.MKTP.KD (download on October 2, 2017)

representation (Figure 2.1). In comparison, we can clearly observe the economic growth performance of each economy and the stories behind it, which will help us better understand the process of overtaking the Chinese economy and its effectiveness. Overall, the average annual growth rate of China's real GDP during this period was 9.6%, South Korea's was 6.2%, the United States' was 2.6%, Japan's was 2.1%, Russia's (the data for 1989–2016) was only 0.4% and South Africa's was 2.4%.

There is double significance in comparing the long-term growth performance of China since its reform and opening-up with its neighbors Korea and Japan. One aspect relates to the warning and the demonstration of neighboring economies. In the late 1970s and early 1980s when China turned to the important strategy where economic development is taken as the central task, the party and state leaders including Deng Xiaoping came to the consensus that China was far behind in economic development, after inspecting developed countries and neighboring countries and regions, and that it's very urgent to surpass other countries in a short time.

In the autumn of 1978 when Deng Xiaoping visited Japan, two incidents reflected his upset to the underdeveloped economy and his determination to improve Chinese people's livelihood. According to Fu Gaoyi,[1] Deng Xiaoping told the host when getting off the car that one of his visiting purposes was to find the "mesona" following the example of Xu Fu, namely the magic code to modernization. When he took the shinkansen, he couldn't help saying "Fast, so fast!" The comparison with neighboring regions unquestionably inspired Deng Xiaoping to come up with the proposal that "poverty is not socialism."

On the other hand, the successful experiences of these neighboring countries and regions with similar historical starting points not only give us confidence but also provide useful development experience. In fact, the experience of these countries and regions is an important reference for China in formulating the "quadruple" and "three-step" strategies in the early 1980s.

An unforgettable memory is linked with Hong Kong. In the period of planned economy, the political movements and rigid systems in mainland China hindered economic growth and the improvement of people's living standards. In sharp contrast, Hong Kong, one of the famous "Four Asian Tigers," had substantial improvement of the living standard after its economy took off. This contrast indicated that mainland China didn't get rid of poverty and demonstrated no superiority of the "socialism" system in the economic contest with capitalist Hong Kong.

In those years, many residents from Guangdong Province crossed the border illegally and "escaped to Hong Kong." Guangdong Province's incomplete statistics indicate that from 1954 to 1980 the officially documented "escape to Hong Kong" involved 565,000 people.[2] Thus, it's meaningful to compare the development pace of mainland China after the reform and opening-up with that of Hong Kong.

Another significance of this comparison is that South Korea, Singapore, Hong Kong Special Administrative Region (HKSAR), and Taiwan, China are part of the "Asian Miracle" that was later commonly referred to as the "Four Asian Tigers" that succeeded in achieving economic catch up – and once the regions with the fastest economic growth in the world. Besides, as East Asian countries and regions, these economies have many similarities with mainland China in aspects of cultural tradition, geographic environment and resources. Therefore, another effect implied in this comparison is to better reflect the economic growth performance of mainland China afterwards. From a global perspective, the growth performance of the three Asian economies of South Korea, Singapore and Hong Kong Special Administrative Region (HKSAR) was barely satisfactory, if not rare, but they had already moved into the high-income stage; their economic growth rates of course didn't match with China, which was still in the process of catching up and surpassing economically.

Japan is not only an Asian neighbor but also represents the most developed country at the time and has historically served as a world center of manufacturing. In particular, when China's reform and opening-up started, the United States and Japan ranked No.1 and No. 2 respectively in economic aggregate among the countries listed in the World Bank's statistics. Therefore, comparing China's economic growth performance with it, we can observe the catch-up characteristics of China's economy more clearly. For these two highly mature economies that were on the neoclassical growth stage, each step of substantial growth must rely on technological progress and productivity improvement, and in the long run, it cannot be expected that there will be a growth rate comparable to catching up with the country. However, after 1990, Japan's average annual economic growth rate was less than 1%, and it fell into the "three lost decades." It has its own reasons. We will explain it in other chapters of this book.

In 2003, from the perspective of nation scale and economic growth, Goldman Sachs Group identified BRIC – Brazil, Russia, India and China – which had influential effects on the world economy and gained special attentions from investors.

In 2010 BRIC allowed South Africa to join the BRIC collaboration. Now BRICS represents the important emerging economies, but the other four members are much superior to China in economic growth. During the period 1978–2016, except for South Africa and Russia, which were shown here, the average annual growth rates in Brazil and India were 2.5% and 6.0% respectively. It's noted that these countries suffered heavy losses in the 2008 and 2009 global finance crisis and were not stable in their recoveries afterwards.

In addition, social tension issues in South Africa – as well as labor conflict, backward infrastructure and insufficient laborers in India and political instability and over-dependence on primary product export in Brazil – reflect the tendency toward "deindustrialization." Most analysts and investors are pessimistic about the long-term growth of these economies.

Some countries are globally perceived during the transition from planned economy to market economy, including China and Vietnam in Asia, as well as former Soviet Union and Eastern European countries. Hence, we compare China's growth performance with that of Russia. As the latter started late in the reforms and adopted radical reform measures, it had rapid drops of economic growth, and its overall economic performance was not as good as expected in the last 20 years. For most of these transitional countries, we can graphically describe the L-shaped growth trajectory, that is, the economic transition has led to a serious recession, GDP has fallen into negative growth for many years and subsequent recovery is not enough.

It can be seen that whether it is compared with itself prior to the reform and opening-up or with various representative economies, the rapid economic growth that China has achieved in the past 40 years is definitely an unbelievable miracle. Chinese and foreign people are inclined to use emotional expressions like "outshining others" or "the scenery here is exceptionally beautiful" to describe China's outstanding economic growth. No one would deny that 1.38 billion Chinese people would not enjoy the improvement in their living standards today, nor would they have the comprehensive national strength of the world's second largest economy that would break double technological records reaching sky-high and abyss-deep, without such extraordinary economic aggregate growth.

2.2 "China collapse theory"

Just as China's economic growth miracle attracts worldwide attention, skeptical attitudes toward this miracle dominated for a while and even come back every time after the prediction that China is declining fails. The economics is usually viewed as "depressive science." One of the reasons is the economists act as hoodoos of economic outlook and love to reveal the future that ordinary people are unable to predict or reluctant to face. As participants in the economics, some economists are willing to tell good news, but some dare to tell bad news. All serve different purposes.

When Paul Krugman won the Nobel Economic Prize in 2008, some media went wild with the statement that he was the one who successfully predicted the

1997–1998 Asian finance crisis. This statement lack evidence and persuasion, but Krugman is indeed famous for his questions about the so-called Asian Miracle and his criticisms of the Southeast Asian economy model. If analyzing from the philosophical perspective that "things must be corrupted before they get grubby," we believe his insight into inherent defects and potential economic risks of the Southeast Asian model. His opinions may not be 100% correct, but they are not contradictory and involved countries and regions prefer to believe them.

For example, after experiencing questioning and criticisms of Krugman et al. regarding Singapore's growth miracle and a wide dispute among economists about the Southeast Asian economic growth model and total factor productivity (TFP), the Singapore government doesn't approve the economists' criticisms to its growth model, but recognizes TFP importance to economic growth sustainability and formalizes this complicated and twisted productivity index as its national goal measurement, requiring 2% increase per year. Maybe this is why Singapore's economic outcomes go beyond those economists' prediction.

Krugman and another American economist Alwyn Young insisted on playing the role of cursing the East Asian economies and China's economic growth. After referring to the "Four Asian Tigers" as "paper tigers" predicting that their economic growth was not sustainable, they denied that China's economy had substantial progress in productivity and predicted that the Chinese economy would eventually hit the wall.[3] After predictions of these scholars became wrong again and again, they still insisted on and repeated the same predictions. It was a bit like the "boy who cried wolf". It was a bit puzzling.

What makes people particularly unable to reflect is that there is still a type of prophecy that is not constructive and simply criticizes for criticism. As to China's economic prospect, there is always a "China collapse Theory" school, whose most reputable scholar is Gordon Chang. In 2001 when Gordon Chang published his English bestseller *The Coming Collapse of China*,[4] two far-reaching historically influential incidents happened, one is good – China was accepted into the WTO, the other is bad – the World Trade Center in New York was hit by terrorist-hijacked planes. Both incidents are incorporated to be evidence of the collapsing Chinese economy by Gordon Chang.

His logic is basically that China's economy has had rapid growth for a while but still has potential risks due to its inherent institutional defects like official corruption and low efficiency of state-owned enterprises (SOE). Once China was accepted into the WTO, the broader competition became inevitable. Insufficient oversea market demands could hardly fuel economic growth when Western countries like the US remained in economic downturn after 911. It is impossible for China to have sustainable growth; hence its coming collapse is within expectation.

None of those astounding predictions in this book have come true in more than a decade after the book is published. The author's strong ideological bias and affection make many data sources look quite dubious. Among serious scholars, few agree and applaud. In the following chapters, we will explain how the facts contradict with Gordon Chang's opinions from every perspective. Interestingly the author who quits an "iron rice bowl" for a free-lance commentary would pay high prices if he admitted his misjudged opinions. Gordon Chang keeps speaking his statements aloud again and again, bad-mouthing the Chinese economy and advocating the moribund "China collapse Theory" as a leading thinker.

Any country has to overcome various difficulties at different stages of its economic development. Take demographic transition for example. Chinese demographic transition moves into a new stage that working-age population stops growing after China leverages demographic dividend to achieve 30-year rapid economic growth, so the Chinese economy is moving into a new stage with increased labor cost and disappeared demographic dividend in the second decade of the 21st century. Brand-new challenges cause China to give up factor input oriented mode and turn to technology advancement, productivity improvement and innovation driven mode to stimulate its economy.

In the face of these challenges, there is no doubt that it's essential and welcome that serious scholars reveal issues, warn the public from experience and lectures at home and abroad and present policy proposals to the policymakers. Gordon Chang keeps his pace with the times. It's of great significance that he discovers China facing such challenges from its demographic transition trend, but he is neither the only nor the first discoverer. He becomes a representative of new "rust belt," asserting that China will displace Michigan in the US. I'm worried the "wolf is coming" tragedy will return.

My suggestion is that one should at least understand demographic transition theory and demographic dividend experience before he gives opinions about population, especially the relation between population and economic growth. We will discuss this issue in the following section. The term "rust belt" refers to earlier manufacturing centers in the American Northeast that declined in industrial restructuring. This phenomenon reflects inevitability and impact of comparative advantage changes. Many general rules and the special phenomena behind them are worthy of deep research and cannot be clearly explained in one or two columns. We will provide answers more precise than Gordon Chang's in the following chapters.

2.3   The source of rapid growth

If we look at the characteristics from the perspective of demographic transition, the period from 1978 to 2010 coincided with the period when China's reform and opening-up and labor-age population grew faster than the non-working-age population increased. We view this period as a population opportunity window or a demographic dividend harvest period. Therefore, during the dual economic development after the reform and opening-up, China's economic growth obviously benefitted from the demographic dividend. It meets the expectation of economic theory, has Chinese characteristics and is statistically proven. From the following aspects of the source of economic growth, we analyze how the beneficial demographic structure created from demographic transition is cashed into demographic dividend in China's economic growth.

First, stable drop of population dependency ratio makes a favorable population base for capital formation during rapid economic growth and helps the national economy keep a high saving rate. Early in the planned economy, China's saving rate – fixed capital formation to GDP ratio – was very high, kept ascending after the reform and reached a record high in the first ten years of the 21st century. From 1995 to 2010, the nominal value of this ratio was increased from 32.9% to 69.3%, almost doubled. But if GDP and fixed capital formation were corrected according to the price index, the increase of this ratio would be higher and the absolute value would be much larger, as GDP shrink index is more than fixed capital price index.

Besides, sufficient labor supply hinders diminishing returns of capital input to some extent. Neoclassic growth theory is based on the law of decreasing return on capital with an assumption of labor shortage. This assumption is undoubtedly essential to Western developed economies but inconsistent with Chinese reality. Therefore, over a long time, infinite labor supply results in high investment ROI in China. High saving rate and high investment ROI are contributions to capital input in the analysis of the source of economic growth.

Second, sustainable increase of the working-age population assures sufficient labor supply. The favorable demographic structure guarantees the continuous entry of new growing labor force. For the backward countries, the improvement of the overall labor force's human capital is mainly achieved through this incremental approach. As the education level of workers increases, China still has low cost advantage in the process of economic globalization. In other words, over a long time, China's competitive strengths include sufficient laborers, low payment and comparatively higher labor quality compared with other developing countries.

For example, in 2005 the average education years of the Chinese working-age population was 33% higher than India. High education improves labor productivity. The analysis of Chinese manufacturing enterprises indicates that for each additional education year the employees have, the labor productivity increases 17%. Double advantages – number and quality of laborers – endow China with the unit labor cost advantage in the long run.[5] The positive effects of these factors on the economic growth contribute to the increase of variable factors including labor investment and human capital accumulation in the production function.

Third, the rural falls behind the urban in demographic transition. A plentitude of surplus rural laborers accumulated in the planned economy are transited during the reform, so resource reallocation efficiency is created where laborers flow from low productivity departments to high productivity departments. This is the main source of labor productivity improvement during this period (this conclusion also applies to total factor productivity). From 1978 to 2015, China's labor productivity (GDP per worker) actually increased by 16.7 times, of which the labor productivity of the primary industry, the secondary industry and the tertiary industry increased, and the total contribution rate was 56%. The change in the allocation structure resulting from the labor force shift contributes 44% to the improvement of labor productivity.[6]

Fourth, not all demographic dividend contributions created due to demographic transition are covered by the variables mentioned above. If population dependency ratio is statistically taken as the explicit proxy variable of the demographic dividend, its contribution to the economic growth is actually the demographic dividend or the residual of demographic dividend related factors. In historic economics documents, most quantitative analyses of demographic dividend, no matter whether in China or other countries and regions, select the population dependency ratio – the comparative ratio of pure consumer population (age 15– 65+) and productive population (aged 15–64) – as the proxy variable of the demographic dividend.

For example, American economist Williamson takes the population dependency ratio as the variable and estimates that from 1970 to 1995 the demographic dividend contributed to 1/4–1/3 of Asian economic growth. In addition, he analyzes the economic growth and demographic structure data of 17 European and North American countries during 1870 to 1913 and discovers that lower dependency ratio almost always accounts for the superior per capita GDP growth rate of the New World to the Old World.[7]

We try to make further decomposition of the economic growth since the early 1980s by the production function, in order to observe all factors' comparative contributions to the economic growth since the reform and opening-up. Among the factors in these theories that are contributive to the economic growth, we select fixed capital formation, gross employment, education years of employees, population dependency ratio and residual as the variables, respectively representing the contributions of capital input, labor input, labor capital, demographic dividend and TFP to GDP growth rate. Further, we can also decompose the contribution of total factor productivity into resource allocation efficiency and residuals generated by labor transfer. Figure 2.2 shows such a disaggregated result, and it can

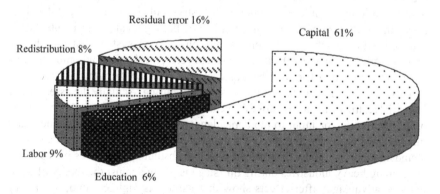

Figure 2.2 The Source of Economic Growth during the Reform and Opening-up

Source: Cai Fang, "Transfer and Reconfiguration of Agricultural Labor in the Reform Period," *Chinese Rural Economy*, No. 10, 2017

clearly show the various sources of economic growth and the relative contribution made by China's economic miracle, the rapid growth of GDP, during the period of reform and opening-up.

2.4   Toward new development concept

The skepticism toward "development is an unyielding principle" is proven wrong. This point of view is held by the minority but makes some sense. After all, these people observe and express concern that China's economy has a GDP-oriented tendency whose highlighted characteristics include: local governments once took the gross economic growth as the core of economic work – even the sole target – and spare no efforts to seek to increase the GDP gross; as a result, serious problems like unbalanced, inharmonious and unsustainable economic development are too difficult to solve. In the following, we will summarize and discuss these issues in economic development.

Economic development has inconsistencies with resources, environment and ecology. For a long time, the pressure to maintain high growth rates has contradicted the relative limitations of resources and the tolerance limits of the environment. Over-dependence on high input and high consumption production, duplicated industrialization of industrial structure, introduction of high energy consumption and pollution of foreign direct investment (FDI) and the vicious cycle of poverty during the production manifest the conflicts mentioned before.

GDP-oriented political achievement philosophy heavily valued by governments at all levels of the local governments and heavy industrialization resulting from value-added tax (VAT) encouragement contradict the unsustainable energy supply of China. Many districts, especially those that have depended on labor-intensive industries to achieve rapid growth since the reform and opening-up, recognize that they have moved into the heavy industrialization stage and start to encourage the prioritized development of heavy industries or intentionally raise the heavy industry ratio by the implementation of industrial policies and regional development strategies. Heavy industrialization is impelled by local governments' GDP-oriented political achievement philosophy on the VAT system that high heavy industry ratio will increase the taxes. In recent years, mechanical, automotive, steel and other heavy industries are the major impetus for GDP growth.

This is a misunderstanding of industrial restructuring. Actually the essentials of industrial restructuring are to move the economic growth from the over-dependence on productive factor input to the dependence on productivity improvement and innovation. For a very long time, China used to be in the developing stage with abundant laborers, relatively scarce capital and absolutely scarce resources. First, developing heavy industries during this stage is going against the theory of comparative advantage; after-effects show that its cost is high. Second, this heavy industrialization is unsustainable. When China has absolutely scarce resources, the international politics of resources restricts our development. The economic growth depending on heavy industrialization will consume a great deal of energy and raw materials. Finally, even after the disappearance of the demographic dividend, economic development has entered a new normal, and it is imperative to adjust the industrial structure and change the mode of development. The principle followed should be productivity-oriented instead of choosing according to the lightness and weight of the industrial structure.

The unsustainability of economic growth is enhanced due to local governments' hunger for FDI and encouragement for and even compliance with the transfer of high energy consumption and pollution industries from developed countries to China. China's rapid growth and potentials attract FDI import. No doubt FDI output countries value the rich and cheap labors, the huge market and its potentials, but they also intend to transfer high pollution and energy consumption industries into China. This intention and tendency is increasingly intensive under the conditions of the world's tight energy supply and boosted emission reduction pressure.

What's worse, the neglect of the environmental price is likely to occur during the transfer of labor-intensive industries from the coastal regions where labor cost has increased to the Midwestern regions. If we indiscriminately attracted investments, the high pollution and energy consumption industries would swarm into China's Midwest regions as never before, and their industrial structure would therefore be far from sustainable.

The concerns about tolerance of economic development enable some people to have questions about "development is an unyielding principle." People are too desperate for adequate food and clothing and income increase to consider environmental pollution before introducing investments or injuries and damages during the employment behavior, so pollution incidents, injuries and major accidents happen frequently. The dangers of pollution are underestimated on one hand, and the safety is neglected and the lives are despised when pursuing production expansion on the other hand. As the society advances and network media develops, environmental pollution incidents, employment injuries and mine disasters are reported without delay, attracting wide attention and receiving wider supervision from the whole society.

In addition, the social development is relatively lagging behind the economic growth. Governments are not so powerful in providing public services to construct social protection mechanisms as in promoting the economic growth, resulting in great disparities in the actual social protection level and demand. Over a long period of time, various types of income gaps were in an expanding trend, and the development achievements have not been evenly shared by all people.

To address the phenomenon existing in social economic development, the Communist Party of China (CPC) proposes a brand-new philosophy – the outlook on scientific development. Further, at the Fifth Plenary Session of the 18th CPC Central Committee, five development concepts were proposed: innovation, coordination, greenness, openness and sharing. As the 18th CPC National Congress concluded, "in contemporary China, the essence of adherence to 'development is an unyielding principle' is to adhere to the outlook on scientific development." In order to understand and practice the five major development concepts, we should also focus on persisting in development and giving them the nature of innovation, coordination, greenness, openness and sharing.

First of all, the Chinese dream of building a Moderately Well-off Society and realizing the great rejuvenation of the Chinese nation will inevitably be supported by the improvement of economic development and national power. In 2016, China's per capita gross national income (GNI) exceeded $8,260. According to the World Bank Grouping Standard, it ranks among the middle-income and upper-income countries.[8] However, it still needs more efforts to move into the rank of higher income countries, and per capita income of $12,235 is not the only thing to be done. The lessons of economic development in many countries show that this is a development stage that easily falls into the middle-income trap. To rejuvenate the magnificent vision of the Chinese nation, China must maintain a reasonable and moderate rate of economic growth before it can step over the middle-income stage successfully.

Not everyone understands this principle of insisting on development. At a meeting in 2010, when discussing how to step over the middle-income stage and avoid the middle-income trap, one scholar stood up to deny the proposition itself, arguing that it is impossible for a country as large as China to reach the so-called high-income industrialized countries. Moreover, the world's resources cannot support China's becoming a high-income country. In order to avoid depleting resources, ecology and environment, China should not pursue higher-income targets. Therefore, he suggested that after reaching the middle-income level in China, as long as the distribution of the whole society is fairly fair, everyone can live fairly well.[9]

This can be described as a typical statement based on good intentions and naive conclusions. The experience of countries falling into the middle-income trap tells us that it's impossible to improve the income allocation under the condition of sluggish economic growth, and people are unable to "live a fairly good life" in such a society. The social equity of course is what we strive for, but the premise of fair distribution of the "pie" of social wealth is to have a "pie" and make it bigger. If there is no circulating social wealth, any commitments to improve people's living standard and income allocation are just lip services, impossible to fulfill.

It's said the Kingdom of Bhutan located in the South slope of the Eastern Himalayas ranks top in a list of sense of happiness. The fascinating TED speech of the Prime Minister of Bhutan is also very popular. This seems to be a typical case that demonstrates people's sense of happiness is totally irrelevant to per capita income. But a further observation indicates this globally No. 129 country had only $2,380 per capita GDP in 2015 and still suffers from inadequate food and clothing or poverty, not to mention meeting material and cultural demands. So it's at most a country contented with poverty and devoted to things spiritual, far from the objective assessment of happiness.

Besides, the essence of the resource, ecology and environment issues is not whether to develop or not but which way to depend on for the economic development. Depending on "zero growth" of "the club of Rome" to solve the resource and environment puzzle is more like giving up eating for fear of choking. A typical example attracting worldwide attention is the destruction of the Amazon Rainforest. With the richest biodiversity and material influence on the global weather, this area happens to cross 8 Latin American countries including Brazil. These countries have lingered in the middle-income phase for long that their widespread poverty imposes great pressure on resources and environment, and their economic growth deviates from sustainability, so they are unable to protect this biological treasure but intensify excessive deforestation, leading this ecological place called "lungs of the earth" into dangers.

In a speech in 2016, President Xi Jinping proceeded from the idea of development centered on the people and explained that protecting resources, ecology and environment are not just means of development but also the purpose of development, which has achieved the new height of the development concept. He pointed out that there is no substitute for the ecological environment, and it is hard to miss it. The environment is people's livelihood, green mountains and blue sky are beautiful, clear waters and green hills are mountains of gold and silver; protecting the environment is protecting productivity; improving the environment is the development of productive forces.[10]

Second of all, the purpose of economic development is to meet the people's growing needs for a better life. What needs to be addressed is the problem of inadequate and uneven development. The development should be tolerant, sharing, comprehensive and harmonious. The earlier development theories prioritize efficiency improvement and production expansion with the ultimate goal of increasing the economic aggregate and per capita welfare. However, economic growth has not naturally led to the so-called turbulent effects, which do not necessarily lead to the fair enjoyment of development by all people. In many countries, it has brought with it various economic and social problems.

Chinese and foreign scholars establish different development theories after observing the issues brought by economic growth itself from perspectives of different subject schools. The contents of development outlooks range from the philosophical human society evolvement to the pains individuals suffer during the evolvement. As the development outcomes contradict with the original intentions, people come up with essential issues like how to define and plan the development. Meanwhile, the metrics for development outcomes are questioned, and new measures are tried.

Malthus is the first one to rethink the development from restrictions of population growth. In his view, the true cause of poverty is "the Law of Nature," where the population is geometrically increased and the supply of living materials is hard-pressed to catch up with the population growth. Eventually the sustainable increase of population makes people fall into the low-level balance trap. The Limit of Growth, a report for the Club of Rome in 1972, extends the Malthusian "population-food" crisis into a "population-resource-environment" crisis.

Some economists use the economic analysis to criticize new Malthusianism and make a clear statement that in developed countries the population growth has positive significance on the economic growth through knowledge advancement and economies of scale. They discuss the diversity of the earth's resources from many aspects and indicate that only if politics, institution, management and market mechanisms are well played will the population growth be favorable for economic development and technical advancement in the long run.[11]

The sustainable development thoughts seek a new development path, which is illustrated in *Our Common Future* published by the World Commission on Environment and Development (WCED) in 1987. The new development path emphasizes people first and coordinates population, resources and environment from intergenerational relations, so that "mankind's advancement lasts not only a few years in a few regions, but for the remote future for the whole earth." The sustainable development is defined as the "development that meets the needs of the present without compromising the ability of future generations to meet their own needs."[12]

French economist Francois Perroux distinguishes "growth" from "development." He believes that development contains more than per capita GDP increase. He emphasizes the structural reform and evolvement where "all types of human resources have potential to gain efficiency and capabilities."[13]

Todaro concludes three core connotations of development: basic living needs, self-esteem and freedom. He proposes the goals of development should include: the increase of basic necessities of life, the improvement of human dignity and cultural values by more employment and education opportunities and the increase of economic and social choices for both individuals and nations.[14] The economist Stiglitz says development means a series of economic and social changes, but these changes themselves are just measures to fulfill goals, and the intention is to make individuals and the society have better control of their own destinies.[15] Amarty Sen indicates that development is a process for people to enjoy freedom, and the ultimate purpose is to seek welfare for people.[16]

Different definitions of development lead to different views on the relation of growth and allocation, and further the relation of equality and fairness during the development process. The core of income allocation is measurement and assessment of developed welfare. Kuznets finds in the earlier phase of economic growth the increased income deteriorates the income allocation, but when income further increases and reaches a turning point, the distribution of income gradually improves. There seems to be a summary of experience supported by statistical data, constituting an inverted U-shaped curve named after Kuznets.[17] The so-called laws implied in this curve are proven to be not 100% correct by the development experience of some countries and regions. Besides, this relation, as a development concept, is already abandoned by most scholars and policymakers.

In the earlier planned economy, Mao Zedong attempted to manage the coordinated but contradictory dialectical relation between fairness and efficiency well. But in later economic systems and years of construction practices there are no effective incentive mechanisms, so the production enthusiasm of individuals, community and enterprises is inhibited. The bad management of this relation ultimately hinders the development of productivity.

The key of balancing fairness and efficiency is how to utilize policies and incentive mechanisms to manage the relation between getting rich first and common prosperity. When Deng Xiaoping advocated "some people get rich first," he emphasized allowing some regions, enterprises, workers and farmers to gain more incomes by their hardworking; he also pointed out the purpose of letting some people get rich first is to set an example and drive other regions, enterprises and people to work hard and eventually achieve common prosperity among all nationalities.[18] Some people getting rich first is the inevitable outcome of efficiency when incentive mechanisms come into full play and would happen in any system. Therefore, Deng Xiaoping's wave-like theory of common prosperity conforms to the law of social development.

The concept of achieving innovative, coordinated, green, open and shared development fully reflects the new ideas, new thoughts and strategies of the Chinese Communist Party's governance of the country since the 18th National Congress of the People's Republic of China. Its purpose, approach, path, focus and measure of development are discussed. A comprehensive response has been made to issues such as sharing, which specifically reflects the unity of goal orientation and problem orientation. Among them, innovation and development focus on cultivating a new impetus for economic growth under the new normal; coordinated development focuses on the health of development; green development focuses on the sustainability of development and conforms to people's pursuit of a better life; open development focuses on making good use of international and domestic markets and two kinds of resources, to achieve internal and external development linkage; shared development focuses on solving social fairness and justice issues, reflecting the essential requirements of socialism with Chinese characteristics and development purposes.

2.5 Transforming economic development

Imbalance, inharmony and unsustainability always exist in China's economic development. The question is not whether we need GDP but what kind of methods we use to promote economic development. To address this core issue, the historical rapid growth has successful experience and useful lectures deserving second thoughts.

Chinese and foreign economists have various interpretations about the "China Miracle" created in last 40 years after the reform and opening-up. Economists correlated the post-assessment of China's economic reforms and development effects and conducted separate discussions on the reform target pattern such as Washington Consensus and Beijing Experience; with the discussion on the reform mode such as progressive reform and radical reform and with the discussion on the relation of government and market such as authority institution and neutral government.

Interestingly, economists usually come to tit-for-tat or opposite conclusions from the same Chinese experience. While most economists demonstrated the "Washington Consensus" to be no longer effective using Chinese experience, some economists still believe the success of China's reform lies in the appropriate application of standard economic theory (in other words, the compliance with "Washington Consensus").[19] But actually in this recognition, the concept of "prescription" of treatment is confused with the concept of "therapy outcome." Speaking of China's reform, there is no evidence of doctrinal principles that we follow from the very beginning, but what we achieve surprises the world.

The reason for ambiguous concepts and contradictory observation results is that, compared with other countries, China's reform concepts and practices have the features including determined goals of China's reform but undetermined, diversified and ever-changing goal patterns and means to achieve the goals. Obviously, if we fail to realize that the CPC tenet of serving the people heart and soul and the outlook on "People First" scientific development provide fundamental guidance to the reform, opening-up and development with Chinese characteristics, it would be impossible to truly understand the "China Miracle."

When assessing the outcomes of China's reform, opening-up and development, Western economists get used to start from some doctrine and compare China with a fixed and priori reference frame,[20] but later discovered this reference frame was not what China takes the initiative to comply with and pursue during the reform. Actually it manifests the philosophical differences in the reform between China and other countries. In other words, the purpose of China's reform is not to transcendentally fulfill some preset goal patterns but to improve people's living standard and national power ultimately. Reform steps and paths are selected and definite goal patterns are gradually settled according to its ultimate purpose.

Starting from this ultimate purpose, we have gradually explored a path suitable for China's national conditions to realize the transformation from the planned economy to the market economy; however, there are no constant or standalone patterns to realize the market economic system, which actually serves the improvement of people's livelihood and national power. Just because of this reform philosophy and direct starting point, the guidance principles and the advancement means of China's reform are not restricted within any transcendental doctrines.

The reform is to improve productivity, most people's livelihood and national power. This principle is throughout definite and should be unswervingly insisted on. Under the guidance of this reform philosophy, reform, development and stability would be integrated into a whole. Reform is for the purpose of development – but subject to stability – while development outcomes are evidence to verify the reform path, and stability creates favorable conditions for deepened reform.

The central government's request for the acceleration of the economic development mode of transformation reflects the party's tenet in economic development thought. At the beginning of the reform and opening-up, China had only $150 per capita GDP and was a typical low-income country. Once the reform stimulated the enthusiasm of laborers and business operators, the first priority was to accelerate the economic development, change poverty and backwardness and significantly improve people's living standard. As Deng Xiaoping repeated, neither poverty nor slow development was due to socialism. In fact, the acceleration of economic development and the improvement of GDP, per capita GDP and people's living standard are touchstones to verify the correctness and the success of the reform and opening-up policy. Therefore, within a certain period of time, the development speed is most critical, so "fast" takes priority over "good."

In last 40 years since 1978, China has achieved nearly 10% average annual GDP growth rate and over 8.6% per capital GDP growth rate. When the Chinese economy moved into a new phase, especially in the 21st century, China was listed as one of the lower middle-income countries and then above-average income countries; its productive factors have been tremendously changed. Meanwhile, more "unbalanced, inharmonious and unsustainable" issues in economic development have emerged than ever before. It becomes more urgent to transform economic development and achieve coordination of economic development and social development. So after a long period of time when rapid economic growth is achieved under the compromise of resources, environment and balance, "better" development is becoming the first choice.

Economists and policymakers have had wide discussions on economic growth modes for a long time and come to consensus that economic growth should be transformed from the extensive pattern to intensive pattern. When making the "9th Five-Year Plan," the Party Central Committee and the State Council officially proposed the requests for fundamental transformation of the economic growth mode. As many issues arising from economic growth were correlated to growth modes, after long-term discussions within the economic circle, the "11th Five-Year Plan" emphasized "accelerating promoting the economic restructuring and transforming economic growth mode" and its critical significance to Chinese economic development.

The "11th Five-Year Plan" said "the crucial reason of many issues arising from China's current economic development lies in unreasonable economic structure and extensive growth mode." So China set forth a series of targets, especially obligatory targets, transforming the extensive and expansive growth mode featuring "high input, high consumption, high emission and low efficiency" into the resource-effective growth mode featuring "low input, low consumption, low emission and high efficiency."

The 17th National Congress of CPC defined the transformation of the mode of economic development as to

> propel three transitions in the mode of economic growth: the transition from relying mainly on investment and export to relying on a well-coordinated combination of consumption, investment and export, the transition from secondary industry serving as the major driving force to primary, secondary and tertiary industries jointly driving economic growth, and the transition from relying heavily on increased consumption of material resources to relying mainly on advancement in science and technology, improvement in the quality of the workforce and innovation in management.

Changing the "economic growth mode" used in the past to the expression "economic development mode" itself reflects a more comprehensive, coordinated and people-centered development.

Since the Party's 18th National Congress, it has become more aware of the changes in the mode of economic development and has become more conscious in practice. In 2014, President Xi Jinping proposed that China's economic development has entered a new normal, and high-household construction has summarized the characteristics of speed change, structural optimization and power conversion that the new normal has. This deep judgment has become a fixed-star for understanding the economic situation, identifying major challenges and focusing on policies. Under the new normal, the main features of economic development are: the growth rate should shift from high-speed to medium-high speed, the development mode should shift from the scale-speed model to the quality-efficiency model and the adjustment of economic structure must shift from incremental expansion to the adjustment of stock and optimization. Incremental and simultaneous, the driving force for development must shift from relying primarily on resources and low-cost labor to innovations.

Reviewing the growth theories and the international experience, we know that the main sources of economic growth are different in different phases, and the suitable development mode inevitably exists within a certain period of time. Only when a growth source is fading and dying is it urgent to transform the development mode in order to find out new growth sources. The sustainable development overcoming the growth restriction factors is formulated due to the growth requirements on the basis of the transformation of the mode of economic development. When the Chinese economy moved into such a phase, the huge growth impetus caused by the institutional reform and opening-up motivated the existing growth sources to their greatest extent and exhausted their potentials. If the economic growth is not transformed from relying mainly on input expansion to relying mainly on productivity improvement, the potentials of economic growth ell decline until drain out.

Economic development has entered a new normal, bringing with it both new challenges and rare opportunities. Responding to challenges and seizing opportunities not only require us to profoundly understand and actively adapt to the new normal but also to actively lead the new normal in accordance with the inherent logic of the new normal, that is, to speed up the transformation of development methods and economic restructuring through comprehensive deepening of reforms, so as to drive economic growth from being driven by investment. To push the innovation (productivity)-driven transformation, maintain high-speed sustainable economic growth and increase the industrial structure into mid-to-high-end and economic efficiency, China will complete the construction of a well-to-do society by the year 2020 and realize the first centennial mission goal of the Party's 18th National Congress.

Many domestic and foreign scholars believe that one of China's greatest challenges is how to avoid falling into the "middle-income trap." President Xi Jinping pointed out: for China, the "middle-income trap" is overdue, and the key is when to step forward and move forward. Under the premise that the economy maintains high speed growth, suppose that after 2016 China's per capita GNI will grow at a rate of 6% and will increase from the current 8,260 US dollars to $12,420 in 2023, that is, we will cross the dividing line from the above average incomes of the middle to the high incomes among countries.

However, due to the concept of the middle-income trap of the economic implication rather than statistical significance, we must be prepared for the long-term response given the following factors. First of all, the World Bank's division criteria for the country groupings are dynamic and may be adjusted upwards in the future and will also be affected by exchange rate changes and change our rankings. Second, the average per capita GNI of high-income countries is much higher than the income level on the threshold, which is currently as high as 41,046 US dollars. To reach this level of per capita income, China still has a long way to go. Third, the concept of the middle-income trap itself is not merely a judgment or prophecy. It is a reminder to a country that the transition from a middle-income to a high-income stage can no longer be simply followed when it crosses the low-income trap. Many of them are effective ways of doing things at the time. Based on the analysis of the causes of this phenomenon and the reasons for the slowdown of the Chinese economy, the first task is to treat the disease symptomatically, stabilize the speed of economic growth, solve the income distribution at the same time, increase the sharing level of development and make all aspects more systematic, mature and stereotyped to support the economic and social development.

In as early as 2010, China's per capita GDP calculated according to the official exchange rate exceeded 4,000 US dollars, ranking among the above-average income countries. Take the middle-income stage as a unique stage of development, and respond to unprecedented new challenges on the basis of this new stage of development, which is the significance of attaching importance to this concept. It is critical for whether it is possible to achieve a change in the way of economic development. The report of the 18th CPC National Congress pointed out that deepening reforms is the key to accelerating the transformation of economic development. At the same time, reforms in related fields will not be smooth and will require greater political courage and wisdom. The system reforms and policy adjustments needed to change the economic development model include: the shift of economic growth momentum to productivity growth requires the removal of a series of institutional obstacles to the free flow of production factors between urban and rural areas, departments and production units; the transition from economic growth demand factors to a more balanced combination of export, investment and consumption, which relies on the reforms of investment and the financing system and income allocation system, and so on.

Notes

1 See Fu Gaoyi's. (2013). *Deng Xiaoping and the Transformation of China* (Chapter 10). Beijing: SDX Joint Publishing Company.
2 "Escape to Hong Kong" in Baidu Encyclopedia. Retrieved October 2, 2017, from http://baike.baidu.com/view/4136265.htm
3 See Alwyn Young. (2003). Gold into the Base Metals: Productivity Growth in the People's Republic of China during the Reform Period. *Journal of Political Economy, 111*(6), 1220–1261; Paul Krugman. (2013, July 18). Hitting China's Wall. *New York Times.*
4 English version: Gordon Chang. (2001). *The Coming Collapse of China.* New York: Random House; Chinese version: Gordon Chang. (2002/2003). *The Coming Collapse of China.* Taibei: Yayan Culture Publishing Co., Ltd.
5 Cai Fang, Du Yang, and Wang Dewen. (2009). Research on Issues of Chinese Education Reform and Development Strategy. In Cai Fang (Ed.), *Report on China's Population and Labor (No.10): Reforming the Education System to Promote Human Capital* (pp. 1–26). Beijing: Social Sciences Academic Press.

6 Cai Fang. (2017). Analysis of the Effects of China's Economic Reform: A Perspective of Labor Reconfiguration. *Economic Research Journal*, 7, 4–17.
7 Jeffrey Williamson. (1997). Growth, Distribution and Demography: Some Lessons from History. *NBER Working Paper Series*, 6244.
8 According to the latest classification standard in 2017, the per capita GNI is less than US$1005 in low-income countries, between 1006–3955 US dollars in middle-lower income countries, and between 3956–12235 US dollars in upper-middle-income countries, exceeding US$12,235 in High-income countries.
9 Yu Yongding (Ed.). (2011). *China's Sustainable Development: Challenge and Future* (p. 43). Shanghai: SDX Joint Publishing Company.
10 Xi Jinping. (2016, May 10). Leading Leaders at the Provincial and Ministerial Level to Study and Implement the Party's 18th Five Years Speech at the Plenary Symposium on Spiritual Practitioners. *People's Daily*, A2.
11 Julian L. Simon. (1984). *The Economics of Population Growth* (Trans. by Peng Songjian, et al.). Beijing: Peking University Press.
12 World Commission on Environment and Development. (1987). *Our Common Future*. New York: Oxford University Press.
13 Francois Perroux. (1987). *A New Concept of Development* (Trans. by Zhang Ning and Feng Ziyi). Beijing: Huaxia Publishing House.
14 Michael P. Todaro. (1999). *Economic Development*, 6th Version (Trans. by Huang Weiping, Peng Gang, et al.). Beijing: China's Economic Press.
15 Joseph Stiglitz. (2000). A New Concept of Development: Strategy, Policy and Process. In Hu Angang and Wang Shaoguang (Eds.), *Government and Market*. Beijing: China Planning Press.
16 Amarty Sen. (2002). *Development AS Freedom* (Trans. by Ren Ze and Yu Zhen). Beijing: China Renmin University Press.
17 Simon Kuznets. (1955). Economic Growth and Income Inequality. *American Economic Review*, *45*(1), 1–28.
18 Document Editorial Committee of the Central Committee of the Communist Party of China. (1983). *The Selected Works of Deng Xiaoping*, Vol. 2 (p. 152). Beijing: People's Publishing House.
19 Yao Yang. (2008). *The Economic Reform in the Process of Institutional Innovation* (p. 1). Shanghai: Truth and Wisdom Press and Shanghai People's Publishing House.
20 For example, an American published work on China's reform quotes Deng Xiaoping's famous saying "crossing a river by feeling the way over the stones" as "how far across the river?" Nicholas C. Hope, Dennis Tao Yang, and Mu Yang Li (Eds.). (2003). *How Far across the River: Chinese Policy Reform at the Millennium*. Stanford, CA: Stanford University Press.

3 Reform is the fundamental driving force

As China's economy has created the miracle of development and increased 1.38 billion Chinese people's average income level to be 16 times higher than that 40 years ago, China's reform and opening-up has also attracted worldwide attention. In fact, the achievements of economic growth and higher living standards are strong proofs of this policy's success. However, China's goal of establishing the perfect system of socialist market economy and the tasks of reform have not been completed yet, and all aspects of the system have not yet been matured and established. Also, as a process of institutional evolution and policy adjustment complying with the demands of the system, reform is also never-ending. Therefore, in order to cope with all sorts of challenges in the future journey of deepening reform, it is necessary to review the reform logics to date and summarize experiences and lessons in the process, thus revealing the unfinished reform tasks.

3.1 Logics of China's reform

Theoretical economists tend to split themselves into two camps in explaining the performance of nation's economic growth. Economists in the first camp start from the premise that the system is given. They emphasize the accumulation of a single factor of production or the improvement of productivity. This camp includes the physiocrats (emphasizing the unique role of land), early growth theories (emphasizing the key role of capital accumulation), development economics (considering the role of labor on the precondition of capital accumulation), demographic dividend schools (highlighting the role of population structure) and neoclassical growth theories (taking total factor productivity as the only sustainable source of economic growth).

Economists in the other camp focus all their attention on institutions' effects on economic growth. Their theoretical explanations are multifarious, including attributing the success of economic growth to the protestant spirit of abstinence and saving, clearly defined property rights, mechanisms restraining interest groups' activities and the perfect market mechanism or governments' active and proper roles and so on, to name just a few.

Obviously, it is not accurate to simply classify these multifarious economic theories into two camps; however, when empirical economists are trying to integrate the accumulation of various factors including production, improvement of productivity, system arrangement, government functions and other variables into econometric models, theoretical economists have indeed failed to form consistency and continuity in logics. Therefore, they are unable to put forward theoretical models that can give unified explanations of the effect factors of production, productivity and economic institution on economic growth. This kind of mainstream economics' tendency makes itself incompetent and deficient in guiding the development and transition of countries' practices or in explaining the success and failure of their economic growth performances.

Hollis Chenery, the former chief economist of the World Bank, believes that once a key obstacle is discovered and eliminated, a country can accelerate its economic growth even if it does not have the necessary conditions for economic development.[1] This view emphasizes the importance of institutional change. However, suppose that a country can still grow at a high rate without development conditions, which is obviously unconvincing.

Therefore, before discussing the importance of reform, we may temporarily set aside institutional factors and only observe the necessary conditions for development, especially the basis for the accumulation of production factors. In fact, we can say that before reform and opening-up, China had already possessed many conditions for high-speed growth. We can make some observations on the accumulation of labor, capital and human capital variables, which are often selected by econometric models of economic growth.

First, before the 1980s, China had entered the transition process from the second phase (high birth rate, low mortality rate and high population growth) to the third phase (low birth rate, low mortality rate and low population growth). Starting from the late 1960s and lasting through the 1970s, the total fertility rate had dropped rapidly. Accordingly, the growth rate of the 15–59-year-old working-age population has already begun to grow faster than the entire population, while the proportion of working-age population began to rise and population feed rates began to drop.

Second, relative to the level of per capita income, China had already possessed good human capital accumulations before reform and opening-up. For example, no matter according to what kind of data source, China's GNI per capita or GDP per capita ranked the last four among more than 100 countries with statistics worldwide in 1980s. However, as one of the human capital indexes, China's average years of education of population of more than 25 years old ranked 62 among 107 countries with data, while another indicator of human capital – life expectancy at birth – ranked 56 among 127 countries with data.

Finally, although low level of per capita income represents lower capital endowment, China still realized quite a high capital accumulation as a result of its strong ability of resource mobilization in the period of planned economy. Compared with the level of per capita income, before the start of reform and opening-up, China had already formed an industrial system with a relatively complete range of categories but an excessively high proportion of heavy industries. This pattern of industrialization was no doubt inefficient, and the industrial structure formed by it deviated from comparative advantages, which, however, profited from the high accumulation rate. During the period from 1953 to 1978, China's average accumulation rate reached 29.5%, higher than the world average.[2]

However, as a result of several major policy blunders and commonly existing institutional drawbacks, a favorable trend of demographic changes, which had already appeared before the reform and opening-up, did not turn into demographic dividend, which was shown during the period of reform and opening-up. Accumulation of human capital and material capital did not turn into substantial economic growth in the period of planned economy; thus people's living standard had not been improved for a long time.

Economists who have recognized the economic system's influences on the performances of economic growth are always eager to create a criterion that should be followed to realize economic growth and name it "consensus." Therefore, when invited, they are eager to recommend to transition countries a packaged reform, known as shock therapy. However, China did not accept the "Washington Consensus," which was once quite popular, not to mention shock therapy, yet it has so far achieved better reform results than countries following the criterion of free market economy.

Many foreign observers and researchers have noted that China's gradual economic reform took several steps, which started without an overall blueprint, in the way of solving urgent problems at that time and taking the pursuit of direct effect as the starting point. For example, that many economists including Coase and Wang Ning think that "a series of events which led China into modern market economy were not purposeful plans" is completely surprising, thus they think that China's economic transformation is an excellent case for Hayek's theory of "unintended consequences of human behavior."[3]

Can China's reform and its success simply be explained by "unintended consequences of human behavior"? In other words, is China's reform a simply spontaneous process or a conscious institutional change or a cooperative game between direct participants in economic activities and senior policymakers under consensus? In fact, behind the reform path with Chinese characteristics, there exists the Communist Party of China's strong desire to improve Chinese people's living standard and explore the practices that Chinese people have made for that. If we realize this fundamental starting point of reform and its characteristics of practice, it is not hard to understand and map out the inherent logics of China's reform in 40 years.

It is well known and can be empirically tested that a series of major policy changes have influenced the direction and promoted the pace of this reform. An important milestone is the Third Plenary Session of the Thirteenth Conference of the CPC convened in the winter of 1978, which established the basic route of taking economic construction as the center of China's reform and opening-up and launched this largest reform with the most far-reaching influence in human history. Another important milestone is Deng Xiaoping's South Tour Speeches at the beginning of 1992 and the CPC's 14th Conference at end of the same year, which established the target mode of building up the system of socialist market economy, leading to the further deepening of the reform. At the turn of the second decade of the 21st century, another important milestone was the 18th National Congress of the CPC and the Third Plenary Session of the 18th CPC Central Committee. It further deployed the comprehensive deepening of economic reforms, brought the reform into an unprecedented depth and breadth and has achieved significant results.

In 1978, when the CPC launched "Theoretically Put Things Right" and reestablished the ideological line of "seeking truth from facts," it faced the harsh reality that 250 million peasants have insufficient food and clothes. While people had not reached the recognition level of completely negating the people's commune system, system forms that could help the rural population to get out of poverty effectively, production contracted to households and work contracted to households were recognized, thus opened the curtain of China's reform. After that, system explorations were propitious for improving the enthusiasm of laborers and microproduction organizations and could be recognized and implemented, while system obstacles that impeded the productivity development were constantly eliminated.

Clear target mode and thought were not formed among the leaders at the beginning of the reform, and the reform's guiding ideology to establish socialist market economic system was not formed until the early 1990s. However, following the evaluation criterion of "propitious for developing socialist productivity, for strengthening comprehensive national strength of socialist countries and for improving people's living standard," it can be said that the reform has formed a solid political consensus from the very beginning, and it has always been widely supported by the people and has an irreversible push.

Economic system is a structure with inherent logical consistency, within which government intention, macro policy environment, allocation of resources, pricing mechanisms, form and structure of ownership system and micro incentive mechanism coordinate and unify to achieve operations of producing activities and economics. Reform is transformation of an existing economic system, involving all aspects of system structure. Also, there necessarily exist internal logics between each local reform. Therefore, before analyzing China's reform logics, it is necessary to review the traditional economic system's formation logics before the reform.

After the foundation of the People's Republic of China, Chinese leaders' strong economic catching-up and transcending desire were embodied in speeding up industrialization, especially in the selection of a strategic target for heavy industrialization. Whether they consciously recognized it or not, the following logics were self-evident, namely that in an agricultural society with low income levels it is necessary to have capital accumulation to realize industrialization, and this could not be conducted by the lead of market signals. Therefore, the planning system pressed down production and producing factors' prices artificially and allocated resources relying on administrative authority and administrative means, while ownership form took direct control of economic surplus's re-allocation through nationalization of the economic activity unit (and the people's commune movement of agriculture). They were both natural results of system arrangements.[4]

Transnational economic research and China's experience in the period of planned economy both proved that under such a mode of economic system, exclusion of market mechanisms led to macro-inefficiency of resource allocation, lack of incentive mechanism resulted in micro-inefficiency of economic activities and absence of a rewards and punishment system harmed workers, farmers and managers' work enthusiasm. The factors of production's growth realized through the government's powerful resource mobilization were offset in large part by total factor productivity's negative growth, failing to turn into good economic growth performance. In particular, mismatch of resources resulted in deformity of industrial structure, thus people's living standard could not be improved along with economic development.

Any institutional change will inevitably encounter difficulties, which is the paradox between reform that must be carried out as well as vested interests it may blow and current ideology. China's reform since the late 1970s did not touch vested interests, nor did it give up immediately the understanding that a planned economy had the socialist economy's characteristics, yet it started using the principle of material benefits to motivate the workers and increase enterprise incentives. With the change of pricing mechanism and the increase of enterprise competitions, the reform started to hit the resource allocation system, and the planned economy system was gradually and eventually given up through reform ways such as double track prices system.

With reforms characterized by only beneficiaries and not impaired and promoted from the bottom up, we have completed the reengineering of incentive mechanisms and governance models for microeconomic units and basically established a system for allocating resources to the market, and the vitality of the market economy system has been rejuvenated. However, with the deepening of reform, Pareto improvement opportunities reduced; it was more and more difficult to avoid touching the vested interests; the requirements for top-level design were put forward for further reforms, and some reforms were also required to advance from top to bottom.

Over the years, in the process of promoting high-speed growth in reform and the opening-up period, the government had played a positive and important role, while at the same time government's behaviors directly intervened in economic activities and not only became the object of reform itself but also became a part of vested interests which impeded this reform. Therefore, on the basis of 40 years of successful practice, deepening reforms must start again at a new starting point. As pointed out by the 18th National Congress of the Chinese Communist Party, with greater political courage and wisdom, the obstacles to the reforms are eliminated through the top-level design.

3.2 Incentive mechanism and governance mode

By the end of 1970s, the most urgent and realistic focuses for the party and nation are to solve the poverty of rural areas and the stagnation of urban workers' wage growth and improve people's living standard. Lack of the principle of material interests suppressed working enthusiasm and thus hindered the development of economy and improvement of productivity. Therefore, an important step to restore people's confidence in the superiority of the socialist system and build consensus on reform was to re-admit the principle of material interests.

Since there is a lack of direct connection between the single laboring stage and final results in the process of agricultural production and agricultural labor's hard-to-supervise characteristics, reform on agricultural economic system took the direction of combing arousing workers' enthusiasm with land use right and land management right, reflecting on the implementation of the household contract responsibility system and the abolition of people's communes. Under the household contract responsibility system, lands owned by villagers collectively were equally distributed to families to farm. After the crop yields paid for agricultural tax and the amount retained by the collective and some agricultural products were sold to the state according to some rules, the family could own and control the remainder themselves.

The household contract responsibility system greatly improved rural workers' productivity enthusiasm. According to Justin Yifu Lin's research, during the period from 1978 to 1984, as a kind of institutional change, the implementation of the household contract responsibility system had a one-time increasing production effect on the total agricultural output, with its growth contribution up to 46.9%.[5] At the same time, farmers got allocation rights of labor resources and long-term accumulation of agricultural labor force's surplus was also liberated, which successively transferred from crop planting to generalized planting industry, business diversification of forestry, animal husbandry, subsidiary business and fishery, township enterprises, as well as non-agricultural industries of cities and towns at all levels.

Since then, with people's dissolution of communes (and thus production teams), decline of collective unified management, abolition of state monopoly for purchase and supply, and later cancellation of agricultural tax, collectively-owned lands were in fact permanently contracted to peasant families, who actually enjoyed the management right and earning right and even part of disposition right. Family-run became the agricultural industry's basic management system by law. In terms of agriculture, micro-incentive problems were once and for all solved. In order to promote moderate scale operation of agriculture, after the Party's 18th National Congress of the People's Republic of China, under the premise of insisting that the collective property of rural land remains unchanged, the "three-power separation" reform of rural land ownership, contracting and management shall be implemented to promote the orderly circulation of rural land management rights, which is another major reform after the household contract responsibility system.

In cities, reform of state-owned enterprises initially took the form of the state's decentralization of power and transfer of profits to enterprises. Around 1978, enterprises and public institutions gradually restored the bonus system, which was cancelled during "Cultural Revolution." In fact, the main purpose and effect of bonuses was not rewards and punishments according to workers' performances but a means of increasing workers' income to mobilize the enthusiasm of the workforce after the long-term wage had not been changed. At that time, bonuses of regular production reward were generally paid from wage-funds, equivalent to 16% to 25% of standard wage.

Relating wage and reward to the performance of enterprise management synchronized with allowing enterprises to retain some of the additional revenue's autonomous disposition right, namely retained profits. In addition to the rights to pay salaries and bonuses, enterprises had successively gained the rights of selling and pricing product, options for production factors, right to use their own capital, right of joint management, options for technological progress directions and other rights. Also, they were allowed to engage in a variety of business operations. These measures created incentives for enterprise production and management, and at the same time they also inspired government departments' and local governments' immediate attentions to enterprises' management performances.

In order to further straighten the relations between enterprises and the state and make enterprises the main management bodies on the market, two reforms also took place in the 1980s, which were "Tax for Profits" and "Loaning Instead of Allocating." The reform of "Tax for Profits" was to draw a clear line between government financial income and enterprises' disposable income and form the mechanism that linked national finance income with tax and enterprise income with profits. The reform of "Loaning Instead of Allocating" was to improve use efficiency of fiscal fund and change investment in capital construction of the national budget from allocations to loans. Although the legal relations formed by "Loaning Instead of Allocating" did not belong to loan relationships but were the use relationship of the fiscal fund, the reform laid an important foundation for finally building up enterprises as the main player in the market.

The state's decentralization of power and transfer of profits to enterprises gave birth to a reform form with Chinese characteristics – the contract system, which was described as "once contracted, efficiency improves." In early 1980, Shandong province took the lead to change retained profit to contracted profit, namely dividing enterprises' profits between the state and enterprises according to a quota or a proportion and forming a responsibility system of industrial economy, which gained national recognition and was widely promoted across the whole country. Since then, circling around enterprise management mechanism, various forms of responsibility systems were created and various reform tests were conducted. These forms include large and medium-sized enterprises' contract systems, as well as small and medium-sized enterprises' pilot projects of rental systems and joint-stock systems.

The core of the enterprise contract system is that enterprises gain autonomous management rights delegated by the state and residual claim rights through their obligations of committing to pay profits (tax) to the state, conduct technological transformation, earn economic benefits, increase their assets' values and their management responsibility of self-sustaining. Different enterprises had different motives, and the forms of the enterprise contract system were multifarious; however, generally this was a beneficial attempt of the state taking indirect regulations and control under the condition that the direction of market-oriented reform had not been determined and people's understanding of state-owned enterprises was still limited. This system focused on making enterprises manage themselves independently and sustain themselves through pushing them to the market, and it was an important step of the reform.

It is worth pointing out that, in the period of reforming state-owned enterprises through the contract system, the government proved the reform principle of separating enterprises' ownership right from management right, and under the guidance of this theory it promulgated and implemented the Law of the People's Republic of China on Industrial Enterprises Owned by The Whole People in 1988, which legally determined principles of separating ownership right from management right, separating government functions from enterprise management, enterprises' independent management and self-sustainment, increase of asset value etc., giving enterprises necessary management autonomy. At the same time, the Law of the People's Republic of China on Enterprise Bankruptcy (Trial Edition) passed in 1986 legally consolidated enterprises' budget constraints and laid a necessary legal foundation for enterprises to eventually enter the market.

The urgency of state-owned enterprises' reform came ultimately from more and more fierce competitions, especially from the non-state-owned economy's pressures. With the manifestation of a rural surplus labor force and the increase of urban unemployment pressure, township enterprises rose rapidly, urban individual economy got recognition and encouragement, and the non-state-owned economy was no longer regarded as disaster, although for a long time the government took the non-state-owned economy as a necessary complement to the state-owned economy. In fact, a more important role the non-public economy's development played was putting competing pressures on state-owned enterprises and strengthening the necessity and urgency of reform.

Signaled by Deng Xiaoping's South Tour Speeches in 1992 and the CPC's Fourteenth Conference, Chinese leaders' understanding of reform entered a new height. While determining that reform was to build up the socialist market economy, they also absorbed and learned all the advanced management ways and methods that reflected the rules of modern socialized production from countries worldwide including capitalist developed countries. And it is the only way for socialism to win the advantage compared with capitalism.[6] With the convening of the 14th National Congress of the Communist Party of China, the enterprise reform shifted from simply delegating power and transferring profits to the reform of the governance structure of the state-owned economy.

This round of state-owned enterprises reform aimed to establish a "modern enterprise system" with clear property rights and well-defined rights and responsibilities as well as separate the government functions from enterprise management and scientific management. Based on academic discussions and some enterprises' piloted reform on joint-stock system, policymakers adopted a corporate form, reforming the governance mode of state-owned enterprises according to the principle "manage large enterprises well while relaxing control over small ones." Particularly speaking, large and medium-sized state-owned enterprises with single investors in special production industries were restructured as wholly state-owned companies, and enterprises with multiple investors restructured as the limited liability companies or joint-stock limited companies and developed a number of nationwide shareholding companies and cross-industry enterprise groups. Small state-owned enterprises respectively adopted contracted management, lease management or joint stock cooperative system or they were sold to a collective or individuals.

After that, enterprise reform generally continued the path of "manage large enterprises well while relaxing control over small ones," with main effects reflecting on the rapid decrease of state-owned economy's proportion, great increase of non-state-owned economy and non-collective-owned economy's proportion, strengthened competition and hardening of enterprise budget constraint. From a statistical point of view, the pattern of coexistence of multiple ownerships and mixed ownerships and competitive development has basically taken shape. As of 2015, among the industrial enterprises with an annual main business income of over RMB 20 million, enterprises registered with the nature of state-owned industrial enterprises only created 4.1% of all main business income, and other parts (i.e., 95.9%) were created by 29 kinds of registered companies including private industrial enterprises, industrial companies with limited liability companies, foreign-invested industrial companies, Chinese-foreign joint venture industrial companies etc. (see Figure 3.1).

Under the condition of enhanced competition, state-owned enterprises indeed improved their efficiency significantly. At that time, the urgency of state-owned enterprises' reform was mainly reflected in the lack of competition pressure for a long time, and the autonomy was not truly implemented, resulting in serious losses. For example, in the late 1990s, one third of national state-owned industrial enterprises suffered serious deficit. Aiming at this situation, through the implementation of "manage large enterprises well while relaxing control over small ones," reducing staff to improve efficiency and hardening budget constraint and other reform measures, state-owned enterprises turned losses into gains gradually. After 1998, the management performance of state-owned enterprises improved significantly,

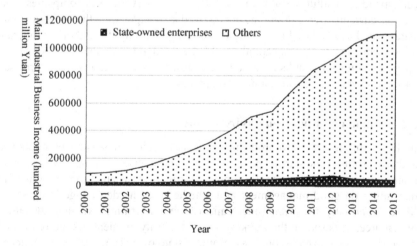

Figure 3.1 Proportion Changes of State-owned Industrial Enterprises' Output Value

Source: *China Statistical Yearbooks* Published by National Bureau of Statistics

and total factor productivity also sped up greatly. At the same time, the situation that diversified economic sectors that coexisted and competed with each other had formed. Generally, enterprise governance structure had been improved, and micro efficiency had improved significantly.

It can be seen from Figure 3.1 that the once popular saying in society that "state advances, while the private sector retreats" was neither a fact nor the key to this problem. The problem was that state-owned economies were not limited to public welfare industries and non-competitive fields. They were also given monopoly power in pricing, workers' income, preferential financing, excluding competition and other aspects. The profits derived from this kind of monopoly do not have to be paid in accordance with its state-owned nature and used for expenditure on public welfare undertakings and social undertakings. Instead, they are invested in a competitive industry that competes with the people for profit, resulting in monopolistic profits and excessive incomes. We can see that the problem of state-owned enterprises has been transformed into how to manage state-owned assets and how to form equal competitive conditions for all kinds of enterprises.

Redefining the relationship between state-owned enterprises and the state has always been the key to enterprise reform and continues to this day. The initial reforms were characterized by the state's transfer of profits to enterprises. They adopted reform measures such as profit retention, profits and taxation and transfer of loans, which enhanced the company's responsibility as a market economy subject and adjusted the way in which the state managed state-owned enterprises. In 1988, the State Council established the State-owned Assets Administration Bureau. On March 16, 2003, the State-Owned Assets Supervision and Administration Commission was established to perform the investor's duties on behalf of the State. The scope of supervision is the state-owned assets of the centrally-owned enterprises (excluding financial enterprises). Local governments also set up corresponding institutions to manage state-owned assets of local companies. The reforms currently being promoted are directed at strengthening the supervision of state-owned assets based on managing capital, reforming the authorized operating system of state-owned capital, establishing a number of state-owned capital operating companies and supporting the restructuring of state-owned enterprises into state-owned capital investment companies.

3.3   Market competition environment

In the condition that micro production units have gained management autonomy and take profits as the starting point, whether price signals are proper or not determines whether enterprises really produce for market, whether they gain profits depending on good management and whether they harden budget constraint. More importantly, the pricing mechanism in fact determines whether allocation of resources is based on the market so that it is truly efficient. As the reform of enterprises took two paths, one was reform of state-owned enterprises' own incentive mechanism and governance mode and the other was bringing competitions through non-public-owned economy's development; reform of pricing mechanism also takes a double-track transition path. Early domestic and foreign observers saw this reform path focusing on the characteristics of the old and new convergence, giving high attention and positive evaluation. For example, Norton, an American economist, has a famous statement that the new system of the Chinese economy is "growing from the plan."[7]

In the condition that state-owned enterprises obtained autonomy for some self-marketing products and self-purchasing inputs and non-public enterprises participated in competitions, the mode of distributing means of production and selling products uniformly by state planning opened a gap. Some purchasing and selling were conducted on market outside planned distribution. Therefore, besides prices determined by planning, price outside planning was determined by market supply and demand, and its formation mechanism appeared. Its formation mainly reflects the relationship between market supply and demand, and it depends on the market mechanism. With the constant decreasing of planned production's share and increasing of the non-public economy' proportion, the share of prices determined by the market also expanded increasingly, and the double-track system gradually unified to the track of market-determined price.

In the course of economic transition in the former Soviet Union and Central and Eastern European countries with planned economies, many of them had shock therapy of suddenly liberalizing prices, which caused vicious inflation and led to stagnation or even regression of economic growth. China in the late 1980s once also tried to use package reform to correct distorted price signals. However, China soon suffered the threat of inflation, and China's price index of retail goods increased 18.5% in 1988, achieving the highest inflation rate during the period of planned economy and reform and opening-up. Therefore, this reform was called to a halt immediately, and reform and development entered the period of governance and reorganization.

At the same time, the double-track price system's pace of transition had not stopped, and a few years later, namely in the mid-1990s, parts of social retail goods priced by the government or by its guidance became quite small. In the formation of prices of agricultural products and means of production, the proportion of market mechanism also improved to a great extent. Since then, the pricing mechanism has been finally affected by the product market.

It is generally believed that the Chinese means of production market lags behind products' production. The pricing mechanism of means of production, especially capital, labor and land, has not been fully determined by the market. Although this judgment that reforms in different fields are in order has some basis, we should not deny the extent of the growth of the production factor market so far and the reform achievements in the formation mechanism of the factor of production. Especially since the 18th National Congress of the CPC, the depth and breadth of reforms have been unprecedented, and the situation has undergone fundamental changes.

The development of capital market can be observed from three aspects: reform of bank system, development of capital market and interest rate liberalization. Taking implementation of "Loaning Instead of Allocating" as timing and a logical starting point, the reform of the bank system began.[8] An important clue of progress for this kind of reform was to change the situation that the People's Bank of China governed the world and operated all financial businesses to successively separate the commercial banks from central banks, commercial banks from policy banks and then the securities industry and insurance industry from banking. At the same time, the joint-stock banks, local commercial banks and foreign banks gradually entered, having greatly increased competition factors. After joining the WTO, China completed the reform of major state-owned commercial banks for the shareholding system based on the principle of building "modern financial enterprises."

Although in the early 1990s, marked by two stock exchanges' establishments in Shanghai and Shenzhen, the capital market's development broke through the ideology confinement of "belonging to socialism or capitalism," the proportion of direct financing has been improved. However, the role of stocks in corporate financing has not been significant so far. The indirect financing of bank loans is still the main form of financial markets. For example, in the total amount of funds obtained from the financial system in the real economy in 2016, that is, 17.8 trillion Yuan of total social financing, RMB loans accounted for 69.8%, corporate bonds accounted for 16.9% and the ratio of financing through domestic stock markets only accounted for 7%. Between direct financing and indirect financing, although there is a certain proportion of reasonable relations based on specific national conditions, the actual existence of such a proportional relationship also reflects the development level of financial markets to a certain extent.

However, under the premise of indirect financing, the degree of interest rate liberalization determination is an important benchmark reflecting the development level of the financial market. In 1993, the central government established a market interest rate management system that set up a market interest rate system based on the supply and demand of market capital, the central bank's benchmark interest rate as the core of regulation and market capital supply and demand that determined various interest rates. Since liberalizing interbank lending rates in 1996 and taking the first step toward interest rate liberalization, China had successively liberalized bond market interest rates and gradually established an interest rate formation mechanism of the monetary market and government bond market, setting a benchmark interest rate for the government's interest rate adjustment, which was another important step to promote interest rate liberalization. After that, the People's Bank of China gradually called off the upper limit of the RMB loan interest rate, relaxing restrictions on the upper limit of deposit rate and lower limit of loan rate, and in July 2013 comprehensively liberalized financial institutions' lending rates control. In 2014, the upper limit of the floating range of deposit interest rates was significantly increased. Until then, the degree of interest rate liberalization had been greatly improved.

The development of the labor market is promoted through the two stages of incremental stock and related approaches, initially manifested in the late 1980s, cross-regions, cross-industries and cross-urban and rural areas' large-scale transfers. Enterprises absorbing these transfers of labor forces included non-public enterprises and some public-owned ones that produced for the market. As a result, these labor employments were market-allocated from the beginning, and workers' wages were close to market equilibrium level. At the same time, the youth in rural areas who had settled in the cities to return to urban areas for employment of knowledge-based youth and the new growth of the urban labor force were increasingly relying on unplanned and independent ways of choosing jobs.

Many people think that determination of migrant workers' wages is affected by institutional factors. Therefore, it is a kind of discriminatory wage rather than a market wage. Admittedly, due to the existence of the household registration system, migrant workers did not obtain an urban house account after entering the city, and their employment was often restricted by the policy. Moreover, under the conditions of the dual economic development, because the large-scale surplus labor has not yet been settled by the market, the wages of agricultural transfer labor do not fully reflect their marginal productivity. However, compared with state-owned enterprise employees' wage determination, migrant workers' wages are mainly affected by labor supply and demand, thus market-oriented.

Another path of the labor market's development is under competition pressure from migrant workers and newly emerged laborers; state-owned enterprises have mainly changed mechanisms of labor allocation and wage formation incrementally through employment system reforms of cutting down stuff to improve efficiency and "break the iron rice bowl." In the late 1990s, China suffered macroeconomic downturn, Southeast Asian financial crises as well as overall loses and mass layoff of state-owned enterprises, resulting tens of millions laid-off workers. Under the premise of obtaining certain policies and assistance, laid-off workers and unemployment laborers could only go to the labor market as self-employed persons. Thus market-oriented allocation of labor sources was formed.

After entering the 21st century, especially with China's accession to the WTO, its economy growth recovered. All kinds of enterprises restored their capability of creating employment, and state-owned enterprises helped laid-off workers find re-employment. At this time, they adopted a market-oriented wage determination mechanism and way of employment. At present, migrant workers, urban workers and all kinds of graduates are no longer assigned work by the government. Instead, they look for jobs in the labor market, negotiate wages and working conditions and sign labor contracts. With the emergence of the labor shortage phenomenon, the wage level is significantly closer to the marginal productivity of labor. At the same time, major breakthroughs have been made in the construction of the labor market system. Labor legislation and law enforcement, the minimum wage system and collective bargaining systems have clearly enhanced the formulation of the labor market.

In the early 1980s, when the system mode of collective-owned land and family·management were established, the constitution revised in 1982 specified that urban land was owned by the state. The market-oriented process of land resource allocation was based on these two kinds of ownership systems, following the basic agricultural management system and in accordance with the principle of usufruct in property law.

First of all, the household contract system, especially after the second round of contracting, clearly defined farmers' land contract rights, stabilized their management expectations and also promoted re-allocation of rural land resources, showing a "Soto effect."[9] For example, under current forms of rural land property rights, subcontracting and subletting of farmers' contracted lands have widely existed between farmers, thus support labor's transfer to municipal departments. Farmers give their contracted land to companies to manage in the form of taking stakes and receive agricultural economies of scale. Farmers use the management right of contracted land for mortgage loans and to improve their financing ability. In general, farmers' land usufruct is guaranteed, and at the same time, land resource allocation efficiency is improved.

The 19th CPC National Congress made two major deployments to the rural land system. The first is the requirement to deepen the reform of the rural land system and improve the system of separation of ownership of contracted land, contracting rights and operating rights. The second is to maintain the stability of the land contract and remain unchanged for a long time. The second round of land contracting will be extended for another 30 years. This not only guarantees the stability of farmers' expectations and business enthusiasm but also provides a mechanism for re-allocation of land resources, which has created the necessary institutional conditions for the construction of modern agricultural production methods.

Second, rural land's transferring to non-agricultural use within the framework of laws, regulations and planning has effectively supported the industrialization and urbanization process. Based on the rural collective construction land, in the 1980s and 1990s township enterprises surged up rapidly, while small towns had also developed by leaps and bounds, both of which became important driving forces of industrialization and urbanization at that time. By strict examination and approval in accordance with the planning, rural collective land was turned into state-owned land for public use or commercial development, which was important for land guarantees to greatly develop the non-agricultural industries, speed up infrastructure construction and prompt urbanization in the whole reform period.

The current land system has also been criticized by many participants and observers. Existing problems include that local governments are over dependent on GDP growth and fiscal income gained by developing land; compensations farmers get from land development are too low, while developers and investors make lots of money quickly; land circulation speed lags behind the requirements for labor transfer, and legal obstacles of using land management for mortgages and stock management still exist; the consensus on problems of whether the red line for guaranteeing food security is reasonable or not and how to maintain it has not been reached yet.

In recent years, a series of local tests on land system reform have been conducted, and some reform measures have also been authorized by the law to conduct trials on a wider scale. The first is the collective rural land right registration throughout the nation, aiming at solving land ownership disputes, safeguarding farmers' land rights, confirming and safeguarding farmers' land property rights in accordance with the law and creating conditions for construction of urban and rural unified land markets. The second is a test for land circulation tickets system; some of them have also achieved accelerated land transfer and enhanced farmers' use of land rights. The third is that some regions attempted to use the contracted land management rights as collateral for loans and were promoted. These trials are undoubtedly useful attempts to solve the previous problems, although the effect remains to be tested by practice and time.

3.4   Development-oriented government

During the entire economic reform process in China, the government's economic functions have realized important changes, from control of all economic affairs, such as allocation of resources and factors of production, determination of prices for products and factors of production, unified collection and expenditure of enterprise finance and direct replacement of enterprise for management decision-making, to manage economy indirectly through macro-control means, industrial policies and regional development strategy, forming a specializing and complementing relationship with the market. At present, the allocation of product circulation and production factors mainly depends on the market mechanism, the enterprises independently and autonomously making operational decisions and whether the government has fulfilled its responsibility to provide public services.

At the same time, it is widely noticed that in China's rapid economic growth the extent to which and ways in which central and local governments have played their roles are obviously different from the commandment of governments' economic functions written in the standard textbook. This kind of government role with Chinese characteristics is quite active, having effectively promoted economic growth so far, while also inducing many problems; these problems have become more prominent as the stage of economic development changes. Therefore, the Chinese government's performance in economic growth is not only a product of reform but also to a great extent should be the subject of further reform.

The urgent desire to develop economy and improve people's standard of living, along with local fiscal decentralization and the cadre assessment system, have induced in local governments strong motives of GDP growth and tax revenue growth, stimulating local governments' competition for pursuing development speed. As any observer can see, the local government usually plays the role of entrepreneur, directly involved in investment promotion, planning and construction, "seeking favor from ministries" and other activities so that some scholars straightforwardly call this type of government development-oriented government, entrepreneur government or competitive government respectively.[10]

For this reason, some observers marvel at the Chinese government's resource mobilization capability, while some are critical about that, totally negating the government's behaviors of pure pursuit of GDP growth. Professor Zhang Wuchang thinks that the system inducing fierce competition among local governments, which specifically refers to governments at the county level, has created "economic growth almost of wonders," thus "it is the most effective system for economic growth in human history."[11] Whether we accept any research conclusion or not, we must admit that competitive government is indeed an important factor of

China's rapid economic growth. Therefore, even if it is a deviation needing to be corrected, fairly exploring its rational foundation is also necessary.

First of all, only economic growth can improve total economic output and the level of per capita income, thus reflecting the performances of local governments with hard indicators. No matter how many disputes exist, GDP is still the most important tool to fully measure economic growth. Besides, for countries and regions with a very low starting point, development is indeed the absolute principle. Therefore, it is understandable that pursuing GDP becomes the direct target of competitive government.

Second, many government officials once believed that the relationship among economic growth, employment and the income of residents has a straightforward correspondence. Therefore, promoting growth is also ensuring people's well-being. For quite a long time, governments at all levels believed that economic growth could automatically bring employment growth, thus improving people's living standard. Therefore, every time economic fluctuation and downward trend appeared, even when central government deliberately regulated the phenomenon of an overheated economy, local governments always righteously or secretly maintained their expectations for economic growth in the name of ensuring employment.

Finally, some leaders of local governments still think that only when GDP increases can tax revenue increase and social policies such as basic social insurance and minimum living allowance be implemented, providing better public services in compulsory education, indemnificatory housing and other fields so as to realize coordinated development between economy and society. This is why after the Party Central Committee put forward people-oriented scientific concepts of development, especially after emphasizing the requirement of coordinated development between economy and society, different regions did not lose any enthusiasm for GDP competitions.

It can be seen that, at least from a superficial point of view, if sparing no effort to pursue and compare the speed of economic growth is for the local government and its officials a way to make the central government and the people be satisfied, why not?

In breaking through the confinement of neoclassical economics, we have sufficient reasons to say that the government has played a positive role in the process of reform and opening-up as well as economic development. For example, promoting reforms needs a government to build consensus as well as design and implement specific programs; during the process of gradual transformation from planned economy to market economy, the mechanism of market-allocating resources cannot reach the designated position with one step, therefore, specific government functions are needed to compensate for the vacuum of the market. Under the condition that the credit system needed by market economy is not completed, especially when the system vacuum is formed in the shifting process from planning method to market mechanism, the lack of market transaction parties' integrity needs to be complemented by corresponding government functions. When pure entrepreneurship is not provided, it is necessary to depend on government officials' human capital to seize the opportunity for economic development.

However, in the areas where government functions promote economic development, it is also easy to cause problems of "too much of a good thing" so that an eternal topic about the relationship between government and market is formed in economics. In the period of China's reform and opening-up, excessive interventions indeed existed in some governmental measures of promoting rapid economic growth, such as industrial, regional and macroeconomic regulation and control policies that produced excessive intervention. Therefore, the market mechanism's efficient allocation of resources was hampered, which even hindered further reform of the economic system.

First of all, the policy measures aiming to support certain strategic industries and government strategies were implemented to balance regional development generally relying on large projects as well as the state-owned enterprise's leading role and "influence" to implement. Besides, macro-control policies tend to stress "protect and constrain," which originally meant protecting investment favorable for employment and optimization of industrial structure and constraining investment for industries with high energy consumption, high pollution and overcapacity. However, in the case of using administrative means excessively, it is easy to fall into the situation that big projects and state-owned enterprises are protected, while private investments and the non-public economy are constrained.

Correspondingly, these large-scale construction projects, "strategic" industries and state-owned enterprises that are actually protected have their own policy dependence and are unwilling to face market competition and influence local governments with their impact on GDP and tax revenue growth. Decisions of government and government departments, in turn, capture policy development and policy tendencies, safeguarding their privilege of obtaining subsidies and monopoly status and soft budget constraints. The result of this pattern is to restrain the development of small and medium-sized enterprises and the private economy, hinder the free entry and withdrawal of industries, reduce the efficiency of the allocation of production factors and injure the competition mechanism for survival of the fittest. Finally, some projects and enterprises are also placed in a situation where they lack efficiency and viability.

Second, government-led and investment-driving industrial policy and regional policy gradually evolve into a kind of surpassing strategy, which has some similarities with the strategy of "heavy industry as development priority" in the period of planned economy, namely giving preference for financial support to large projects and large state-owned enterprises, suppressing small and micro enterprises financially and hindering financial system reforms. For example, state-owned commercial banks must also provide sufficient and low-cost loans to large state-owned enterprises, and they are reluctant to bear the investment risks of small and medium-sized enterprises and start-up companies. At the same time, in order to maintain its own profitability, it is also necessary to lower the deposit interest rate, which in effect forms a situation in which the depositors subsidize enterprises and distort the distribution of national income.

Third, government fiscal funds, which play an important role in this type of investment, also have soft budget constraints, since the distribution lacks market assessment. Therefore, they become a kind of institutional rent, contributing to rent-seeking incentives of local government, investors and corporations, which also lead to failure in prohibiting corruption and to corruption flourishing. For example, the widely criticized financial transfer payment is generally due to the fact that there are few general projects and special projects, and the situation that has not been changed for a long period of time is the result of renting and rent building by departments that have the power to allocate resources. Due to the existence of this situation, not only does the allocation of resources deviate from the efficiency principle and inhibit potential innovation activities, it also causes the high debt of local governments, and the direction of reform of the fiscal system to public finances is hindered. The progress of the reform is not satisfactory in a period of time.

In addition, economic growth competitions between local governments have indeed motivated government officials' working enthusiasm; however, linking investment performance to officials' personal economic interests and promotions distorts evaluation and incentive mechanisms of officials' working performances. An early study by Zhang Wuchang found that in some county-level governments, 1%–2% of the amount of foreign capital can be used as rewards for officials who have contributed.[12] The phenomenon of government officials taking commissions has undoubtedly ruined the corporate culture and worsened the business policy environment. Although this is not necessarily a common phenomenon, local government officials do receive such benefits by directly participating in the allocation of resources. At the same time, they don't have to be responsible for investment effects, so it is easy to get things alienated to the situation of attracting investment only for getting commissions.

Finally, this kind of local governments' competitions for attracting investment and capital will inevitably lead to their competitions for lowering prices in the factors of production, resulting in artificial distortion of cost of production. Land expropriation compensation for farmers is pretty low, so there is a huge space between land cost and auction price. In order to attract investment, many local government promise land prices far lower than the market level and provide land for free. Even "Zero premium" of offering "three supplies and one leveling" is very common. Even so, local governments still benefit a lot from selling land, and many of them earn big on land, thus local finances depend seriously on land sales.

In response to the implementation of a large-scale stimulus package to cope with international financial crisis, such as in the period after 2009, local governments used land revenue as a guarantee for bold debts. According to the audit investigation of the National Audit Office, local governments' debt reached 10.7 trillion Yuan in 2010. Then it further accumulated and may have exceeded more than 12 trillion Yuan in 2012. This kind of government debt grows too fast and depends too much on land revenue; therefore there exist big risks. For example, some local governments' debt of repaying capital with interest in 2012 may have reached 1.25 times the size of disposable land income, and a large part needs to be repaid by raising new debt or financial income. In addition, there are many violations and corruptions in the management of such debt.[13]

Since the party's 18th National Congress, the Central Government has been making great efforts to take effective measures to resolve the risks of debt and has achieved remarkable results. The level of China's debt is generally controllable. However, there is still a phenomenon that some local government debts are growing faster and are borrowed illegally. According to the audit results, by the end of March 2017, from the perspective of the audited regions, the government's debt risk at this level was generally controllable, but the government's commitment to repay the debt balance with fiscal funds was still 87% higher than at the end of June 2013, among which the grassroots district counties and the Western region have more than doubled its growth; in some places, large amounts of bank debt, trust financing and other forms of bank loans have been reserved.[14]

Economic growth competitions between local governments also tend to underestimate the cost of resources and environment, making it difficult for economic growth income to compensate for the cost of resource exhaustion and environmental damage it caused. Although the labor price has been determined by the market, due to the existence of institutional barriers such as the household registration system, migrant workers do not enjoy equal basic public services, the coverage rate of social insurance is very low and some companies deliberately evade the implementation of labor contract law and other labor. The basic social insurance and other requirements stipulated in the regulations have also led to artificially depressed labor costs. The enthusiasm for competition among local governments, as well as the inequitable responsibilities and capabilities of basic public services and the incompatibility of incentives for reforms, have become an intrinsic motivation to hinder the reform of the household registration system.

The development-oriented government with Chinese characteristics formed during the reform process has undoubtedly made important contributions to the rapid economic growth that has been achieved so far, and we can indeed draw some useful lessons from it. However, should we accept Professor Zhang Wuchang's conclusion that the competition between local governments is a "most effective system"? Although economics is an empirical science, the conclusions drawn from the study should not be too absolute. However, the previous issues concerning the government-led growth model apparently do not support Professor Zhang Wuchang' conclusions.

How to treat a situation where local governments competing with each other and pursuing the model of economic growth not only involves evaluating the effectiveness of past reforms but also has a close relationship with the direction of how to choose further reforms? Apart from saying nothing, Zhang Wuchang's argument is that a competitive government can reduce corruption and that the labor force should not be protected by labor contracts, and it is neither a correct conclusion nor a choice of the right direction and agenda for reform. Moreover, a series of major reforms since the 18th CPC National Congress and its effects have also shown a new mode of government action and its effectiveness.

The Third Plenary Session of the 18th CPC Central Committee held in 2013 revised the "basic role" of the market in the allocation of resources to "decisive" and stressed the "better role of the government." This principle has also become an important part of Xi Jinping's socialist ideology and basic strategy with Chinese characteristics in the new era. To better play the role of the government, it is not necessary to play more of the role of the government. Rather, it must manage those things that the market can't control or manage, while ensuring that the market plays a decisive role. The responsibilities and functions of the government are mainly to maintain macroeconomic stability, strengthen and optimize public services, ensure fair competition, strengthen market supervision, maintain market order, promote sustainable development and common prosperity and remedy market failures.

Notes

1 Referred from Loren Brandt and Thomas G. Rawski. (2008). China's Great Economic Transformation. In Loren Brandt and Thomas G. Rawski (Eds.), *China's Great Economic Transformation* (p. 9). Cambridge and New York: Cambridge University Press.
2 Justin Yifu Lin, Fang Cai, and Zhou Li. (2003). *The China Miracle: Development Strategy and Economic Reform*, Revised Edition (p. 71). Hong Kong: The Chinese University Press.
3 Ronald Coase and Ning Wang (2012). *How China Became Capitalist* (Preface). New York: Palgrave Macmillan.
4 Justin Yifu Lin, Fang Cai, and Zhou Li. (2003). *The China Miracle: Development Strategy and Economic Reform*, Revised Edition. Hong Kong: The Chinese University Press.
5 Justin Yifu Lin. (1992). Rural Reforms and Agricultural Growth in China. *American Economic Review*, *82*(1), 34–51.
6 This is an important view of Deng Xiaoping in his Southern Tour Talks. See Dong Fureng (Ed.). (1999). *The Economic History of PRC*, Vol. 2 (p. 351). Beijing: Economic Science Press.
7 Barry Naughton. (1995). *Growing Out of the Plan: Chinese Economic Reform, 1978–1993*. New York: Cambridge University Press.
8 Yi Gang. (2009). Internal Logic on Reform of Bank Industry in China. In Cai Fang (Ed.), *30 Years of China's Economic Transition (1978–2008)* (pp. 101–120). Beijing: Social Sciences Academic Press.
9 Peruvian economist Soto points out that land used by the poor but with no clear property rights has big potential value, which foreign investment, credit and all kinds of aids cannot match. See Hernando De Soto. (2007). *The Mystery of Capital*. Beijing: Huaxia Publishing House. Therefore, we call land value increment and capitalization realized by utilizing the right for land potential profitability generally the "Soto effect."
10 For example, Carsten Herrmann-Pillath and Xingyuan Feng. (2004). Competitive Governments, Fiscal Arrangements, and the Provision of Local Public Infrastructure in China: A Theory-Driven Study of Gujiao Municipality. *China Information*, *18*(3), 373–428.
11 Zhang Wuchang. (2009). *China's Economic System* (pp. 146 and 165). Beijing: CITIC Publishing Company Limited.
12 Zhang Wuchang. (2009). *China's Economic System* (p. 158). Beijing: CITIC Publishing Company Limited.
13 Liu Jiayi. (2013). *Report of the State Council on Auditing Work of 2012 Central Budgetary Execution and Other Financial Revenues and Expenditures*. Retrieved June 27, 2013, from www.npc.gov/cn/npc/cwhhy/12jcwh/2013-06/27/content_1798983:html
14 Hu Zejun. (2017). *Audit Report of the State Council on the Implementation of the Central Budget and Other Fiscal Revenues and Expenditures for the Year of 2016*. Retrieved October 29, 2017, from http://politics.people.com.cn/n1/2017/0623/c1001-29359662.html

4 Globalization and the Chinese factor

Ever since economic globalization originated, since China's reform and opening-up in the early 1980s, especially since China joined the World Trade Organization (WTO) in the early 21st century, undoubtedly China has been deeply involved in this historical process, and it has become a globally recognized beneficiary and promoter of globalization. With regard to economic globalization, politicians, entrepreneurs and scholars have admittedly agreed that not all countries can benefit equally from globalization, and not all groups in a country can equally benefit from that country's participation in globalization. In many aspects and many cases, globalization has even caused the Matthew effect of "the poor poorer and the rich richer."

Indeed, no experience has demonstrated that globalization can benefit all participating countries and all groups unconditionally. However, China can maximally benefit from economic globalization. It is also a globally significant experience that can raise China's wisdom and provide developing countries with an alternative solution. The root cause is that China has made full use of its own favorable institutional advantages and economic development conditions while deeply participating in and taking full advantage of the external conditions provided by globalization. In other words, China sets foot on its national conditions, adheres to reform and opening-up and promotes development and sharing, making full use of the positive factors of participating in global economic division, avoiding the negative factors as it can, thus becoming a classical example of giving full play of comparative advantages to realize economic catch up and benefits to all people.

4.1 Meaning of globalization

It is generally believed that globalization arose in the 1950s. However, there are also some people who think that globalization should be traced back to an earlier date, for example, Britain in the middle and late 19th century, since Britain was the world's largest economy at that time, with its GDP accounting for nearly 10% of the world as a whole, the ratio of exports to GDP exceeding more than a third and about 60% of textile products being exported. By the late 19th century, about 40% of British domestic savings were used to invest overseas. However, it was more like a scene in the monologue with the title "globalization of one country." The basis of taking this phenomenon as the origin of globalization is not enough.

Combining the definition of economic globalization, which is focusing on the expansion of goods and services, foreign direct investment and significant geopolitical changes, taking into account the breadth of participating countries and the performance of China in embracing the world economy in high-speed growth, we can approximately take the year 1990 as the beginning of this round of globalization. On the one hand, China began its reform and opening-up in the early 1980s as a catalyst for its inevitable progress and further advancement. In 1986, it applied for the restoration of the contracting party status in GATT and joined the World Trade Organization (WTO) in 2001. On the other hand, the disintegration of the Soviet Union in 1991 marked the end of the world-wide Cold War which had lasted for more than 40 years; subsequently, the countries of the former Soviet Union and Central and Eastern Europe began to undergo economic transformation. It was precisely at that time that the global flow of world trade and capital took a new step, marking the use of these historic events as a tipping point, and the globalization has entered a new climax since then.

However, the globalization with real worldwide impacts and brand new contemporary characteristics did not become a phenomenon of world universal attention until the turn of the 21st century from the 20th. Westerners believe that the New York Times represents the focus of global opinions; therefore someone made a statistical analysis and found that the articles on globalization debates published by this newspaper reached the largest number in history in 2000, never before and never again. Famous journalist Thomas Friedman argued that about at this time huge changes of the world political landscape and a series of brand-new technical inventions and applications made the world smaller and smaller; at the same time, the starting line of the competition in various countries was constantly leveled out.

Opinions about whether globalization is the Gospel or disaster are various and have brought a lot of debate. On January 30, 1999, tens of thousands of protesters gathered in Seattle to interrupt the WTO trade ministers' meeting. It was the first anti-globalization protest. Some protesters climbed onto the flagpole that morning and did not come down to declare their protest against globalization. And some protesters dismantled the McDonald's fast food restaurant which was taken as a symbol of globalization and had fierce conflicts with the police. Since then, any world-wide conference or forum on globalization has hardly encountered strong or even violent resistance. Although this kind of anti-globalization movement can be cracked down on by the police, and street protesters do not have real discourse power after all, conferences aiming to reach consensus on various conferences of globalization are mostly aborted in this protest atmosphere.

In the public opinion circles and the theoretical circles for globalization, to a large extent there is no unanimously defined definition. At that time people participated in activities that opposed and resisted globalization and all of them had their own motivations respectively. For example, some are for refusing the invasion of the capitalist system and way of life, some are for their fear of foreign competitors, some are for defending labor interests from the harm of industrial decline, still there are others equaling globalization with environmental degradation or simply blaming all their dissatisfactions of reality on globalization and regarding it as the root of all evils or scapegoat, to name but a few.

Let's return to the economists' understanding of globalization. As soon as economics was born, Smith saw the productivity difference between countries, the so-called absolute advantage or absolute inferiority of productive capacity, while Ricardo found that even if a country's productivity of all products was lower than another country, it could still have comparative advantages in the production of certain goods. Since then, modern economists including Heckscher, Ohlin and Samuelson have put this idea into theories and models, forming the well-known comparative advantage theory that we must study in the economics class.

Therefore, we have got the first definition of globalization in economics. A relatively narrow statement commonly accepted is that globalization means mass global flow of goods and services. Since every country has comparative advantages and can benefit from trade, more and more countries participate in international trade of products and services, and expanding their scales unprecedentedly. This is naturally a process that generates global benefits.

Economists not only are concerned with economic globalization but also recognize that globalization can contain broader content. For example, Stiglitz defines economic globalization on the one hand as "leading to greater economic interaction among countries in the world through the expansion of the flow of goods and services, capital, and even labor" and acknowledges on the other hand that globalization also includes international flow of creativity and knowledge, cultural sharing, global civil society and global environmental movement.[1] Krugman believes that globalization is an all-inclusive expression of the increasing world trade, the connection of financial markets in various countries and many things that make the world smaller.[2]

China's reform and opening-up since the 1980s was undoubtedly involved into globalization. And then China actively participated in negotiations and applied to join the General Agreement on Tariffs and Trade Organization – which is the World Trade Organization (WTO) today – and eventually entered the WTO in 2001, meaning that it has a more active stance in joining globalization. For China, the entry into the WTO means opening to other contracting countries, as well as enjoying more favorable accesses to goods and services, platforms to solve trade disputes and say on the rules of international trade under the premise of a necessary transition period, thus it can gain a better environment for trade development.

Located in East Asia, China also enjoys a regional advantage, allowing it obtain the benefits of economic globalization more significantly, that is, to become a part of the so-called Flying Geese Model. At Nagoya University in the 1930s, Kaname Akamatsu was about to begin his career of economic research after studying in Europe and the United States. Soon he put forward a theory that is well known later and was called the "Flying Geese Paradigm" in English.

At first, this theoretical model was only used to describe how Japan, as a recently developed economy, had used the changes of dynamic comparative advantages to complete a completed "import-import substitution-export" catch-up process. Since then, owing to the contributions of several Japanese economists, such as Kojima, it has become popular gradually and is used to explain and understand the East Asian economic development mode, which is according to the dynamic change of comparative advantage; labor-intensified industries have been transferred among the Four Asian Tigers, East Asian countries and then China's coastal provinces to promote the whole region's economic development and catch up.

Therefore, many researchers take China's participation in globalization, the process of turning rich and cheap labor forces to competitive manufacturing industry products, as a part of the "Flying Geese Pattern" formed in East Asia. In this way, globalization's connotation is extended, which means globalization is not only the expansion of products and services around the world but also the unprecedented expanding of capital flow. It was just in the 1980s that the more developed economies in East Asia gradually gave up the production of labor-intensive products and realized an even more capital-intensive and technology-intensive upgrade of the industry. At the same time, starting from the establishment of special economic zones and opening of coastal cities, China gradually realized its overall economic opening-up, received labor-intensified industries and introduced foreign direct investment. It finally became a global manufacturing center and was called the workshop of the world.

Paul Romer, who is widely known as the father of the endogenous growth theory, emphasizes people's role of intentionally conducting research and exploration to promote technology advances in economic growth. As a result, in his opinion, globalization is more an idea's flow globally. In fact, this definition has not contradicted the principle of comparative advantage.

First, it is an extension of comparative advantage theory in concept. As Bernard Shaw says, if you have one apple and I also have one, we each still have one after we exchange them, yet if you have one idea and I also have one, we can both have two ideas after we exchange them.

Second, the flow of ideas usually needs to depend on forms as global trade and flow of factors of production. Through trade of products and services, as well as introduction of foreign capital, developing countries can learn advanced technologies and administrations. Human capital flows across the countries in a scale never seen before through negotiations, visits and studying abroad, which is a greater chance of widely exchanging and absorbing ideas.

4.2   Catch up and convergence

According to the traditional definition of globalization with the scale of trade in goods and services, China's opening-up has undoubtedly made marvelous achievements. In addition, China has attracted large-scale foreign direct investment as well as exchanges of people and ideas; it has broken through the supply bottlenecks such as lack of capital, management, technology and human capital gaps, inadequate resource allocation capacity and other resource supply capacity shortages. Other countries have demand for products with comparative advantages in China, but these also helped China fill the gap in demand that is necessary for high-speed growth.

Much research has proved that the process of lately developed countries' catching-up with developed countries is not as easy as early neoclassical growth theory had expected. Theoretically, due to the law of diminishing returns of capital, recently developed countries can gain a higher return on capital than developed countries. Once they have necessary system conditions, policy preparations and factors of production supply needed for economic growth, they can achieve the goal of convergence with faster growth. However, although convergence is not without precedent in reality, it is as rare as morning stars in human economic history.

Some studies on growth have found that the long time needed for convergence is depressing. Even if recently developed countries in the economy have possessed all conditions of economic growth the same as advanced countries and enjoyed late-starting advantages in technology and the system, thus being able to implement economic catch-up strategy with faster growth, the process of convergence is still prolonged. This is because there is a huge economic development gap in today's world, which is the result of economic growth difference over a long time. For many typical rich and poor countries, if we want to explain the huge difference between them in the overall economy, per capita income and quality of life, we need to trace back to the industrial revolution in the late 18th century and early 19th century, as well as the "great divergence" worldwide caused by it.

In other words, the gap formed in hundreds of years might need the same length of time to be eliminated. Economists Robert Barro and Xavier Sala-i-Martin have given an example to explain the long time to realize catch up. America's GDP per capita was $18000 in 1990, which was 285 times of Ethiopia's $285. They imagine, if America no longer grows and Ethiopia keeps its average annual growth rate of 1.75%, which has been maintained by America for a long time, it needs 239 years to realize convergence. Even if Ethiopia's growth rate rises 1%, meaning it keeps Japan's long-term growth rate 2.75% to catch up, it still needs 152 years to catch up with the invariable America.

The above theories and experience tell us that it is impossible to achieve economic catch up with the same growth rate as spring rain, and a high-speed increase like rainstorm is enough to produce substantial convergence effects. A well-known rule of thumb in statistics is the "rule of 72," namely, if an economy grows at 1% a year, it needs 72 years to double itself; if it grows at 7.2% per year, it needs 10 years to double itself and if it grows at 10% per year, it needs only 7 years to double itself. During the period from 1978 to 2011, China's average annual GDP growth rate approached 10% and then was expected to maintain a growth rate of around 7% in many years after the first decade in the 21st century. Therefore, we have got an interesting "Summers Assumption."

Lawrence Summers is an economics talent not punctilious, who likes to imagine how future historians view the age we live in. He thinks that 300 years later, when the people of the future write our history today, they may not remember the end of the Cold War, nor will they remember the "9 • 11" event, but it will inevitably be a big book that China is in the history of mankind because of its rapid economic growth. Living standards in a person's life cycle can be improved for the first time in human history: a person's life cycle can witness a 100-fold increase in living standards and its impact on other people in the world, the important impact of the global economy and its significant impact on the world's population and the global economy.

A strong desire to catch up is the original intention of the birth of development economics, and revelation of the reason of convergence is the driving force of economic growth theory's evolution. The story of China's economic catch up and convergence, as well as its relationship with globalization, will inevitably make important annotations for economic growth and globalization as well as related theories. In particular, for a recently developed country, the constraints of catching up developed countries in the economy are both supply side and demand side factors. To understand how China benefits from globalization during the period of reform and opening-up, we can focus on factors from two aspects – supply and demand.

4.3   Break the bottleneck of supply

Let's first look at how globalization helps China break through constraints of economic growth on the supply side. Factors of economic growth on the supply side generally mean factors of production supply and productivity improvement capabilities, which usually constitute a recently developed country's growth "bottleneck," including supplies of capital, technology, labor and human capital as well as the improvement of total factor productivity.

More specifically, in a growth account or production function that describes the economic growth process, when you put GDP growth on the left side of equal sign as variables to be explained, all independent variables explaining growth performances on the right side of the equation are factors of economic growth on the supply side. Most of the studies conducted in this quantitative analysis of economic growth generally choose the variables such as capital accumulation, labor supply, human capital (workers' education standards), total factor productivity etc. to explain economic growth rate. Participation in economic globalization's forces on these variables, or the opening-up factors' promoting effects on supply and utilization of factors of production as well as on productivity improvement, could be described as globalization's contribution to the potential growth rate.

For early development economists, the supply side bottleneck for any country to achieve economic take-off is capital accumulation. Traditional economic theories emphasize a lot capital accumulation's decisive role in the process of economic development. The Famous Harrod-Domar growth model, which has dominated economic growth theories for many years, just focuses on one factor-saving rate. And some development economists simply take a certain level of savings rate as a necessary condition for economic take-off.

For instance, Lewis and Rostow respectively put forward the necessary rate of capital accumulation to realize economic take-off. Lewis believes that the core issue of economic development is a certain level and rapid increase in capital accumulation or how to increase saving rate and investment rate from 4%–5%

or even lower to 12%–15% or even higher. In Rostow's view, economic growth usually proceeds along five stages: (1) stage of traditional society, (2) stage to create premises for take-off; (3) stage for taking off, (4) mature stage, (5) stage of large amount of mass consumption. He takes saving rate and investment rate's increases from 5% to 10% or higher as a necessary condition for the key stage of economic take-off.

Starting from the neoclassical growth theory, technological progress and productivity improvement are more emphasized. Solow finds that the economic growth performance includes a part that cannot be explained by input of production factors. For example, when both capital and labor input increase by only 2%, the output may increase by 3%, and there is one percent growth rate that does not know where it comes from. When it is not yet understood what this additional growth component is, it is statistically referred to as the Solow residual. Later, economists found that this residual reflects various factors that can increase productivity, such as technological progress and allocation efficiency. From this point on, it is called total factor productivity (TFP).

Solow's research shows that under the condition of diminishing returns on capital, total factor productivity is the only sustainable source of economic growth. Starting from this Solow dogma, many economists have doubted the "East Asian miracle" and predicted its economic growth cannot be sustained since these economies lack productivity and only rely on capital and labor inputs.

Here is an interesting story. The World Bank published a report in 1993, which first introduced the world to the "East Asian miracle" represented by the Four Asian Tigers and other economies' economic growth performances with its authority. After this report, not to mention debates about the causes of the East Asian miracle, opinions were various on whether the so-called miracle itself existed or not. A number of scholars good at econometric analysis such as Alwyn Young and Lawrence Lau find the reason that those countries and regions having created the "East Asian miracle" have achieved good performance of high-speed economic development is in fact by input increase, rather than by productivity improvement. They all agree that, excluding the factors of investment, "miracles" disappear immediately, as "falling from the top of Mountain Olympus to the plain of Thessaly." This is also the conclusion drawn from factors on the supply side.

However, after the Four Asian Tigers and Chinese mainland's successful economic catch up, seen from today, it seems that this view is wrong. As for why economists have made errors in judging the East Asian miracle and whether their theoretical and empirical studies have some reasonable parts, we will continue to discuss them in later chapters. Here, we only need to observe one fact: that owing to the high cohesion of China's demographic transition stage and economic take-off stage, it has not only broken the "bottleneck" of capital accumulation successfully but also broken through the assumption of neoclassical growth theory – diminishing returns to capital.

For a backward country in economy, low per capita income means capital accumulation that can be used for investment is insufficient. This truth has long been clearly explained by the "Vicious Circle of Poverty" Hypothesis. It is based on

Malthus' Poverty Trap Theory, which assumes that in poor countries, regardless of what causes the increase in income, it usually leads to a corresponding increase in population, which in turn pulls per capita income back to a level that can only survive.

When China began its reform and opening-up in the late 1970s and early 1980s, its per capita GDP was less than $200, thus it undoubtedly met the standard for backward countries. Therefore, according to "Double Gap" Theory in development economics, which means that larger domestic investment than saving leads to capital insufficiency and trade deficit leads to lack of foreign currency, introducing foreign direct investment undoubtedly helps China to break the "bottleneck" of capital accumulation significantly.

However, this is not globalization's main contribution. Or we can say, before understanding globalization's positive role on capital accumulation, we need to first understand how globalization turns China's special population factors into demographic dividend, which promotes economic growth directly. Since the mid-1960s, China's dependency ratio of population (i.e., the ratio of dependent population to working-age population) began to decline as a result during the period of reform and opening-up, China's accumulated potential energy for demographic dividend could be fully released.

Under China's special circumstances, cashing potential demographic dividend is the most important factor of participating in economic globalization. Under the condition of possessing a large number of labor force surplus, only when transforming cheap labor force into resource comparative advantage condensed in labor-intensive products through international trade and then gaining international competitiveness and market share can the demographic dividend be fully cashed. Once provided with this condition, demographic dividend's manifestation of working-age population's increase will also have an important influence on this growth factor capital accumulation, meaning not only is the low and declining dependency ratio of the population a benefit for achieving high savings rate, but also the infinite supply of labor force can play an inhibiting role in decreasing returns to capital. Therefore, we can say that if there is no extensive participation in economic globalization, demographic dividend is only a potential gift rather than growth factor, and the growth condition of capital accumulation cannot be fulfilled.

Of course, there's no doubt that introduction of foreign direct investment also has positive effects. In addition to investment in scarce capital itself, foreign direct investment enjoys looser policy privileges; especially that it has less government interventions in the management process, which becomes a kind of system advantage. Combined with technology, management and market brought by foreign investment, they usually have a higher resource allocation efficiency, which is also a globalization factor more important than capital itself.

As early as in the period of planned economy in the mid-1960s, China's dependency ratio of population began to drop down, and in the mid-1970s growth rate of working-age population was significantly faster than the whole population growth rate. That is to say, demographic factors had potentially possessed the conditions for generating demographic dividend.

It can be seen that due to lack of necessary institutional conditions for economic growth, favorable demographic factors not only have not been converted to the source of growth but also have been accumulated into redundant rural labor forces and urban enterprise workers due to stagnant growth and institutional constraints. Only under the conditions of reform and opening-up can this surplus labor can be released and become a source of economic growth.

In the process of export-oriented labor-intensive industries' development, a series of important labor force transfers have appeared. Since industries participating in globalization are necessarily export-oriented, most concentrate in economically developed areas taking the lead in reform and opening-up and are mainly dominated by the non-public economy; the transfer of agricultural labor force surplus follows the modes as from agricultural to non-agricultural industries, from the Midwest China to coastal areas, as well as from previous state-owned enterprises to non-public economic enterprises. Realization of such a labor transfer process means more efficient allocation of resources. In the period of China's reform and opening-up, this efficiency of resource re-allocation constitutes an important part of total factor productivity.

Krugman once quoted a fable in economics textbooks: an American company claimed to have made a mysterious "technology innovation" and put it into practical application, transferring this country's abundant wood and wheat into consumer goods of huge market demand, thus earning a great deal. However, after investigating seriously, people found that this company did not have any real technology. It just carried wood and wheat to Asia and then exchanged them for manufactured goods needed by consumers. After all, this company just simply used the principle of comparative advantage to do trade. Krugman's intention in telling this story is to show us that trade is not mysterious; it is only a management process just like producing and manufacturing.

However, we can extend from here a different but more useful meaning. The company in this example exchanged back products needed by the domestic market with the help of international trade rather than technological innovation to realize the target for profits. In the same way, a country can absolutely achieve the same economic growth as technology innovation or productivity improvement through using comparative advantages to participate in economic globalization. That is to say, the realization of comparative advantage in the international division of labor has the same effect with technology progress, which promotes productivity and economic growth.

It can be seen that the participation in economic globalization helps China break through the "bottleneck" of factors of production's accumulation and obstacles of productivity improvement, ensuring that in more than 30 years of reform and opening-up China's economy has obtained unprecedented rapid economic growth. When reviewing how globalization promotes China's economic development positively, we can observe the miracles created by GDP's actual growth over the past 30 years not only from the statistics but also through analyzing these data, making more in-depth observations on the formation of higher potential output capacity owing to the factors of production being more fully developed.

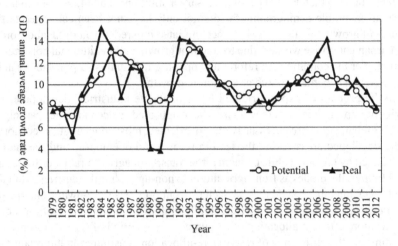

Figure 4.1 Potential and Real Economic Growth Rate

Source: Cai Fang and Lu Yang, Population Change and Resulting Slowdown in Potential GDP Growth in China, *China & World Economy*, Vol.21, No.2, 2013, pp. 1–14.

In Figure 4.1, we have given the average real GDP growth rate realized per year on average for the 30 years from 1979 to 2012, as well as the estimated average annual GDP growth rate. The latter is due to the full use of labor, capital and land resources and the output capacity that can be obtained by continuous productivity improvement. Once demand-driving factors can meet the requirements of this output capacity, consistent real growth rate can be realized.

4.4   Is this "toil just for the benefit of others"?

Domestic scholars have always been critical of China's great involvement in international division of labor to become the factory of the world and its manufacturing center. They think the exportations of low-end manufacturing products are working for multinational companies, toil just for the benefit of others. In the absence of in-depth, objective and scientific economic analysis, this criticism seems undoubtedly logical and quite consistent with Chinese people's feelings. Therefore, no matter in media or in theory circles, this view is very popular. Let's first look at the three links included in this understanding.

First, a large number of facts indicate that the exportation process of manufacturing products is mostly controlled by multinational corporations. In fact, manufactured products claiming to be "made in China" just put the simple machining parts in China, while the parts with the highest value-added ratio such as product brand, design, marketing, after-sales service and other such processes are controlled by foreign companies. Factories in China only earn a negligible fraction of profits. For example, according to the report of the *New York Times*, researchers in Silicon Valley broke down the iPhone 4 to find that in this product from Apple Inc. the manufacturing process with the smallest fraction of costs is in an assembly plant in Shenzhen, while more than 100 kinds of components with high profits are respectively microchips made by Germany and South Korea, mobile phones chips for wireless Internet or cell phone signals made by America, touch screens made by Taiwan and so on, not to mention the huge profits earned by Apple Inc. as product developer.

Second, China's massive exportation fed by these low-profit enterprises causes huge surplus with the United States and Europe, thus to forming the largest foreign exchange reserves worldwide. In the absence of safe and reliable investment purposes, these foreign exchange reserves are in turn invested in developed countries, especially in the fields with low rate of return but big risks such as United States Treasury bonds, which generally have negative returns. Such investments not only bear the losses of dollar depreciation, some even go down the drain in the case of financial crisis.

Third, although China's high saving rate and America's high debt rate are complementary, helping America to maintain a low-saving and high-consuming mode, nevertheless it is China that is endlessly criticized, such as being given the bad name of manipulating exchange rate, setting up sweatshops, having high carbon emissions, as well as being the source of global economic imbalance etc. Accordingly, these moral frame-ups often transfer into constraints in action. As an active participant in world trade, China has increasingly become a direct target of various trade protection measures and encounters increasingly powerful obstacles in opening-up to the outside world.

It is clearly seen that China being the workshop of the world is not always full of glory, but experiences difficulties and hardships everywhere. A necessary analysis on international misunderstandings and wrong actions that some countries have adopted will be conducted in the next section to clear the facts on the basis of theory and reality. Here, we need to have a look at whether China can avoid the big tide of economic globalization from the beginning. In other words, once China's participation in the international division of labor is combined with the necessary conditions needed by high-speed growth in the period of reform and opening-up, the conclusion will be quite obvious.

In the condition of having higher potential growth rate, we still need some demand factors for support to actually achieve high growth. Even when factories, machines, workers and technicians used for producing some products are all ready and transportations and other infrastructure capacities are sufficient to ensure energy supplies and product transportations, still, the actual manufacturing process of a product cannot get started if buyers of this product are lacking. In the same way, potential producing capacity with no support from demand cannot be transformed into real economic growth. In general, the demand factors of economic growth are summarized as final consumption demand, investment demand and export demand, namely "the Three Demands," among which the level of consumer demand depends on state financial resources, residents' purchasing power and consumer willingness.

China was in the queue of low-income countries defined by the World Bank not only in the early years of reform and opening-up but in most years throughout the 1980s and 1990s. According to the World Bank statistics, when China ended 10 years of turmoil of "cultural revolution," its GDP per capita, according to the constant price of 2000, was only $149 in 1977, $771 in 1997 and didn't break through the $1,000 mark until 2001. According to the World Bank's dividing standard in 1998, $760 per capita is the demarcation point between low-income countries and below-average income countries, while according to the dividing standard in 2000 $996 is the demarcation point.

By constriction of lower consumption level due to residents' lower income level, residents' final consumption demand is obviously not sufficient to support high economic growth rate for a long time. Therefore, the dependence of economic growth on investment demand and export demand will inevitably increase over time. From this perspective, the large-scale and fast-growing exportations of manufacturing products and the resulting large-scale investment demand have not only helped to realize the comparative advantage of labor abundance and cash dividend but also delay the phenomenon of decreasing returns to capital, making investment-driven economic growth continue for a long time, at the same time creating unprecedented external demand.

It can be seen later that from the reform and opening-up to the present, except for some extreme years, the contribution of final consumption has remained relatively stable. In 2001, China's accession to the WTO had been declined for some time. At the same time, the fluctuations in investment demand and net export demand were relatively large, and they had been growing rapidly after China's accession to the WTO. Therefore, the actual situation of the annual average growth rate of GDP at around 10% during this period in each year depended mainly on the performance of investment demand and export demand and the fluctuation between the two. This trend was reversed after the international financial crisis of 2008–2009; the contribution rate of consumer demand to economic growth increased, and the contribution rate of investment demand and export demand decreased.

Although from a statistical point of view, since 2001, China's net exports of goods and services have not contributed much to economic growth. Except for the importance shown in the years before the financial crisis, the overall contribution to GDP growth is even a negative number. However, this GDP-based estimate reflects only the contribution of exports as an added value. If export-oriented production is used as an economic activity, it should be measured from the used factors of production, such as the scale of labor input or employment, and it can be seen that net exports contribute to the Chinese economy's ability to realize its potential growth.

We can see that the positive effect of exports on economic activities and thus employment is significant. The existence of a large-scale surplus labor force means that China enjoys a low wage competitive advantage in the period of reaping dividends. In other words, a rich labor force has been condensed into labor-intensive manufacturing products and has become the basis of international competition – comparative advantage. As a result, China has not only become a trading power but

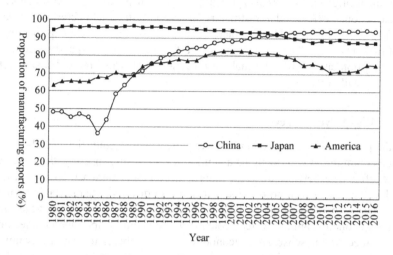

Figure 4.2 Comparative Advantages of Manufacturing in China, Japan and America

Source from: http://stat.wto.org/StatisticalProgram/WSDBViewData.aspx?Language=E, download on November 25, 2017

also gradually overtaken and even replaced the traditional manufacturing export-ing countries such as the United States and Japan in the international market, and China has become a world factory and a global manufacturing center. From the perspective of total manufacturing exports, China surpassed Japan and the United States in 2003 and 2006 respectively; in terms of the ratio of exports of manufac-turing products to total exports of goods, China surpassed Japan and the United States in 1992 and 2006 respectively. (Figure 4.2).

Through the observation of the manufacturing industry's export proportion and export-related employment proportion, it can be seen that while the degree of dependence on international market demand factors has deepened, employment has expanded. For example, the proportion of total exports in all manufacturing sales was 23.9% in 2004 and 18.9% in 2008. In all employment in manufactur-ing, the proportion of labor working for export was 26.4% and 22.3% in the two years respectively. Besides, in export-oriented enterprises of coastal areas such as the Pearl River Delta Region, due to their extensive use of liquid migrant workers and service dispatching workers, many workers in reality have not been reflected in staff statistics, thus the actual employment figure is seriously under-reported. If taking these factors into account, China's economic dependency on export demand measured by employment will be undoubtedly higher.

We can say that, since China's reform and opening-up, especially after its acces-sion to the WTO, China has been called the factory of the world or the world manu-facturing center. This phenomenon itself reflects that the factors of foreign demand have played an important and indispensable role in breaking the demand "bottle-neck" of economic growth. Not only that, the development of the export-oriented manufacturing industry has also pulled the developments of energy, raw materials, construction, services and infrastructure through industry agglomeration and externality effect, as well as location factors. Besides, as employment expands, urban and rural residents' income increases, and the purposes of expanding domestic consumption and continually making it economic growth's main demand factor are eventually realized.

4.5 Big-power effect

In the process of world economic development, while countries usually follow some common laws, showing us a similar development trajectory, there are also huge differences between different countries, presenting many varieties of the road to development. An important factor leading to different characteristics among countries is the differentiation between the big country economy and the small country economy, among which economic scale is most important and meaningful in an economic sense. Also, economic scale closely relates with many unique properties that we care about. Total economy and trade – and further total endowment of production reflected in them – both have significant impacts on a country's participation in globalization and the role of international division of labor.

China as a huge economy, once joining the economic globalization as a producer and trader, has inevitably changed the traditional international economics, although it may not necessarily change the comparative advantage theory. If we do not understand this, it will be difficult to understand why economists cannot be consistent between theory and policy suggestions or to understand why China faces so many criticisms and has become the top target of trade protectionism.

Winner of the Nobel Prize in Economics Paul Samuelson has always been dedicated to promoting Ricardo's theory of comparative advantage. It is said that when he was studying, he was once defeated by his classmates and failed to answer which theory could be considered the most accurate and important theory in the social sciences. Thirty years later, he gave the answer that the theory of comparative advantage is in line with this standard. Another American winner Paul Krugman even declares that if there must be some creed for economists, the following oaths must be included, which are "I believe in the principle of comparative advantage" and "I believe in free trade." However, when their country – the United States – is no longer the absolute beneficiary of globalization, their claims on policy are obviously inconsistent with their theories.

A new situation noticed by Samuelson is that productivity improvement makes China's comparative advantage no longer limited to the original export industry, while this comparative advantage with dynamic changes transfers China into a strong competitor of America's related industries, therefore in fact, free trade will not make the United States and China benefit equally from it. Obviously, whether as a US leading economist or as a centenarian familiar with growth and decline of countries and regions led by comparative advantage shifts in history, Samuelson will not easily give up the theory of comparative advantage nor recommend protectionist policies of any forms.

However, Samuelson has no alternative but to admit that since the beneficiaries of globalization within a country will not automatically make necessary compensations for the damaged, American workers whose jobs are replaced by Chinese competitors have undoubtedly paid the price for globalization. Another winner of the Nobel Prize in Economics, Michael Spence, draws a startling conclusion from experience studies of American employment changes, in which industry outsourcing has destroyed the American economy. US economist Paul Romer admits that free trade can fundamentally reduce inequalities among countries. However, what tangles him a lot is that sympathy for the disadvantaged people in the world is a good thing, while unfortunately inequality within the United States is rising constantly.

Facing conflicts between national interests and the principles of economics, Krugman, who has paid constant attention to income inequalities in the United States for a long time and has always been famous for being outspoken, has claimed without scruple that China's huge trade surplus is the result of official manipulation of RMB exchange rate rather than completely the result of comparative advantage. This understanding leads him to come up with policy proposals beyond the bottom line of science and even to suggest the US government taking punitive measures against China.

Blaming other countries' policy distortions for dynamic comparative advantage changes and national competitiveness decline and taking arbitrary interventions and punitive policies is not a new matter and is not happening for the first time. I was on a business trip to New York in 2010 and was set to stay at the Plaza Hotel. I vaguely felt that I had heard of this hotel before suddenly remembering that a remarkable historical event happened here, which was the signing of "Plaza Accord." On September 22, 1985, in order to get rid of the dilemma of trade and finance "Double Deficits," the United States, along with France and the United Kingdom, forced Japan and the former Federal Republic of Germany to agree to appreciate their currencies substantially.

The principle of comparative advantage has never changed, however, an important factor one is unable to neglect is the so-called big-power effect, which relates to China's status in the world economy. The traditional theory of comparative advantage assumes that there are two countries, two products and two kinds of production factors, thus demonstrating that both countries can benefit from trading. The implicit assumption here is that countries, products and elements are all homogeneous and equal. However, since China's economy is a leviathan, once it involves itself in the international division of labor, its own factors of production such as labor force and manufactured products have a scale large enough to submerge some smaller economies on the one hand and lead to some big powers' industries' decline rapidly on the other hand in international trade of certain products.

It is true that China also imports products from other countries with the same overwhelming scale, such as its strong demand for machinery and equipment from developed countries and minerals from resource-rich countries. However, due to many factors including political prejudices, the situation that each country can equally benefit from international division of labor is no longer an unalterable principle. For example, out of political preconceptions, the United States and some Western countries have imposed restrictions on China. Many high-income countries have rejected the necessary domestic redistributive policies and lacked effective social protection mechanisms, placing their social groups with sufficient competitiveness in globalization in a marginal position. It can be seen that since the problem is not unilaterally attributed to China the heavy burden of resolving the imbalance in the world economy cannot be accomplished by China alone.

First, developed countries, especially the United States', strict restrictions on exports to China have made the latter unable to play the role as the world's biggest importer at the time when it has become the world's biggest manufacturer and exporter of labor-intensive products. The United States is a country with a long tradition of trade protection, whose export restrictions on high-tech products have always been an important part of its trade policy. America's strict constrictions on exports of high-tech products to China have lasted since the establishment of the People's Republic of China, gone through the Cold War till today. Since China's accession to the WTO, Sino-US trade has significantly increased in scale. At the same time, the United States continues to implement export restrictions on China in the name of national security, causing a huge trade imbalance between these two countries. China and the United States are at different stages of development in science and technology, and the latter's more and more export restrictions on China of high-tech products obviously deviate from the principle of comparative advantage, therefore, there is no doubt that the United States' trade deficit with China needs to reflect on its own policy orientation.

Second, a country's competitiveness is ultimately the result of this country's technology progress and productivity improvement. Inhibiting trade partners' economic development environment and hindering them from playing the role of dynamic comparative advantage are not helpful for solving one's own problems. American economist Robert Gordon lists a number of factors that slow down the economic growth of America at present and will in the future keep it from innovation and the trend of its diminishing effects on promoting economic growth. Respectively, these factors are disappearance of demographic dividend, wandering of education development, worsening of inequalities, interactions between globalization and information technology, energy and environment, family and government debt etc. It is obvious that attributing economic growth, which is mainly due to domestic factors, to trade opponents, even if it is to shift people's attention politically, will ultimately lead to desperation.

Third, the United States is the absolute beneficiary of globalization after all. However, the wrong tendency of domestic economics and social policies lead to a large number of workers lacking skills for employment, and the country goes further and further along the road of unequal distribution of incomes. Blaming industry transfer and competitions brought by outsourcing to hide domestic policy mistakes will not be an effective cure for their system's ills. Yet Krugman sees the crux of the problem in this regard. He reviews the relationship between Democrats and Republicans' different policy tendencies for income distribution and the actual inequality degrees in the process of the two parties' alternation in power, and comes to the conclusion that the expansion of the income gap is closely related to the adoption of a certain kind of domestic income distribution policy. The facts will soon prove that if domestic social policies cannot be changed, even if a different kind of government is selected, getting more and more objectionable to other countries, the situation will not be fundamentally improved.

4.6 "Goose" or "tiger"

In addition to distinguishing between the economies of large and small countries from the perspective of the size of the economy, we can also look at it from another perspective. The core feature of a small country's economy is its internal resource endowment structure and the homogeneity of its industrial structure. Since there isn't production factors' flowing obstacles in system, the constant differences between regions' resources endowment structure are none, or that these differences soon disappear in the process of development. As a result, national economy as a whole obtains comparative advantages on one or some industries owing to the relative abundance or scarcity of its factors of production. Once comparative advantage changes, economy will enter a new stage of development as a whole.

Big country economy's characteristic is the heterogeneity between different regions. Influenced by institutional factors, the flow of factors of production encounter obstacles of the system, namely there exist huge differences of resource endowment structure between regions, and convergence of economic growth can't be formed for a long time. Therefore, when some regions enter into new stages of development, their endowment structures of factors of production change correspondingly, thus comparative advantages and industrial structures change. At the same time, other regions may still remain in their original development stages and can't show the corresponding structural changes.

The large- and small-country economies that are differentiated by regional homogeneity or heterogeneity will have different performances in long-term economic development. In particular, at the crucial stage of economic development, the economic performance of the two economies may present huge feature differences. According to this definition, China is the most typical big country economy. In addition to her economic aggregate ranking second in the world, the most consistent feature of the earlier definition is that, due to the absence of a nationwide integrated production factor market for a long time, the resources are relatively resource-constrained and the production factors are relatively scarce. There are huge differences in prices as well as the level of economic development.

Observing China's major economy effect in this sense, regional characteristics reflected in the process of its economic development also show its prominent uniqueness through the period of regional economic development stage shifts. That is to say, in the economically developed regions, the endowment structure of production factors changes its comparative advantage. If labor costs increase significantly, the change in relatively backward regions is not significant or even has not yet occurred. It still maintains relatively low labor cost characteristics.

Recognizing and fully understanding China's economy as a giant country's giant effect will help us judge the key turning point in the economic development stage. For example, for China, it is the disappearance of the demographic dividend, which in turn increases the cost of labor and the direction of the manufacturing industry in China or the shifting direction and transfer path of the global manufacturing center. This special regional effect of China demonstrates that although economic growth theory has summarized many economic principles and revealed many laws, every country has its own special national condition, thus can more or less be an exception of economic models. This point can be fully illustrated by comparing this big-power effect of China with the small-power effect of Singapore.

US economist Paul Krugman once criticized the East Asian model using the example of Singapore. He thought Singapore's experience showed that this country's high-speed economic development is mainly driven by the input of production factors rather than supported by improvement of productivity. Therefore, he predicted that Singapore's economic growth could not be sustainable. Many years after he made this unconfirmed prophecy, he was introduced to Prime Minister of Singapore Lee Kuan Yew at an international conference. Prime Minister Lee Kuan Yew always remembered Krugman's criticism in his heart and he said to the latter: you think what we have are all accumulations of factors of production, which cannot be supported without technological progress. Then, I ask you a question, Singapore's savings rate has been nearly 50% for the past 40 years, which can be counted as the highest in the world, but our return on capital has not decreased. If there is no technological progress, how will the return on capital not fall?[3]

If this dialogue between these two persons really happened rather than being made up, I want to clap for the question proposed by Prime Minister Lee Kuan Yew. Krugman was wrong about the East Asian model, since he took the hypothesis of the new classical growth theory as an unalterable principle, not knowing the demographic dividend and not willing to admit the existence of a development stage as a dual economy. We will explain this point in later chapters. Here what I want to say is that the challenge of Prime Minister Lee Kwang Yew certainly makes sense, but he may not be able to give a reasonable economic answer.

First of all, Lee Kuan Yew confused the difference between the marginal return rate of capital and the return rate on investors. The diminishing return on capital, which refers to the marginal remuneration of capital in the general analysis of economic growth or a specific econometric analysis, will decrease with the increase of investment. For economies with technological progress and productivity improvement, capital contribution of economic growth is replaced by corresponding improvement of total factor productivity, so that economic growth can be sustained. At this time, investment on economic process is still profitable. When Lee Kuan Yew said "return on capital has not decreased" he actually referred to the latter. As Singapore becomes a more mature economy, the phenomenon of diminishing returns on capital in the former sense will inevitably occur, which is also in conformity with the neo-classical theory of growth without exception.

Second, there is a special condition in Singapore, which Lee Kuan Yew had not mentioned to Krugman. And it was also not necessary to do so since Krugman did not understand the meaning. That is, due to a large number of Singapore's introduction of foreign labor force, the arrival of the Lewis turning point was delayed, thus the harvest time of the demographic dividend was extended. In East Asian economies, many countries and regions have used foreign workers to keep labor supply and delay the Lewis turning point. As a result, some researchers have used the shortage of labor in international or regional areas rather than in one country as a sign of Lewis's turning point. However, Singapore is an exception of using foreign workers all the time, so that about 40% of this country's GDP has been created by foreign workers till today. More or less, there is no doubt that this is an important reason why Singapore's labor supply is more abundant and then the diminishing returns on capital's delay.

For a small-power economy like Singapore, the practice of depending on foreign migration labor in great scale to keep a labor supply is feasible. However, for a big-power economy like China, this is not realistic. Let's imagine that China intends to introduce a 20- to 29-year-old labor force from other developing countries in order to increase the total employed population in 2010 by 40%; a rough calculation shows that the total demand will account for nearly 40% of the population in all other developing countries in this age group.

However, as a big-power economy, China has its own unique advantage. It can also, like Singapore, continue to carry forward the talents of being rich in labor, delay the changes in comparative advantage and gain time for its own adjustments, that is, to form a domestic version of the Flying Geese Model and thus continue to benefit from globalization for some time. On the surface, the emergence of the "labor shortage" caused by the disappearance of the demographic dividend and the rapid rise in the wages of unskilled workers seem to indicate the end of the comparative advantage of labor-intensive industries in China.

That is to say, if labor costs continue to increase, and if we follow the previous experience of the geese model, as in the process of East Asian economic development, labor-intensive industries have shifted from Japan to the four Asian dragons and then to other Asian countries and the coastal areas in China. The shift of China's labor-intensive industries to other countries seems to be logical. In fact, this conclusion is not necessarily logical, and in fact it is not accurate. At least for a certain period of time, the potential of resource re-allocation efficiency will still exist in China and is mainly reflected in the transfer of labor-intensive industries among regions.

In other words, as a big-power economy, China is not a lonely leading goose but a huge tiger which cannot be traced. We can see a number of factors which will strongly support the "Huge Tiger Model" of industries transferring in different domestic regions. Before the potential of this process is exhausted, industrial transfer can occur, but it is not sufficient to quickly obliterate the comparative advantage and competitiveness of Chinese manufacturing. And this time it means the upgrading of China's industrial structure.

One of the factors contributing to the transfer of industries between regions is that we have so far failed to see which country or group of countries has sufficient scale and power to replace China's manufacturing power. There have been some reporters who saw the arrival of investors in places like India and Vietnam due to rising wages in the coastal areas of China. They followed these investors to the new investment areas and made interviews. As a result, they were surprised to find that the wages of ordinary laborers in these countries are also rising, and they are in line with the timing of rising wages in China, and the rate of increase is almost the same.

Actually, it is not strange. Since China's cheap labor force curbed global wage increases in the past 20 years to 30 years, China's wages have risen significantly at present, and it can naturally drive wages to increase in other countries, especially those who follow China and wait to harvest demographic dividend.

As a kind of strategic thinking for investment, Goldman Sachs created the concept of "BRICS," then "Next 11," which has economic growth potentiality and is related to demographic dividend. These countries are South Korea, Indonesia, Mexico, Pakistan, the Philippines, Bangladesh, Nigeria, Iran, Vietnam, Turkey and Egypt. Since South Korea is a high-income country whose demographic transition process is similar to China, actually it should not be put in this group. However, India, which was not included in the "Next 11," is instead more compliant to the standard of being able to compete with China in labor supply potentiality and wage level, therefore, we replace South Korea with India in the comparison with China. There is no doubt that the potential manufacturing undertaking countries are far beyond this scope. Here we are just taking these countries as an example. The reasons that we want to explain will be general.

Some of these countries above undoubtedly have advantages over China in labor costs. For example, in countries such as India, Vietnam and Bangladesh, per capita GDP and wages are significantly lower than in China. However, according to the purchasing power parity, the per capita GDP of Turkey and Mexico is higher than that of China, therefore they have not formed great competitiveness from the perspective of labor costs. One important fact that needs our attention is that China is a big country in population and labor, whose status cannot be replaced by all these countries above adding up together.

For example, among the total population of working age from 15 to 64 years old of all the 12 countries in comparison in 2010, China took the absolute majority of 38%. If the world's second most populous country India was excluded, China's proportion of working-age population reached 55%. Even by 2020, the proportion of the working-age population in China remains higher than many other countries.

The large size and proportion of dominant advantages of China's labor force determine that these countries' possibility of replacing China to become the world manufacturing center is still not enough, at least for the moment. In other words, even if a smaller proportion of China's labor-intensive industries transfers to a certain country or countries, it can cause the obvious increase of related countries' labor demand, resulting in insufficient labor supply and then reducing their competitiveness because of rising wages.

It has been found in recent years that the trend of labor shortage and wage increase is very obvious in countries trying to undertake China's labor-intensive industries. Here we take India as an example. Although both its population size and working age population size are very large, the number of average years of education of the population over 25 years old in this country was only 4.4 in 2010 due to their low education levels. Since many of them cannot meet the requirements of their jobs, India's effective labor supply is actually not sufficient. This may explain why, according to certain standards, India's wage increase has been the highest in Asia for 10 consecutive years.

Obviously, labor supply not only depends on its absolute quantity and relative quantity but also on whether the skills of workers can meet their job requirements or not. In other words, the quantity of labor and human capital determine the end-result of the manufacturing industry together. Let's look at the average number of years of education for people over the age of 25 years old. Among the 11 countries that are compared with China, only Mexico and the Philippines have more educational years than China, about 13 to 14 months. And more countries' per capita years of education are much lower than China, such as that of Bangladesh, which is 33 months lower than that of China. If we calculate the product of total population over 25 years old and the average number of years of education per capita as the amount of a nation's human capital, then China accounted for more than 50% in 2010 among the 12 countries (Figure 4.3).

According to the forecast of the growth rate of per capita education of the above-mentioned countries during the period 2000–2010, the average number of years of education for people aged 25 and over in China will reach 8.63 years by 2020. At that time, China's total human capital will still account for 45% of all these 12 countries.

This prediction has several implications. First, at least until 2020, China's total human capital will still maintain a huge advantage. A certain share of labor-intensive manufacturing will be transferred to other developing countries. However, China's position as a manufacturer of such products cannot be completely

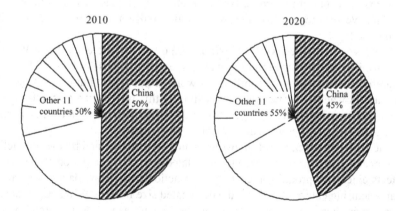

Figure 4.3 China and Other Competitive Countries' Share of Total Human Resources

Source: Calculated according to the United Nations Data

replaced. Second, the key to China's maintaining its status as a major manufacturing country is the speed and quality of human capital accumulation or educational development. The demographic transition is an irreversible process. The first demographic dividend will eventually disappear, but the quality of the workforce can be accelerated and the second demographic dividend can be unlimited. Third, countries will experience the challenge of replacing labor with capital and replacing workers with machines. The higher the human capital endowment is, the easier it will be to win in this robot-human race.

Another factor that helps industries transfer among regions is the expectation that wages in central and Western regions will continue to be lower than in the Eastern region within a certain period of time. With the emergence of a shortage of migrant workers and the creation of more employment opportunities in the development of the central and Western regions, the wages of migrant workers tend to be convergent among Eastern, central and Western regions. In 2003, the average wage of peasant workers in the central and Western regions was only equivalent to 74% of the Eastern region, and this proportion increased to 96% in 2009. It seems that wages in the central and Western regions have already reached a convergence with the Eastern region.

However, I have always believed that we can still expect that wages in coastal areas will increase faster than in the central and Western regions. Because of the total number and occurrence rate of labor dispute cases, the Eastern region accounts for an overwhelming majority. For example, 72% of the country's labor disputes on file occur in the Eastern region. The incidence of labor disputes in such regions, that is, the number of labor dispute cases per thousand employees, is 5.2, which is much higher than the 1.5 cases and 2.0 cases in the central and Western regions. Since the main controversy in labor disputes is the wage, which means the current wage level in the Eastern region is less satisfactory for workers, continuous quick wage rise can be expected in order to attract workers; it is expected that wages will continue to rise rapidly. Facts have proved that this expectation is correct. By 2016, the ratio of peasant wages in the central and Western regions to the Eastern region will return to 90.7% and 90.2% respectively.

Moreover, compared with the current wage level in the central and Western regions, it is still attractive to local workers, especially those older rural laborers. Therefore, when they are mobilized to work in non-agricultural industries, the increase in wages may be relatively stable. In this way, we can see the shift of labor-intensive industries to the central and Western regions from the perspective of regional wage differences and potential labor supply.

The regional allocation of industries is not only determined by the production factors and cost factors but also closely related with the aggregation effect, which affects enterprise production cost and transaction cost. Using data from China's manufacturing enterprises above the designated size from 1998 to 2008, (namely, prime operating revenue more than 5 million Yuan), as well as research findings of fiscal and tax data by counties,[4] the effect of industry agglomeration dominated labor-intensive industries' regional allocation before 2004, leading to more

Table 4.1 Distribution of Main Business Income of Manufacturing Industry (%)

	Eastern Region	Central Region	Western Region
First Census (2004)	72.23	18.53	9.24
Second Census (2008)	67.38	22.34	10.28
Third Census (2013)	59.64	27.93	12.44

Source: State Statistics Bureau website: www.stats.gov.cn/, download date: November 25, 2017.

concentration of the latter in the Eastern region. After that, this effect declined gradually, while increases in enterprise comprehensive management costs and factor cost gradually become important factors that affected the industry allocation.

Therefore, since the shortage of migrant workers occurred in 2004 and the subsequent increase in wages, the transfer of labor-intensive industries from the Eastern region to the central and Western regions (mainly the central region) began to take place. According to the data of three national economic censes, it can be seen that the proportion of the Eastern region in the national manufacturing industry has been significantly reduced, with an annual average rate of 2.1% during the period of 2004–2013; the proportion of the central and Western regions has increased significantly, and the average annual has increased by 4.7% and 3.4%, respectively (Table 4.1).

Notes

1 Joseph Stiglitz. (2006). *Making Globalization Work* (p. 4). London: Penguin Books.
2 Alex MacGillivray. (2006). *A Brief History of Globalization: The Untold Story of Our Incredible Shrinking Planet* (p. 5). London: Robinson.
3 The story was quoted from Yifu Lin's speech, see also Yifu Lin. (2013). Talk about Economy. *Discussion Memoir, 36*, 33.
4 Qu Yue, Cai Fang, and Xiaobo Zhang. (2012). Have the "Flying Geese" in Industrial Transformation Occurred in China? In Huw Mckay and Ligang Song (Eds.), *Rebalancing and Sustaining Growth in China*. Canberra: The Australian National University E-Press and Social Sciences Academic Press.

5 Development stages and turning point

Bob Dylan asked in his lyrics: how many roads must a man walk down before you call him a man? Economic development of any country, if not always stagnant, will surely experience different development stages. For economists and policymakers, judging such economic development stages is most easily confused with the unchanged economic development stages in which economy fluctuates. There exist closely related connections between the economic cycle and economic growth process. They not only exert important influences on each other but also are determined by different factors respectively. Therefore, if we want to understand the Chinese economy, we need to combine short-term perspectives with long-term ones. Only by doing so can we make the right judgments on economic development stages and macroeconomic situations and form a targeted responding train of thought and policy measures.

Fundamental changes have taken place in China's economic development stages. Not only was the Lewis turning point stepped over, but also the demographic dividend began to disappear rapidly, which would eventually present as decreased potential output capacity on the supply side. If this cannot be realized in the long-term aspect, judgment on the short-term macroeconomic situation will also be an inevitable mistake. If we think that growth slowdown is caused by cyclical factors, thus we adopt policies to stimulate growth from the perspective of demand, it will undoubtedly produce the opposite effect. We can see from international experiences that such policy failures often lead to disastrous consequences.

5.1 Economic development stages

Many early development economists have a common characteristic. They were keen to divide economic development into different stages. According to the logics of this theoretical tradition, latter countries tend to follow the paths and corresponding laws that former countries have experienced. It is for this reason that comparative study on economic development becomes meaningful. Among the division of economic development stages, the most famous is Rostow's Five Stages of Economic Development Theory, stating that a country becoming rich from being poor needs to experience five stages of development, which are the stages of traditional society, preparation for take-off, take-off, becoming mature and mass consumption.

However, opinions have been varied on the division of development stages from the day the theory was born, and it has caused fierce debates among scholars. Besides, with gradual fading out of development economics after the 1970s, neoclassical growth theory has occupied the mainstream status correspondingly. Economic development is no longer divided into stages, which seem to have only one type from beginning to end, known as the neoclassical growth. According to Thoreau's analysis, in growth of this kind labor force is lacking, constant capital investment will be impeded by diminishing returns and as a result the only sources of long-term economic growth are technological progress and productivity improvement.

However, such an explanation cannot satisfy economists, because no one can deny that the Malthusian poverty trap has been dominant for the longest time in human history, and this equilibrium trap characterized by the cycle of poverty and hunger has nothing in common with Solow's neoclassical economic growth. Therefore, sooner or later some economists will come forward to admit that, before the status of Solow's neoclassical growth, there indeed existed a status of Malthusian equilibrium, and they have tried to analyze these two using a unified theoretical framework.

It is Prescott and his partners who have made this contribution, namely admitting the Malthusian stage into mainstream economic analysis and actually returning to the division of economic development stages.[1] Not only that, in an article by this winner of Nobel Prize in Economics with another co-worker, he further acknowledged that, in fact, there existed a transition stage from "Malthus" to "Solow," and the key of this transition was how to eliminate impediments constraining labor mobility.[2]

We can imagine without a lot of effort that this economic development stage from "Malthus" to "Solow" should be called the "Lewis" stage. Naturally we know that this stage is also known as the dual economic development stage, which is characterized by agricultural labor force surplus being absorbed by constant living wages of the modern sector's growth until the new phenomena of labor shortage and constant wage increase appear, namely, the arrival of the Lewis turning point.

It is generally believed that the knowledge of property rights of modern economics, including growth theory, should belong to Western economists. However, in the history of Western economics, thousands of years' transition from the Malthus Era to the Solow Era was as slow as a snail, while the demographic transition process was unable to show changes of periodic significance, therefore it was hard to see clearly the Lewis Era between them. As a result, the process of dual economic development is often ignored by Western economics, and Lewis's correct observation is thought to be only a peculiar phenomenon in developing countries; even when people of insight in later mainstream economic circles have observed similar phenomena, they are still unwilling to make appropriate expressions straightforwardly.

For example, Prescott and his partners we have mentioned have never noted this transitional stage being observed, instead, they only pointed it out. Masahiko Aoki, who has made deeper observations based on East Asian experiences, also refused to call it the Lewis stage, yet he called it Kuznet's stage. Obviously, he didn't want to emphasize the transfer of labor surplus, while he was more willing to turn his attentions to changes of economic structure.[3]

However, no economists can deny the existence of the dual economic development process once becoming long-term observers of China's economic development. This is because, during the whole period of reform and opening-up, Chinese economic development has been accompanied by massive labor transfer from the countryside to cities all the time, and the Chinese economy's high speed is just realized by removing institutional obstacles to condense this rich and cheap labor factor into labor-intensive products, thus turning it into a comparative advantage in the international market through participation in global division of labor.

Not only that, understanding of the Chinese economy can only be shallow if we don't understand Lewis's theory and the development states it has described. The existence and transfer of a large amount of labor surplus not only affect economic development process in the long-term but also in the short-term, endowing it with Chinese characteristics, also, the decline and eventual disappearance of this labor surplus lead to changes of economic development stages, determining the future pattern of Chinese economic growth.

An important Chinese phenomenon parallel and closely related to this is rapid demographic transition, presenting as constant opening of the demographic window and its closing down gradually afterwards. When debating whether the Lewis turning point has come or not, researchers with negative views are reluctant to admit the arrival of this turning point even when they have seen the phenomena of labor shortage and wage increase, since the most difficult point for them to convince themselves of is why this turning point came so early in China.

Indeed, the fast speed of China's demographic transition is unprecedented so that people have summarized a general statement, known as "getting old before getting rich." Therefore, breaking people's mindset needs to theoretically put demographic transition into the Lewis framework, which means building an extended theoretical model of dual economy and experientially making observations on the demographic dividend China has gained in the process of economic growth jointly with the transfer of agricultural labor force.

Lewis himself probably didn't notice the demographic transition theory that had already appeared in his era, but he still took demographic transition in the "high birthrate, low death rate, high growth rate" stage as an implicated premise of the dual economy existing in developing countries. Starting from here, the only concerns left for Lewis are just modern sectors' expansion and their absorption of labor surplus, while the demographic transition's turning into the next "low birth rate, low death rate, low growth rate" stage needs not to be taken into consideration.

Once we take these two factors into account: economic growth absorbs labor surplus and demographic transition reduces labor supply, China's exceptional

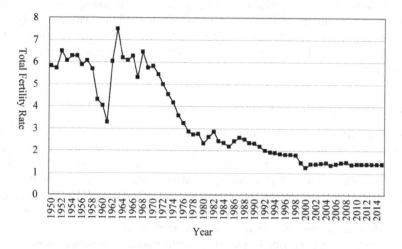

Figure 5.1 Total Fertility Rate during the Period of the People's Republic of China

Source: calculated according to the database of China Population Information and Research Center before 1998, and calculated according to all previous population censes and population sample survey data from 1998 to 2008 and later; the level after 2008 has been generally accepted by scholars

performances in economic growth and demographic transition leading to the rapid arrival of the Lewis turning point is completely logical and can be expected.

As shown in Figure 5.1, the fertility rate in China began to drop down quickly after the 1970s, then in the 1980s fertility rate's decrease was accompanied by the development of a dual economy initiated by reform and opening-up. By the early 1990s, total fertility rate dropped below the replacement level of 2.1. Since the 21st century, fertility rate has basically stabilized at 1.4.[4] A long period of low birth rate level undoubtedly has intrinsic logical relations with the arrival of the Lewis turning point and the disappearance of demographic dividend.

Until now, we could see according to the acknowledged theoretical frameworks that, at least at the beginning of reform and opening-up, along with China's achievements of large-scale poverty alleviation, it had gotten rid of the Malthusian trap and entered into the period of dual economic development, having realized unprecedented and remarkable growth performances. Accompanied by the arrivals of the Lewis turning point and the turning point of demographic dividend's disappearance, the fundamental change that Chinese economic development stage faces is essentially the transition from dual economic development to neoclassical growth.

Whether the right phased judgment on China's economic development can be made or not, as well as whether the nature of challenges the Chinese economy is facing can be realized or not, relates to whether the miracle of Chinese economic growth could be sustained for a long time. If the theoretical framework that combines the long-term period with the short-term is lacking, we are likely to draw a plausible judgment and produce mistaken policy conclusions when facing such a transition without previous experiences to refer to, and this will inevitably lead to the completely opposite policy effect. The Chinese economics community and policy community have failed to make proper and accurate judgment for a very long time.

5.2 Turning point of Chinese economy

When positioning for the Chinese economic development stage, an analytical method commonly used is comparing China with some countries that have experienced a similar development process and have now entered the rank of high-income economies. However, comparing current China with the development period of the reference countries is a rather subtle choice. It is no doubt that naturally researchers can select different development periods as reference points according to the reference conclusions they want to get.

For example, comparison between China and other countries on the same development stage seems to indicate the possibility of China's economic growth as a recently developed country after it has reached the stage of a specific per capita income level or insinuating which country's road of success or failure China might follow in the future. However, when doing so, inappropriate choice of the time for comparison may cause misunderstanding and misguidance. Therefore, we should avoid subjective randomness and make economic development comparisons according to the internal logics of things as much as possible.

For example, to compare mainland China with Japan and the "Four Asian Tigers" is a very meaningful research subject which also needs to be exceptionally careful. Like mainland China, Japan and the "Four Asian Tigers" were once regarded as miracle makers having successfully realized economic catch up. Also, their development path has many similarities with China, including the fact that both countries have benefited from demographic dividend created by demographic transition, while governments have played a more prominent and direct role in the process of economic development. More importantly, however, China, Japan and the "Four Asian Tigers" have undergone the Lewis turning point from infinite supply to shortage of labor, as well as the turning point of demographic dividend's disappearance.

Lin Yifu found that China's GDP per capita in the case of economic slowdown was equivalent to 20% of the United States' in the same period; this development stage was equivalent to Japan in 1951, Singapore in 1967, the China Taiwan Region in 1975 and South Korea in 1977. Data show that these economies achieved economic growth rates of 9.2%, 8.6%, 8.3% and 7.6% respectively in 20 years after reaching this node. Thus the conclusion is China still has potential for high speed growth. However, such an approach for comparing economic development stages neglects the role of demographic factors in economic growth and China's characteristic of "getting old before getting rich." Therefore, this comparison loses two of the most meaningful pieces of information.

First, comparing China with Japan in the 1960s and 1970s, since their per capita income levels are closer, we can undoubtedly conclude that, according to the experience of Japan, China still has 20 years or an even longer period of rapid growth. This conclusion helps people to understand the possibility of China's economic growth, while this reasoning cannot answer the essential question of whether China can avoid the middle-income trap or not. In fact, compared with economies successfully crossing the middle-income stage and entering into the high-income rank, more countries began to stagnate just in the stage where growing possibility still exists or even fell into the middle-income trap. Therefore, identifying the source that determines the sustainment of growth is more targeted for China than just pointing out the possibility of maintaining growth.

Second, it is generally believed that the Japanese economy reached the Lewis turning point of labor shortage and wage increase in 1960; however, the turning point of demographic dividend's disappearance marked by the working age population stopped growing, and the population dependency ratio did not appear to begin to rise until the early 1990s. In terms of the interval between these two turning points, China's characteristic of "getting old before getting rich" has a different performance, namely, after arriving at the Lewis turning point in 2004, it only took a few short years to stop the growth of the working-age population from 15 to 64 years old in 2013. If starting from China's national conditions and selecting the population aged from 15 to 59 as the working-age population, it had already started a significant decline since its peak in 2010.

Through comprehensive considerations, it is clear that comparing China in 2010 with Japan in 1990 is more conforming to the common challenges faced by both economies, so to the original purposes of comparative studies. It was just in 1990 that Japan's economic bubble burst and its economic growth fell into more than 20 years of stagnation. For example, during the period from 1990 to 2010, Japan's GDP's average annual growth rate was only 0.85%. Observing the changes Japan encountered, which are similar to today's China, as well as their relation with the Japanese economy's "20 years lost" will help us to understand the severe challenges China is facing, from which useful policy implications can be derived.

In a typical dual economy's development, since labor supply is almost unlimited, labor needed by economic growth that is constrained by industrial accumulation ability can be provided on the level of constant living wage. As a result, industrialization in this period is accompanied by massive labor transfer from countryside to cities all the time. In terms of this process, China has features different from Japan and other East Asian developed countries.

Besides the aforesaid unique characteristic of "getting old before getting rich," labor mobility still faces greater institutional barriers in China. Under the strict confinements of people's communes systems, the unified purchase and sale system and the household registration system before the reform and opening-up, the transfer process of China's rural labor surplus was delayed for decades. Even after that, when the scale and scope of labor flow had expanded, they were still restricted by the household registration system at the same time. Therefore, labor transfer is not complete, which still belongs to the "come and go" mode, while transferred laborers and their families have failed to become permanent urban residents.

Therefore, the turning point of labor shortage really comes up too early in China, i.e., restricted by the household registration system, labor shortage appears before the remaining rural surplus labor is completely transferred. This also means that the potential of reform to release labor supply really exists. When quarreling over whether China faces its Lewis turning point, whereas economic development stages have long-term features, changes are also reflected in certain time sections, so someone advised to substitute the Lewis turning point with the concept of the "Lewis Turning Section."[5] Considering vast territory and imbalanced regional economic development in China, this advice is undoubtedly reasonable.

However, when constructing such a "period" that helps to recognize problems, we should also pay attention to two things. The first is to prevent this period from being infinitely extended so as to lose this turning's original meaning and inherent regularity. The second is to ensure that its structure has an observable nature in experience so that actual comparisons and judgments can be conducted.

According to the concept of dual economic theory itself, the process from the Lewis turning point's appearance, when labor shortage and wage increase show up, till commercialization point's appearance when labor's marginal productivities of agricultural and non-agricultural industries become equal can be regarded as the Lewis turning period. However, mainly due to the condition that the equivalency of labor's marginal productivities is difficult to grasp in experience, we believe, based on the experiences of East Asian economies, the interval between the Lewis turning point and that of the demographic dividend's disappearance is a turning period much easier to observe, which also has more policy implications. Seen from China's experience, the two turning points above, namely the Lewis turning point and the turning point of demographic dividend's disappearance, have both shown up, thus taking the interval between these two as the Lewis turning period can demonstrate more profoundly its policy implications.

Figure 5.2 shows the whole process of the Chinese working age population from 15 to 59 years old starting from rapid growth to slow growth, then to zero growth and finally to negative growth. Generally the working age population's change and the dependency ratio of the population changing from falling fast to slowing down to rising after reaching the lowest point happen at the same time. Therefore, here we take the change of the working age population as representative of these two processes. As shown in Figure 5.2, we subjectively mark the year 2004 as the Lewis turning point and the year 2010 as the turning point of demographic dividend's disappearance, and the years between these two are the Lewis turning period. It is not necessarily accurate to say this classification is subjective; in fact, it is the product of combining theory with experience.

According to the theory of dual economy, when labor demand grows faster than supply so that the typical phenomenon of constant wage in the dual economic development period no longer exists, the first Lewis turning point is coming. In 2004, China reached the Lewis turning point with shortage of migrant workers and then continuous wage increase as empirical evidence. In 2010 the working age population reached the peak and then began its negative growth after that, while correspondingly the dependency ratio of the population began to increase after

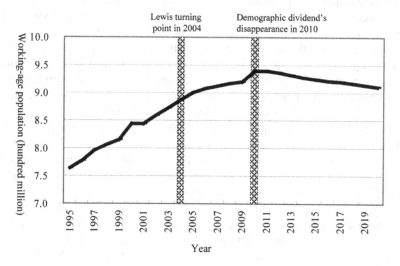

Figure 5.2 China's Lewis Turning Period

Source: China Development Research Foundation (2012) "China Development Report 2011/12: Change of Population Situation and Adjustment of Population Policy", China Development Press, 2012.

reaching the bottom, meaning that the demographic dividend formally ran out. Since China was influenced by the characteristics of "getting old before getting rich," its Lewis turning point was very short, only lasting for 6 years.

Using the same conceptual framework to observe Japan's economy, the Lewis turning period was undoubtedly from 1960 to 1990. During this period, the Japanese economy maintained rapid growth for 30 years, but once it crossed this time point Japan's economic growth came to an end abruptly without inertia.

Seen from the surface, Japan went through the bubble economy in the 1980s, unable to revive after this bubble burst. However, if we can't find other more fundamental factors, it is difficult to convince others that the bubble burst will lead to more than 20 years of economic stagnation. Therefore, we should put aside this direct catalyst of the bubble burst and take a look at what makes a high growth economy come to a halt and even become depressed on that particular stage of economic development. More importantly, we need to understand what lessons China can learn from this.

Once Japan's demographic dividend disappears, it becomes a typical neoclassical economy like all developed countries. At this time, the only source which can support economic growth is total factor productivity, which relates to technology innovation and resource allocation efficiency improvement. Whether total factor productivity improvement can be kept to compete with other developed countries is the key to whether Japan's economy can realize optimum growth, which depends on system vitality, innovation ability, level of human capital and a series of other factors.

In these respects, some fundamental obstacles truly exist in Japan. For example, the protection of enterprises without vitality hinders resource reallocation; the artificial suppression of higher education development delays the adaptability of human capital and the new development stage. In particular, in the face of the potential growth rate's inevitable reduction, the government focuses on stimulating investment through industrial policies and makes macroeconomic policies long-term and normalized, trying to improve economic growth speed by means of demand-driving, yet the result is even further from expected.

With the working-age population aged from 15 to 59 reaching the peak in 2010 and the dependency ratio of the population dropping to the bottom correspondingly, China faces the turn of development stages similar to Japan in those years, mainly marked by demographic dividend's disappearance or the Lewis turning period's ending and then by potential growth rate's decrease.[6]

First of all, labor shortage and wage increase caused by it will significantly and more and more seriously weaken labor-intensive industries' comparative advantages. The most important characteristics of dual economic development are infinite supply of labor and wage stagnating on a survival level for a long time. Therefore, the arrival of the Lewis turning point means constant wage increase due to the shortage of ordinary workers.

This trend has been widely observed by researchers on the Chinese economy. Figure 5.3 shows almost perfectly the complete dynamic state that, before 2004, wages of migrant workers wandered at the survival level and then improved at ever-increasing speed. Ordinary workers' wage increase has played the role of weakening labor-intensive industries' comparative advantages, which is self-evident

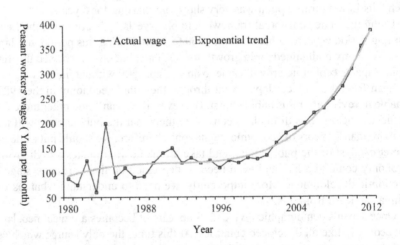

Figure 5.3 Trend of Peasant Workers' Actual Wage Changes

Source: Lu Feng, *Expansion of Employment and Wage Increase (2001–2010)*, China's Macroeconomic Research Center of Peking University, 2011. The original data's closing data is by the year 2010, and the author of this book updates this figure to the year 2012 according to data from National Bureau of Statistics

in theory and can be widely observed in practice. Since the rapid growth in the past 30 years depends on low labor cost, a factor related to population, the disappearance of demographic dividend will undoubtedly lead to inhibited economic growth.

Second, when facing constant wage increase, in order to solve increasing labor cost, many observers think the way out is to substitute capital for labor; such method has been used by enterprises in real life. However, if only substitution of machines for labor is attempted by increasing investment, diminishing returns on capital will soon occur in several cases. First, improvement of the speed of human capital cannot be kept synchronous with the increased speed of capital-labor ratio, so the added machines cannot keep up the trend of increasing returns. Second, facing slower growth, the government tends to adopt industrial policies to stimulate growth, including incentives and subsidies for new industries, resulting in a distorted price of capital factor; this not only encourages too rapid development of capital intensive industries directly, but also lures enterprises to substitute labor with machines using cheap capital.

Increasing capital-labor ratio is a way to improve labor productivity but not a sustainable way. Once beyond the permit of conditions, diminishing returns on capital will occur. In fact, the characteristic of neoclassical growth is that diminishing returns on capital will surely occur if labor supply is no longer unlimited, while the growth rate without productivity improvement is eventually unsustainable.

Finally, with working-age population in rural areas decreasing, the speed of labor's transferring out from agriculture sectors has decreased, which can also reduce the speed of resource reallocation efficiency's improvement, making improvement of total factor productivity more difficult. Since the scale of 16–19-year-old rural population (dominant in migrant workers) already peaked in 2014, then turned to negative growth, the growth rate of peasant workers slowed down greatly, for example, the growth rate in 2016 was only 0.3%. That is to say, under the current system, the rural labor force available for reallocation has already been allocated.

During the reform and opening-up, the increase of total factor productivity mainly relied on labor transfer, which brought resource reallocation efficiency. Therefore, slowdown of the former meant that this source could no longer bring about considerable improvement of total factor productivity. Although the sources to increase total factor productivity still exist, the existing institutional constraints such as the household registration system and monopoly of state-owned enterprises hinder free mobility of the factors of production including labor force between enterprises, ownerships, sectors, regions and between urban and rural areas, therefore it's more difficult to get further resource reallocation efficiency.

In this case, even with no policy misleading, simply development stage change itself will inevitably mean that China's economy will increase on a lower potential output capacity. Potential growth rate is the normal growth rate that can be realized on the premise that capital and labor are both made full use of, as well as under the supply constraints of certain factors of production and within the limits of total factor productivity's improvement. It may be seen that observing potential growth rate from the view of the supply side may be a meaningful empirical footnote to central judgment of the new normal of economic development as well as to the structural reform requirements from the supply side.

Therefore, in general, economists observe this economic development stage change's influence on economic growth rate through estimating potential GDP growth rate. Mainly because the working-age population began its negative growth after 2010, after making necessary assumptions, we estimate that China's potential growth rate will drop down to 7.6% in the "Twelfth Five-Year Plan" period and to 6.2% in the "Thirteenth Five-Year Plan" period from the average 10.5% in the "Eleventh Five-year Plan" period.[7] Although this should not be regarded as a prediction, theoretical expectation fits well with what really happened later.

5.3   Understanding the macroeconomic situation

In terms of discipline framework, macroeconomics originally includes a short-term perspective, namely cycle theory, and long-term perspective, namely growth theory. But in the actual research, these two are not inherently unified, as economists either limit their own study to macroeconomics (narrowly meaning cycle studies) or to economic growth theory, thus restricting themselves to a corner. In judging economic development stages and understanding economic situations in order to determine macroeconomic policies and choose development strategies, this tendency often leads to economic analysis insufficiency.

Although the macro economy will also encounter supply shocks in the short term, such as the influence of the oil crisis in the early 1970s on some developed economies, in general, potential growth rate determined by supply factors is stable in the long term; while demand factors also have a long-term trend, they show characteristics of short-term volatility more often. Based on judging the economic development stage accurately, we need to combine characteristics of long-term supply factors shown by development stage change with demand factors in short-term macroeconomics, thus making a correct evaluation of the economic situation and putting forward decisions for targeted regulation direction, object and signal.

In other words, only by the combination of long-term and short-term perspectives can we have theoretical and practical consistency in judging the macroeconomic situation, thus getting a correct conclusion and making targeted policy choices. Combining these two closely not only helps us judge the macroeconomic situation, but also forms the premise of correct policy measures. Long-term supply factors and short-term demand factors construct four macroeconomic situations through different combinations.

The first is the combination of strong supply with strong demand, namely the formation of a matched state of higher potential output capacity with a stronger level of demand. Generally, this occurs in the economic development stage where the supply of factors of production is sufficient, productivity has significant room for improvement and there is no obvious phenomenon of diminishing returns on capital. It is clearly seen that this is a catch-up phenomenon in the process of dual economic development. Under purely this situation the phenomenon of continuous cyclical unemployment will not appear, neither will serious inflation appear.

The second is the combination of strong supply with weak demand, namely the formation of an unmatched state of higher potential output capacity with a weaker level of demand. The most typical of this kind is as follows: under the condition of economic recession or financial crisis in the process of rapid growth, impacts of cyclical demand make output growth unable to reach the potential level. Usually, this combination causes serious shocks on the labor market, resulting in cyclical unemployment.

The third is the combination of weak supply with weak demand, namely the formation of a matched state of lower potential output capacity with a weaker level of demand. Usually, when the dual economic development stage is coming to an end, the source of traditional growth declines, at the same time, the new source of growth has not been unearthed yet. Both previous situations are normal states of neoclassical growth.

The fourth is the combination of weak supply with strong demand, namely the formation of an unmatched state of lower potential output capacity with a strong level of demand. In fact, this kind of situation only occurs when artificial interventions are implemented, namely stimulating investment or expanding exports through distorted policy means. In condition the that potential output capacity decreases, if strong demand factors are artificially stimulated, real growth rate will exceed potential growth rate, which easily leads to inflation, excess production capacity and even the bubble economy etc.

In fact, the previous theoretical situations formed according to the combinations of long-term supply factors with short-term demand factors' characteristics correspond directly to macroeconomic situations in China's history and reality. With the help of this theoretical abstract, we can understand the past and the present and also predict the future.

First, the first situation was the Chinese economy's normal state before 2010, namely before the Lewis turn was completed. At that time, benefiting from the demographic dividend brought by demographic transition, supply factors were conducive to economic growth and the Chinese economy had a higher potential growth rate. For example, estimates we had made showed that the potential growth rate from 1978 to 1995 averaged 10.3%; the potential growth rate from 1995 to 2009 averaged 9.8%.

At the same time, resident income growth, rapid investment increase and export increase in large scale provided corresponding demand factors. Therefore, in general, macroeconomic balance was formed on high growth potential in this period. The growth rate gap presenting as the difference between potential growth rate and real growth rate has certain fluctuations among different years, but on the whole, its volatility is not large, which is also in a diminishing trend (See Figure 5.4).

Second, the second situation is the state of economy when it encounters serious internal or external hits in the big trend of the first situation. For example, after the mid-1990s, China's domestic macroeconomic downturn and the Asian financial crisis successively caused serious demand decrease and insufficient utilization of

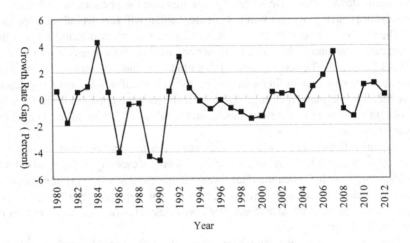

Figure 5.4 Growth Rate Gap in the Period of Reform and Opening-up

Source: Cai Fang and Lu Yang, Population Change and Resulting Slowdown in Potential GDP Growth in China, *China & World Economy*, Vol.21, No.2, 2013, pp. 1–14

production capacity, then mass unemployment. Later, with China's accession to the World Trade Organization and the aid of foreign demand, its economic growth rate rebounded to the potential output level and its macro economy returned to the normal state in the first situation. In addition, countermeasures for inflation from 1988 to 1989 and subsequent regulations, as well as the world financial crisis from 2008 to 2009, used to make the actual growth rate drop below the potential output capacity.

Third, 2012 is a typical year of situation three. Starting from entering the "Twelfth Five-year Plan" period in 2011, China's potential growth rate had decreased more greatly than before. According to our estimation, potential the growth rate in 2012 dropped from the previous year's 8.1% to 7.5%. Under this condition, the level of external demand happened to decline obviously, achieving unintentionally the matching of demand and supply. As a result, the actual growth rate did not obviously exceed the potential growth rate, thus no inflation was caused; also, since the former was not lower than the latter, no employment influence was encountered; instead, the balance of economic growth has been enhanced.

Finally, the main risk of China's future economic growth is the appearance of situation four. Both among economists and among practitioners, there exists a misunderstanding that the key factor determining economic growth is demand. Therefore, each time economic growth encounters obstacles, the most common countermeasures all point to taking some means to expand the internal and external demands. In fact, for China, after the middle 1990s, this understanding makes sense in the transition period from shortage economy to surplus economy. However, once economic development gets over the Lewis turning period and the demographic dividend disappears, the factor restricting economic growth would be potential output capacity, rather than the demand factor over a certain period of time at least.

In fact, contributions of consumption demand, investment demand and export demand to GDP growth rate in 2012 are respectively 4.04%, 3.93% and –0.17%. Yet seen from the average level from 2001 to 2011, generally the contribution rates of these three are respectively 4.5%, 5.4% and 0.56%. Even if in a certain period of time in the future external demand's contribution becomes zero, investment demand decreases by half and consumption demand remains unchanged, the demand factors are sufficient to support the requirements of potential growth rate.

Combining China's economic development stage with the recent situation, we can make a conclusion that the real challenge the Chinese economy is facing does not lie in the short-term macroeconomic demand factors but in the long-term sustainability of economic growth. In other words, the hope of exceeding potential growth rate by stimulating demand is the wrong choice. Instead, improving potential growth rate itself is the correct policy option.

However, insisting that lack of demand leads to sluggish growth in theory and adhering to implement various policy measures aiming at stimulating demand in practice often become reality easily, eventually bringing disastrous consequences. Although the central government has judged economic development to be entering new normality, deployed supply side structural reform to transfer mode, adjusted structure and changed power, governments in some places still take keeping growth as an excuse to attract more investment and increase investment amount so as to stimulate GDP growth.

It was pointed out in the 19th CPC National Congress Report that China's economy has changed from high speed growth to high quality development. At the same conference, the expression "sound and fast development" in the Constitution of the Communist Party of China was changed to "higher quality, more efficient, more fair, more sustainable development." This means that, if "sound" and "fast" in terms of economic growth interacted as both cause and effect and promoted each other at previous development stages, nowadays they have become a pair of contradictory or alternative choices and cannot coexist.

At the current development stage of China, it's impossible and very dangerous to pursue speed. In this aspect, Japan learned a painful lesson. For a long time, it was widely believed in Japan that high speed economic growth in this country mainly relied on overseas market demand, while domestic consumption demand was always weak. Therefore, after Japan got across the Lewis turning point in 1960, labor intensive industries lost their comparative advantages gradually; then demographic dividend disappeared rapidly at the high-income stage in 1990, and performance of total factor productivity was insufficient to support neoclassical economic growth; it has widely been believed that industrial policy characterized by government intervention, expansionary fiscal policy and easy monetary policy and various means should be used to boost domestic demand, especially investment demand. Nowadays, the so-called Abenomics characterized by an easy monetary policy continues such traditional policy.

In fact, the slowdown logic of the Japanese policy community is dead wrong from theory to policy. First, powerful research evidence shows that, in the high speed growth period of Japan, consumer demand was a non-neglectable pulling force, while outstanding export performance was the result of economic growth, rather than reason.[8] Next, research also indicates that economic stagnation of Japan after 1990 was the direct result of poor performance of total factor productivity.[9] Just because of the aforementioned misleading theory and policy and improper policy prescription, Japan's economy suffered the following consequences in the past nearly 30 years: the bubble economy and its burst, zombie firms and zombie banks running wild and long-term economic stagnation.

Regardless of financial risks, the American economy is more sustainable, healthy and prosperous than high-income countries like Japan and even Europe, which also recover faster from global financial crisis. The reason is not various versions of demand stimulus nor states' positive roles as investors but its cheap energy it tries its best to get, cheap labor force realized by the demographic dividend's extension and a relatively flexible labor market, which attract companies all over the world to invest, forming higher growth potential through the efforts of enterprises and society. Of course, with the increasingly divided politics of the United States, economic policy move continuously toward nationalism, its long-term economic development is no longer favored.

In 1990 when economic growth began to stagnate, Japan had already entered the ranks of high-income countries. "The lost 30 years" after that caused various problems for the Japanese economy, and this country's international status of competitiveness and innovation ability significantly decreased; however, generally the Japanese economy still continued to grow slowly in a sustainable way with low carbon emissions, and people enjoyed a rather higher quality of life. Therefore, we can say that the Japanese economy over the past 30 years was in a high-income trap.

However, due to the fact that that China has a "getting old before getting rich" characteristic and is in the above average-income stage, if its demographic dividend disappears and the Chinese economy cannot keep the necessary growth rate or even slows down to an extent as serious as Japan, it will undoubtedly face the danger of falling into the middle-income trap.

5.4   How to avoid "middle-income trap"

When China was in the above average-income stage, it suffered the disappearance of demographic dividend and then encountered the turning point of the traditional economic growth source's exhaustion. Although this was a natural process of economic development, it did not mean that China would inevitably fall into the middle-income trap by then. However, seen from many countries' lessons and experiences in world economic history, this potential risk undoubtedly exists.

For example, some economists use the percentage of each country's per capita GDP in that of the United States to define countries: those higher than 55% are high-income countries, those between 20% and 55% are middle-income countries and those less than 20% are low-income countries. Among the 132 countries in comparison, 32 were defined as middle-income countries in 1960, and this number was 24 in 2008. If we observe this group's characteristics of change, we can find that about half of the middle-income countries have the possibility to remain in the middle-income stage after nearly half a century, while those leaving this group mostly flow down to the low-income group and fewer up to the high-income group.[10]

If here we use Tolstoy's famous saying "All happy families are like one another; each unhappy family is unhappy in its own way," maybe we can say countries falling into the middle-income trap each have their own reason. For example, the International Monetary Fund (IMF) conducted an empirical analysis on the risk of Asia-pacific countries' economic slowdown and thus their falling into the middle-income trap, after that, they ascribed the risks faced by Malaysia, the Philippines and China to institutional factors, thinking that Vietnam, India and Indonesia were facing the risks of insufficient transportation and communication infrastructures, while on the other hand, compared with the Asia-pacific region, the Latin American countries had defects more obvious in terms of regional integration and trade.[11]

However, we can still integrate the related factors according to the logics of economic analysis, observe their causal relationship and find something with regularity and universality, thus we can learn from other countries to avoid repeating mistakes they have made before. In other words, although the similarity between the middle-income trap and poverty trap is that both are equilibrium traps in an ultra-stable equilibrium state difficult to be broken by conventional forces, the difference between them is also very obvious, that is, the poverty trap is a continuation of a long-term Malthus state, whose direct causes are usually hard to suddenly find out, while the middle-income trap is often caused by some visible policy mistakes.

As a result, we can take different countries' policy mistakes in the process of economic development for empirical basis and construct a circular causality relationship for the middle-income trap, thus taking a look at what are the necessary steps to fall into the middle-income trap and which factors make a nation unable to escape from this vicious cycle so that we can find the entry point to break the causal links in policy.

Step one: rapid economic growth slows down in a particular period of the middle-income stage. For a less developed country, a higher growth rate is often easy to be achieved and in the transitional stage of development from poverty trap to middle income through capital accumulation and labor input. However, when it reaches a certain stage of development or its previous sources of growth disappear or it makes some policy mistakes, usually it will experience a sharp drop in growth rate.

One of the most famous studies shows that any growth rate beyond the world average is abnormal and will eventually "regress towards the mean" according to rules. As the author says, "mean value" is the average growth rate of world economy.[12] Some even claim that this is an inviolable "iron law." Through international comparison, some scholars find that according to the purchasing power parity (PPP) in US dollar terms of 2005, when per capita GDP reaches 17,000 dollars, the rapidly growing economy will often suffer a significant slowdown, generally dropping down by 60% in economic growth rate.[13]

Step two: under the condition of sharp slowdown in economic growth, if we have the wrong understanding of the nature of problems, our policy responses are often quite opposite, which is not only far from effective but even causes artificial distortions, probably making the slowdown in growth become economic stagnation. For example, if the reason for slowdown is the decrease of potential output capacity but the government's policy focuses on stimulating growth on the demand side, a series of distortions and negative effects will be caused. Among them, nothing is more serious than the government's excessive use of industrial policy, causing the distortions of factors' prices, while the most severe policy consequences are inflation, the bubble economy, excess capacity and improper protection for backward industries and enterprises. By this time, slowdowns that may be originally normal or temporary will turn into long-term slow growth or even stagnation instead.

Step three: in the face of a series of social problems brought by stagnation of economic growth, the government further takes measures in the manner of drinking poison to quench thirst, resulting in comprehensive distortion of the social economic system. For example, in the condition that economic growth stagnates and the cake can no longer be made bigger, redistribution of this cake leads to common rent-seeking incentives in society and causes corruption. Since the privileged groups tend to get a bigger share of income as well as the existence of the Matthew Effect in income distribution, the situation becomes increasingly worse, thus intensifying social contradictions. At this moment, a government with struggling finance can often and only rely on populist policies for which they have made promises but cannot realize. These policies are not only unhelpful; they hurt the incentive mechanisms in economic activities.

Step four: the serious unequal distributions of resources and incomes accompanied by stagnant economic growth give rise to the vested interest groups, and the latter try their best to maintain this distribution pattern that is beneficial for them, therefore, system drawbacks of the middle-income trap are not easily broken. Once entering into this system state, relevant economic and social policies will be captured by interest groups, and not only will economic growth come to a halt, institutional evolution will be more difficult, thus a system not conducive to economic growth is solidified.

Correspondingly, all kinds of factors of production are no longer allocated according to the principle of maximum productivity but to the principle of maximum vested interests. Once a country falls into this situation, its worst result is that it not only cannot get rid of the middle-income trap but might even drop back to the low-income level.

Since the previous steps have a causal relation in timing sequence and logics, blocking the possibility of its malignant spread from the logical starting point is the most effective countermeasure. At the same time, the phenomenon of each step can also exist concurrently, thus the countermeasures should be comprehensively coordinated. Seen from some countries' experiences, before slowdown or even stagnation of economic growth, usually, system drawbacks not conducive to sustainable growth have already shown up, and the deterioration of income distribution often directly hurts economic growth itself.

It may be seen that the relationship between income distribution and the middle-income trap is: under the condition of economic growth and income growth's stagnations, the income gap often becomes worse. On the other hand, if the gravity of expanding the income gap along with economic growth reaches a certain limit but is not stopped by effective policy measures, it will cause social instability and reduced social cohesion, thus becoming an obstacle to economic growth, as well as the reason for its slowdown or even stagnation.

5.5 How to cope with growth slowdown?

In the case of demographic dividend's disappearance, assuming that other conditions remain unchanged, decrease of potential growth rate down does not mean that China is bound to fall into the middle-income trap. Ultimately, demographic dividend is just the source of economic growth in a particular development stage. Only when it is replaced by a new source of productivity improvement can dual economic development transform into neoclassical growth, realizing the transition to the high-income stage. In fact, when the window of population dividend is closed, the door for more sustainable economic growth is already there, thus the most important thing is whether you can open it or not.

A main purpose of economists' dividing economic development into stages is they hope successors learn experiences and lessons from forerunners so that they can find a more smooth way of studying with fewer detours. According to the previous steps of falling into and being perplexed by the middle-income trap, as well as combining with the reality of China's economic growth, we should plan ahead from the following aspects.

At present, the most important thing for China is to understand accurately the slowdown of its economic growth, to find a really suitable prescription and to form consensus among economists and policymakers. General Secretary Xi Jinping regards the downward turn of economic growth as a feature of China's economic development entering a new normal, reminding policy researchers and developers to recognize and adapt to this new normal and to lead the new normal through supply side structural reform. This idea is to recognize the deceleration from the perspective of the changes in the economic development stage. It provides a way for economists to understand the economic situation and for policymakers to maintain their strategic determination and engage in a streamlined policy approach. China's economy focuses on transforming the mode of economic development and optimizing and upgrading the industrial structure so as to realize the dynamic transformation of economic growth.

In 2012, when decrease in potential growth rate emerged preliminarily, the press circle and theoretical circle were full of misleading arguments. Whether journalists or macroeconomic analysts, almost everyone attributed the problems to underconsumption with one voice. Specific to this year, when talking about underconsumption, it was tantamount to saying sluggish recovery of the United States from financial crisis, sovereign debt crisis in some European countries and other factors impacted China's export demand.

In the troika of demand factors, external demand cannot be controlled by us; consumption demand cannot be greatly improved in a short period of time. Therefore, the next logic is naturally to be expanding investment demand through increasing investment intentions. Some economists form a tendency of exploring a "new economic growth point" for a short while. From a long-term point of view, people put forward suggestions such as speeding up the urbanization process, increasing investment on infrastructure constructions in the Midwest areas and making beforehand investment on emerging industries. Sometimes, people also blur the difference between long-term structural problems and short-term cyclical problems and suggest stimulating macroeconomic policies.

These suggestions are not only based on the wrong judgments of the economic development stage and macroeconomic situation, they also have some dangers specifically. That is, these kinds of suggestions are very likely to be consistent with the policy measures that governments are good at. The intention of promoting urbanization, regional development strategy and industrial policy should serve policy combinations for specific purposes, having their unique meanings and applicable scopes. In this regard, the Chinese government already has mature policy tools and means of implementation and even can be said to be adept, with some good results having also been achieved in the past. However, once these policies are used to drive investment demand in order to achieve the goal of transcending potential growth rate, they will be counter-productive, hurting the Chinese economy's sustainability of long-term growth.

For example, industrial policy is originally for conditions when traditional comparative advantages disappear; the government helps investors and enterprises to search for new comparative advantages in the form of a certain amount of subsidies, which focus on long-term growth sustainability. However, if this policy is turned into a short-term means of stimulating demand, then the government's supportive policy will lose its limitations. Facing government preferential policies and direct subsidies, rent-seeking behaviors will inevitably appear. Investors and enterprises will pour in, not even considering comparative advantages or competitiveness nor caring whether there is market demand or not. The results are undoubtedly deviating from comparative advantage, aggravating excess capacity and causing asset bubble and high debt.

Let's take another example. Regional development strategy focusing on central and Western regions as well as resource-exhausted regions is meant to promote balanced economic development among different regions through the central government's supportive policies. However, if this policy becomes a means of stimulating investment in order to transcend the potential growth rate, industrial developments of regions as objects being supported will inevitably deviate from comparative advantages, lacking competitiveness in both international and domestic markets, while long-term economic growth will be hurt instead.

Excessive use of macroeconomic policies will also lead to the same results. Monetary policy and fiscal policy normally should be used to adjust short-term demand fluctuations. However, economic policies aiming to make economic growth rate higher than the potential growth rate for a long time tend to make loose monetary policy and expansionary fiscal policy permanent and normalized, which will inevitably help to enlarge the distortion effects of industrial and regional policies. Excess liquidity will also encourage a speculative bubble economy and protect enterprises with backward production capacity and less competitiveness as well as sectors with low productivity.

The original meaning of potential growth rate is normal economic growth rate, which can be realized under the condition that factors of production supply are determined by resource endowment, as well as on the basis that a range of other factors determine productivity improvement. Therefore, transcending the potential growth rate in a demand-driven way is like trying to drive athletes' performances above their potential through executive orders, publicity and means of material incentives, perhaps effective temporarily or occasionally, while eventually leading athletes to get injured.

However, we are not helpless in the face of declining potential growth rate, nor should we not do anything. Due to having experienced the turning point of demographic dividend's disappearance, potential growth rate's decline will be unusually sharp at this time, the phenomenon of structural unemployment may occur, government revenue will be suddenly stressed, and the investment circle is also desperate for help. Under the condition that the government clearly sees the situation and tightly controls the monetary spigot, non-substantial economies tend to take unusual means to create money supply due to their lack of capital, thus causing potential financial risks. Therefore, laissez-faire isn't the best policy choice.

Like sports training is not perfect, system determining factors of production supply and productivity improvement also have drawbacks, which leaves us a lot of room for improving the potential growth rate from the supply side. Therefore, when people talk about creating system dividend through reforms, they essentially mean creating better system conditions for factors of production supply and productivity improvement, thus achieving the goal of increasing potential growth rate.

So far, market mechanism has not yet played a fundamental role in the allocation of resources, and the space for improving productivity is still huge, therefore, deepening the reform of economic system and perfecting the system of socialist market economy can bring new source and power for China's economic growth. In the following chapters, we will analyze respectively various system factors hindering factors of production supply and productivity improvement, find out fields urgently needing reforms as well as priorities being promoted and put forward policy suggestions.

Notes

1 Gary D. Hansen and Edward C. Prescott. (2002). Malthus to Solow. *American Economic Review, 92*, 1205–1217.

2 Fumio Hayashi and Edward C. Prescott. (2008). The Depressing Effect of Agricultural Institutions on the Prewar Japanese Economy. *Journal of Political Economy, 116,* 573–632.
3 Masahiko Aoki. (2012). The Five Phases of Economic Development and Institutional Evolution in China, Japan, and Korea. In Masahiko Aoki, Timur Kuran, and Gérard Roland (Eds.), *Institutions and Comparative Economic Development* (pp. 13–47). Basingstoke: Palgrave Macmillan.
4 Guo Zhigang, Wang Feng, and Cai Yong. (2014). *China's Low Birth Rate and Sustainable Development of Population* (p. 21). Beijing: China Social Sciences Press.
5 Ross Garnaut. (2012). The Macroeconomic Implications of Lewis Turning Point. In Cai Fang, Yang Tao, and Huang Yiping (Eds.), *Has China Crossed the Lewis Turning Point.* Beijing: Social Sciences Academic Press.
6 Due to the household registration system and other factors, potential agricultural labor transfer still exists in China and provides a certain time window opportunity for adjustment. This will be discussed in detail later.
7 Cai Fang and Lu Yang. (2013). The End of China's Demographic Dividend: The Perspective of Potential GDP Growth. In Ross Garnaut, Cai Fang, and Ligang Song (Eds.), *China: A New Model for Growth and Development* (pp. 55–73). Canberra: Australian National University E Press.
8 See Lai Jiancheng. (2010). *The Taste of Economic Thought History.* Hangzhou: Zhejiang University Press.
9 Fumio Hayashi and Edward C. Prescott. (2002). The 1990s in Japan: A Lost Decade. *Review of Economic Dynamics, 5*(1), 206–235.
10 Wing Thye Woo. (2012). China Meets the Middle-Income Trap: The Large Potholes in the Road to Catching-Up. *Journal of Chinese Economic and Business Studies, 10*(4), 313–336.
11 Shekhar Aiyar, Romain Duval, Damien Puy, Yiqun Wu, and Longmei Zhang. (2013, March). Growth Slowdowns and the Middle-Income Trap. *IMF Working Paper*, Asia and Pacific Department, WP/13/71, International Monetary Fund.
12 Lant Pritchett and Lawrence Summers. (2014). Asiaphoria Meets Regression to the Mean. *NBER Working Paper*, 20573.
13 Barry Eichengreen, Donghyun Park, and Kwanho Shin. (2011). When Fast Growing Economies Slow Down: International Evidence and Implications for China. *NBER Working Paper*, 16919.

6 Engine for sustainable growth

During the period from 2004 to 2010, China completed its crossing of the Lewis turning period; its growth rate slowed down obviously in 2012 and down year by year from then on. It must be recognized that this trend of growth rate slowdown is a natural result of potential growth rate's decline, rather than the impact of demand factors. In the specific development stage, attributing the slowdown of economic growth to insufficient demand is a common mistake, which easily leads to biased policy orientations and unsuitable policy prescriptions. As a result, referencing relevant economic theories with an open mind, drawing experiences and lessons from other countries, and deeply understanding Chinese economic reality have vital policy significances for understanding the real reason of this slowdown, which helps prevent the occurrence of fishing-in-the-air policy misguidance and leads corresponding policy efforts to the right direction of seeking new growth engines.

6.1 Focusing on the supply factors

Whether athletes can get good grades or not indeed relates closely with encouragements and motivations from society such as sports officials, advertisers, Internet users etc. However, ultimately these impacts from outside can only help athletes to play to their potential, rather than determine their performance, which is not a sufficient condition. Through analogy with economic phenomena, external motivation is only a kind of demand factor, while the key to determining the athletes' grades is the "potential growth rate," which belongs to factors on the supply side.

If a player was given expectations higher than his athletic performance, it is not hard to imagine how he would react. Since strengthening the physical fitness and level of training to improve performance in the short term is an unattainable goal which violates laws, there are only two choices for him: for a man capable of self-constraint morally, he can only desperately go beyond his physical limit and eventually get injured; a man with poor moral self-constraint or lured by unscrupulous coaches or teams might think of other dishonest practices, such as doping.

Economic policies not changing the growth potential but just concentrating on demand stimulus will give inappropriate guidance to subjects of economic activities, namely investors and entrepreneurs. For example, no matter the implementations of loose monetary policy or expansionary fiscal policy or the stimulation of demand through industrial policy and regional policy, both their policy starting points are encouraging investment in real economy. However, investment activities at this time are not in conformity with intrinsic motivations for investing, which almost become a kind of rent-seeking activity induced by government subsidies, usually only leading to overcapacity and economic bubbles.

When we say decrease in overall potential growth rate of an economy, we also mean the decrease in both the comparative advantage and competitive advantage of manufacturing industry; manufacturing enterprises could no longer keep previous production scale or growth rate under the increased supply of factors of production and the increased productivity. Meanwhile, under the condition that potential growth rate declines, the comparative advantage and competitive advantage of manufacturing production are both decreasing; production enterprises whose productivities are below the existing ones can no longer sustain themselves. When the real economy is not strong, enthusiasm for project construction such as infrastructure is not high, either. For example, when Japan tries to stimulate economy through large-scale public investment, it meets the embarrassing situation of difficulty placing investment capital. Isamu Miyazaki, former chief of the Japanese Economic Planning Agency, has found that in the implementation of fiscal stimulating policies, public investment will meet deduction problems layer by layer, starting from "budget has been made but has not been allocated," moving to "budget has been allocated but is not been in place" and finally to "capital is in place while the project has not been started" etc.[1]

After the outbreak of the world financial crisis in 2008, quantitative easing monetary policies with low interest rate and zero interest rate economic growth appear to be the life-saving straw which Europe and the United States as well as Japan have competed to throw out. Among them, Japan has already been on this rugged road for more than 10 years. The problem is, if a country really faces the problem of insufficient demand, easing financial conditions do not naturally turn into companies' and investors' investment desires; if a country is facing the problem of potential growth rate being too low, easing financial policies that stimulate demand will not be suitable for curing the ills of real economy's lack of competitiveness.

It is not only like that. Competitiveness and comparative advantage cannot support the previous growth rate and investment desires. At this time, excess liquidity will inevitably flow to unproductive or speculative fields for investment, such as the financial industry, real-estate industry and overseas real-estate investment etc., first forming the bubble economy, followed by the bursting of the bubble and finally pulling economic growth to the abyss of long-term stagnation, just as what has happened in Japan from the 1980s to the early 1990s.

Just as in the face of athletes' poor performance we should focus on internal factors such as physical conditions, athletic potentials and the levels of training instead of seeking solutions from external motivating factors, when we meet the situation where decline of potential growth rate leads to the slowdown of economic growth, we should focus on factors on the supply side and explore the source to maintain sustainable growth. If physical factors such as age determine that athletic performance must decline to a certain level, we have to accept the decline, yet if there's still potential left untapped, we should focus on improving the efficiency of training, rather than imposing external stimuli on the athlete blindly.

Remember the argument between former Prime Minister of Singapore Lee Kuan Yew and American economist Krugman we talked about in the fourth chapter? From their dialogue full of heated disputes, we can not only clarify what are the factors on the supply side to realize economic growth but also understand what are the Lewis turning point's influences on the supply side of economic growth as well as what policy options we have.

On the basis of other economists' work, Krugman thinks that Singapore's economic growth simply relies on capital and labor inputs (undoubtedly also growth factors on the supply side), while total factor productivity (more durable growth factors on the supply side) is not increased, which has no difference from the Soviet Union under the condition of planned economy, and eventually it cannot be sustained.

Krugmans' judgment cannot be approved by Lee Kuan Yew, whose predictions have not come true. The reason is that before the Lewis turning point's arrival, like other East Asian economies, Singapore had the characteristic of infinite labor supply, which helped it to avoid the occurrence of the phenomenon of diminishing returns on capital; after the arrival of Lewis turning point, Singapore did not make efforts to stimulate demand but focused on increasing the potential growth rate on the supply side, which relied on foreign workers to extend the demographic dividend and avoided the decline of return on investment through improving labor productivity.

Lewis pointed out: "The key of the whole process (of dual economic development) is capitalist sector's use of surplus."[2] According to this train of thought, summarizing Singapore's experience will promote understanding for how to maintain economic growth after the arrival of the Lewis turning point. Here, we use Figure 6.1 to take a look at how to maintain the returns on investment before and after the Lewis turning point arrives respectively.

Before an economy reaches the Lewis turning point, namely the stage of agricultural labor force surplus' transfer represented by OL, its characteristic of infinite labor supply can give capital accumulation the same proportion of labor supply, thus the phenomenon of diminishing returns on capital will not appear, besides, labor transfer among sectors can create resource reallocation efficiency, thus return on investment can be maintained at a high level, as indicated by AQ in this figure. Many scholars' studies prove that China's economy has indeed maintained a high return on capital for quite a long period of time.[3]

Along with economic development reaching the Lewis turning point, meaning the theoretical marginal productivity of agricultural labor is no longer zero, manifested as labor shortage and rise in wages of ordinary workers, relative scarcity and thus relative price relation between capital and labor changes, capital-labor substitution emerges, marginal return to capital starts to decrease; meanwhile rate of return on investment might also decrease accordingly.

Many findings show that significant and rapid diminishing marginal return on capital has already appeared in China. For example, marginal rate of return on

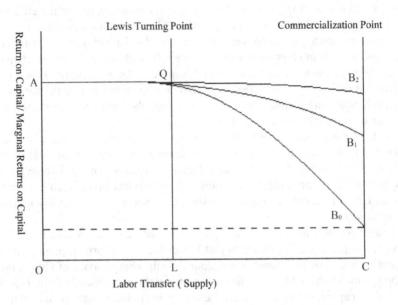

Figure 6.1 Returns on Investment before and after the Lewis Turning Point

capital in China's economy decreased by 18.7% in a short period from 2004 to 2009.[4] From the perspective of rate of return on investment, according to the estimates of Bai Chongen et al., return on capital decreased in China from 24.3% in 2004 to 14.7% in 2013; mean annual decrease rate was 5.7% in that period.[5]

Assuming that other factors are constant, we can expect that the downward trend of diminishing return on capital will continue, as shown by QB_0 in Figure 6.1, until economic development reaches the commercialization point, when marginal labor productivities of agricultural and non-agricultural industries become equal, then the dual economic development stage comes to an end. However, as shown by QB_1 and QB_2 in Figure 6.1, there are some possibilities to slow down or stop the rapid decreases of marginal return on capital and/or return on investment.

Marginal return on capital is the output increase brought by every additional unit of capital input under the condition that other factors remain unchanged. Therefore, it is the basis of return on capital but not the latter's only source. There are two reasons for economists like Krugman to mistakenly think that Singapore's return rate on investment will decrease inevitably: one is that they do not understand that infinite labor supply can prevent the occurrence of the phenomenon of diminishing marginal returns on capital, the other is that they a priori assume that Singapore cannot be transferred into a new way of growth, with which it keeps a higher return on investment through the improvement of productivity.

Lee Kuan Yew can proudly declare to Krugman that Singapore's return rate on investment is still very high, the reason is that Singapore has delayed the arrival of diminishing marginal returns on capital due to its flexible immigration policy and eventually realized its transfer to a productivity-driven way of growth. According to the Global Competitiveness Report 2016 published by the World Economic Forum, Singapore's global competitiveness ranked the second among 138 global economies in the data.

We can draw inspiration from Singapore's experience; we can divide the marginal return on capital and return on investment and take a look at which policy measures can have favorable impacts respectively on these two. In Figure 6.1, we use QB_1's improvement relative to QB_0 to represent the delay of the diminishing marginal returns on capital and use QB_2's improvement relative to QB_1 to represent the effect of maintaining high return on investment, which can be achieved by other factors.

The key for dual economic development to avoid diminishing marginal returns on capital is the existence of the unique phenomenon of infinite labor supply, which can break the neoclassical condition of labor shortage. Therefore, practices that can increase labor supply and ease the phenomenon of labor shortage can slow down the process of diminishing marginal returns on capital. In the example of Singapore, this effect may be generated when a large scale of foreign workers is used (allegedly up to 40% of the total workforce).

However, the period of dual economic development will come to an end eventually, while the neoclassical growth stage is just the destination any late-developing country wants to reach in the end. Therefore, diminishing returns on capital will after all be inevitable, and the key to maintain return on investment lies in the improvement of labor productivity. In other words, labor productivity will not prevent the decline of marginal returns on capital but offset the effect of declining returns on investment caused by the latter, thus maintaining economic growth.

Generally speaking, there are various ways to improve labor productivity, including using machines to replace labor force, improving the proficiency of workers, adopting more efficient technology and process, improving the allocation efficiency of factors of production, etc. In the statistical sense, human capital can be measured; machines' replacement of labor can also be observed from capital-labor ratio's increase, thus other factors become a residual error in an econometric model or are called the total factor productivity under the condition that they cannot be observed directly in the form of statistical variables.

With a econometric method, we can make some simulations to take a look at the increase of labor participation rate, a factor which can delay the phenomenon of diminishing returns on capital, as well as the improvement of total factor productivity, a factor which can maintain the return on investment, thus allowing us to see what effect each has for improving potential growth rate.

Simulation results on China's economy show that, during the period from 2011 to 2020, if we increase labor participation rate of non-agricultural industries to 1% per year, potential growth rate of the annual average GDP can increase by 0.88% during this period. In the same period, if the annual average growth rate of total factor productivity increases by 1%, then potential growth rate of the annual average GDP can increase by 0.99%.[6] The effect of increasing potential growth rate is significant in both cases. There is great potential in China to increase the non-agricultural labor participation rate and total factor productivity, while development of these potentials rely on deepening the reform in relevant fields.

For example, promote the reform of the household registration system, enable more peasant workers to become urban residents, stabilize employment of the transferred rural labor force in urban areas, create conditions to promote the transfer of manufacturing industry from coastal regions to central and Western regions, further develop and improve the labor market, promote more sufficient employment, expand the agricultural business scale and increase agricultural labor productivity so as to increase labor participation rate.

There are also various ways to improve total factor productivity, for example, in the case that the agricultural labor force's proportion remains still high, if we promote the continuous transfer of labor force surplus, we can continuously gain the resource reallocation efficiency. In addition, we can also create resource reallocation efficiency by creating a fairer competitive environment, allowing factors of production's free flow among industries, departments and enterprises, letting long-term inefficient enterprises drop out of business and expanding efficient enterprises accordingly. Finally, we can encourage innovation and promote application of science and technology, narrow the technology gap with developed economies and increase the contribution rate of technological advance to economic growth.

What this simulation we have done here does not mention is that the improvement of laborers' human capital undoubtedly helps to greatly improve the potential growth rate. The ways of human capital accumulation include all kinds of education and training, "learning by doing" etc. The motivation, quality and effect of education and training, along with the learner's adaptive ability to the labor market are related to a series of system factors, which also put forward further requirements for reform.

6.2   Labor productivity

Economists who have paid attention to growth have long found that differences between countries' economic development levels are in the end differences of their productivity. Productivity generally refers to the output capacity level created by a certain level of input, in which "input" can refer to different factors of production such as capital, labor and land, so productivity can refer to capital productivity, labor productivity and land productivity. However, the most frequently used and most comprehensive productivity index, which is also quite meaningful, is labor productivity, namely the index using the output capacity of labor factor to measure economic efficiency.

Statistical departments or researchers measure labor productivity on the overall level, by which they can calculate the GDP produced by each employee, or they can calculate the GDP produced in each working hour. Apparently, there are differences between countries in statistical caliber, data availability and reliability, and different researchers also tend to take different measurement methods; therefore, different research often leads to different results of labor productivity measurement. For this, the attitude we should adopt is admitting the existence of differences between methods and the necessity of diversity, while supporting the issue we try to explain with cross-validations based on different research results.

Wu Xiaoying is good at using unique methods to adjust data like GDP and conducting research related to productivity issues. He emphasized labor productivity's vital importance for economic catch up through transnational horizontal comparison. He also found that recently developed economies' labor productivity improvements were usually much faster than earlier developed countries since they had more technical availabilities. For example, on a comparable economic development stage, the speeds of China's Taiwan and South Korea's labor productivity growths were much higher than that of Japan. However, mainland China did not show a better performance of labor productivity than Japan, South Korea and China's Taiwan in a similar catch-up process.[7]

In fact, this problem is not difficult to understand; we only need to observe how before China's economic reform the planned economy system prevented labor to be allocated to non-agricultural industries, thus to what extent it had accumulated a large proportion of agricultural labor surplus, forming the atypical employment. These observations would be sufficient to explain how big China's employment pressure was before of the reform and opening-up started and how big the scale of labor to be transferred was. In 1978, the proportion of agricultural added value in GDP of China was 28.2%, and the proportion of the labor force was up to 70.5%; the ratio between these two proportions (i.e., comparative labor productivity) was only 0.40, accounting for 14.4% and 20.4% of the secondary industry and tertiary industry respectively.

According to the principle of comparative advantage and the hypothesis of inductive technological evolution, China's economy with serious labor surplus has formed the largest scale of labor migration in human history since the reform and opening-up. During quite a long period, China has focused on developing labor-intensive manufacturing industries and absorbed a large number of agricultural labor surpluses, which are quite rational on both macroscopic and microscopic scales, specifying more clearly that market mechanism has played a good role.

Since joining the WTO, China's labor-intensive manufacturing enterprises in coastal regions have attracted the labor force transferred from rural areas with lower and long-term stable wages, gaining strong competitiveness in the international market. Abundant labor supply with cheap cost is an important factor for China's realization of high economic growth during this period. Therefore, the Lewis turning point and the disappearance of the demographic dividend's influences on economic growth will be demonstrated as labor supply becoming a "bottleneck," along with comparative advantage and competitiveness declining correspondingly under the condition that wage increase leads to higher labor cost in manufacturing industries.

However, theoretically speaking, these disadvantageous factors can be offset by the improvement of labor productivity. The improvement of labor productivity can not only be manifested as the increase of each laborer's output level but can also be manifested as the decrease of quantity of labor force needed by unit output. As a result, even China's economy encountered a labor supply "bottleneck" after experiencing the turning point; if labor productivity can increase according to a certain speed and scale, it is sufficient to make up for the production decrease caused by lack of labor force, thus maintaining the speed of economic growth.

From another perspective, synchronized wage increase based on labor productivity only increases workers' incomes and most widely shares the economic development achievements among inhabitants, which is not destined to hurt comparative advantage and the sustainability of economic growth. Otherwise, do we really hope to never improve the wages of ordinary workers just in order to maintain manufacturing products' competitiveness? In fact, when we talk about synchronizing wage increase with labor productivity improvement, which we are emphasizing to let people share the benefits, we are also emphasizing that wage increase must be based on labor productivity improvement in order to not weaken enterprises' competitiveness and thus to maintain the Chinese manufacturing industry's comparative advantage.

Japanese media and scholars noticed significant backmoving of manufacturing industry production from China to Japan and attributed this to reversal of unit labor cost in these two countries. According to the Japanese media reports, unit labor cost in dollars was three times as much and above in Japan, compared with that in China in 1995. But the cost in China exceeded that in Japan in 2013; this trend still continued in 2014. This statement is not correct thus far, because obviously the cost in China did not exceed that in Japan. In 2013, unit labor cost of China's manufacturing industry was 29.7% of Germany, 36.7% of South Korea and 38.7% of the United States; it was 39.5% of Japan in 2011.

However, it is noteworthy that both labor cost and labor productivity determine the competitiveness of an enterprise, sector and manufacturing industry of a country (tradable goods); they combine to form "unit labor cost," i.e., the ratio of labor cost to labor productivity. Unit labor cost really increases very fast in China, faster than other manufacturing powers. Because first, labor cost increases very fast, average annual growth rate increased from 8.5% in the period of 2001–2005 to 14.8% in the period of 2005–2013; second, increased speed of labor productivity is slower than the increase in wage, from 13.9% down to 9.2%. The acceleration occurs year after year. Therefore, annual average growth rate of unit labor cost increased from –4.9% to 5.2% in the same period (Figure 6.2). At this speed, unit labor cost of China's manufacturing industry will finally exceed that of these manufacturing powers.

The saying that labor productivity can offset labor shortage's effect on weakening growth potential seems to contradict the saying that potential growth rate will inevitably reduce after demographic dividend disappears. In fact, both of these two statements make sense in theory, but after the Lewis turning point appears requirements for improving labor productivity will be greatly enhanced, which also easily generates various misguidance, thus making it more difficult to achieve the effect of improving potential growth rate to a certain extent.

In the stage of dual economic development, since there are a lot of labor surpluses in agriculture, we only need to transfer labors from sectors with low productivity such as agriculture to non-agricultural sectors with higher productivity; thus the

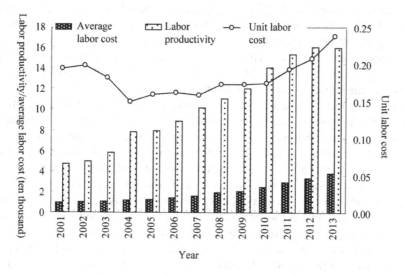

Figure 6.2 Changes in Unit Labor Cost of China's Manufacturing Industry

Source: Attention should Be Paid to Too Rapid Increase of Unit Labor Cost by Cai Fang and Du Yang, New Normality Supply side Structural Reform: Thoughts and Suggestions of An Economist by Zai Caifang, China Social Science Press, 2016.

Chinese economy's labor productivity as a whole will be improved. Therefore, in this stage of development, the opportunity of improving labor productivity is easily available as "low-hanging fruit". For example, according to the estimates of the author, with respect to China's economy between 1978 and 2015, overall labor productivity increased 16.7 times. In which the contribution portion of the primary industry, secondary industry and tertiary industry themselves was 56%, while the contribution of others (44%) came from the reallocation of labor among three industries. As economic development enters a new stage, such opportunities of resource reallocation diminish, and labor productivity can no longer be increased so simply.

Now, let's look at through which ways the improvement of labor productivity is usually realized. If we calculate the output realized by each laborer or labor time, at least four obvious factors have affected the performance of labor productivity. These factors or ways of improving labor productivity will play a big or small role according to time and place, with their difficulty level of achieving good results and sustainability also varying.

The first factor is the laborer's ability, which can generally be gained through developing general education and vocational education, providing on-the-job training, strengthening medical and health protection etc. They can be generally referred to as human capital. Statistically, the most common but inadequate variable of human capital is the average number of years of schooling for workers. Human capital will play a bigger and bigger role in labor productivity improvement as a whole, at the same time being sustainable in the long run.

The second factor is the laborer's capital equipment level, such as the number or scale of machines and equipment each worker can operate, which can be specified by capital-labor ratio in statistics. When labor shortage appears and ordinary workers' wages start to rise constantly, the trend that capital input of the whole economy, especially of the industrial sectors, grows faster than labor input, performs as the improvement of capital-labor ratio.

The third factor is the allocation efficiency of various factors of production, including the coordinated allocation among them, as well as their reasonable allocation among enterprises, industries and regions or among economic activities of different ownership and scale. This efficiency originates from factors of production's full flow, and it is an important component of total factor productivity.

The fourth factor is the efficiency generated by technological progress and system innovation, presenting as typical total factor productivity. For example, if the input of all tangible factors of production (such as capital and labor) increases one percentage, the real output increases more than this percentage point; the additionally increased part is residual error that cannot be interpreted by input, i.e., total factor productivity. Generally speaking, total factor productivity is an eternal source of labor productivity improvement and economic growth. As economic development enters into the neoclassical stage, economic growth depends increasingly on this source of productivity.

6.3   Capital deepening

Which pattern a country's industrial structure presents and what kind of technology type it adopts as a whole are usually determined by the relative scarcity and relative prices of this country's factors of production in a specific stage. Therefore, in terms of a particular stage of development, there exist no problems in which industrial structure and technical structure are better among countries. This is the so-called law of comparative advantage.

In a typical dual economic development stage, labor is abundant and cheap, and enterprises tend to adopt technologies which need more labor and less capital, thus industrial structure has the characteristics of high labor-intensity and low capital-labor ratio. Only in this way can a country obtain comparative advantage and competitive advantage on an enterprise level, industry level and nation level, have higher potential growth rate and achieve faster actual economic growth.

Once an economy crosses the Lewis turning point, relative scarcity of factors of production is reversed. Accordingly, comparative advantage and competitive advantage also vary gradually. Therefore, relative to factors of capital, after labor prices' increase, enterprises tend to use more labor-saving technologies, with their industrial structures being more capital-intensive and capital-labor ratio being increased accordingly. This is the process of capital deepening.

The first to respond to changes in relative prices of the factors of production are enterprises. When entrepreneurs feel the difficulty of recruiting workers and the increase of labor costs, they will usually buy more machines and hire fewer workers. Investors will also react to this new endowment structure of factors of production, and they will start to invest in industries consuming less labor, namely the more capital-intensive ones. Further, the government will follow up accordingly. When the government observes the change of comparative advantage, it often uses some supportive industrial policy measures to encourage investors to invest in industries having potential comparative advantages, which are also relatively capital-intensive or technology-intensive.

If more machines are equipped, labor is appropriately saved and each worker is made to create more output in the case of controlling more machines this means labor productivity is improved. However, simply relying on increasing capital-labor ratio to improve labor productivity may lead to two problems of sustainability.

First of all, the effect of labor productivity improvement generated by capital's replacement of labor is not enough to fill the gap caused by economic growth rate's slowdown. In the dual economic development stage, labor surpluses in agriculture are transferred to non-agricultural industries in great scale, which means labor resources are reallocated from sectors of low productivity to sectors of high productivity, bringing a huge labor productivity improvement and supporting rapid economic growth. After the Lewis turning point, this effect of resource reallocation between agricultural and non-agricultural industries will inevitably weaken gradually, no longer being the main source of supporting economic growth.

At this time, capital (machine)'s replacement of labor is indeed a means of improving labor productivity and sustaining economic growth, while new machines and equipment also embody factors of technical progress; however, if the productivity gap cannot be filled in the condition that there are no total factor productivity's contributions of technological progress and system innovation, economic growth has difficulty maintaining the expected level. Under the effect of the law of diminishing returns on capital, labor's replacement of capital has a limit, especially that it cannot be too quickly conducted in the way of the "great leap forward." For example, in the condition that the operator's human capital is not fundamentally improved, more, more complex and more valued machines cannot be effectively operated, thus return rate on capital input will ultimately drop down. Therefore, an important policy implication of the new normal of economic development is adaptive to the slowdown of economic growth.

Second, there exists another possibility, namely that the cost for improving capital-labor ratio is higher than its economic benefit and therefore labor productivity is not improved. In a normal market environment, prices for factors of production have no distortions, thus we can predict investors and enterprises and keep capital's replacement of labor in control completely and rationally. However, if the government interferes, the situation of capital allocation's deviation from efficiency will appear. Government's behavior, which causes distortion of capital allocation, may originate from the following several different motives.

First, the government hopes to encourage investors to explore new comparative advantages through industrial policies, therefore it offers subsidies to some sectors and enterprises. For example, many local governments have established local pillar industries and leading industries in the future, which they try to include in nation-supported industry planning, and they will build low-cost investment conditions through financial subsidies and preferential loans. However, as private investors may have failure in their choices, this choice made by government does not necessarily conform to dynamic comparative advantage's direction.

Second, the government attempts to implement loose monetary policy to stimulate investment and drive demand, thus forming a macroeconomic policy environment of excess liquidity and causing lack of constraints for investment and financing costs. This financial environment not only encourages excessive investment but also cannot play the role of "survival of the fittest," which eventually leads to the generating of malinvestment, causing a lot of enterprises' and industries' capital intensity to be higher than the normal requirements of comparative advantage. Financial risk is thus accumulated.

Third, the government does not want certain enterprises and industries to perish, thus it tries to help them to survive in relentless competition. A disadvantage of the government's choice of dynamic comparative advantage lies in the fact that, different from a single investor, a government is not willing to accept choice failure. Therefore, for the investments conducted with government support (especially the big projects) or the enterprises being paid the government's special attentions (for example, state-owned enterprises), even if they have made mistakes, the government will not let them be eliminated from the market. Therefore, these enterprises of malinvestment and poor management have captured the government and continue to get capital injections instead, until they become invalid capacity and zombie firms.

These policy motives and policy measures will produce the effect that financing and investment costs are artificially pressed down, thus the price of capital factor is distorted. However, such policies cannot be generally preferential, which will inevitably form an implementation of "government picking winners." For those enterprises and investors being benefited for this or that reason, capital-labor ratio's increase is financially advantageous. Nevertheless, this is seen from the micro level in terms of individual or certain enterprises and investors, while seen from the economy as a whole this does not necessarily lead to the improvement of labor productivity.

On the other hand, selectively providing cheap capital supply actually means deprivation of capital availability for other enterprises, investors and industries. Giving some participants in economic activities a preferential financing environment of capital-availability, from another perspective, is a discriminatory financing environment for other participants. The more abundant, cheap credits are obtained by the protected enterprises, the more serious the difficult and expensive financing problems will become for small businesses and entrepreneurs; these two phenomena just resemble two sides of a coin. Those potential investors and enterprises being neglected not only cannot receive the same equal financing treatment but even have lost fair market environment for factors of production.

In a period of intense adjustment of industrial structure, grasp of a new comparative advantage and improvement of productivity often depend on thousands of small and medium-sized private enterprises' risk investments, thus ultimately making the future industries and technology leaders win out in a kind of competition of creative destructions. Policies which distort capital allocation are meant to protect investments and enterprises of low efficiency, inhibit efficient investment activities and enterprise managements and even kill the potential innovative activities.

Therefore, if such mechanism of creative destruction cannot be developed, potential innovation opportunities will decrease significantly; overall economic productivity cannot increase along with the increase of capital-labor ratio. It may be seen that the increase of capital-labor ratio is not a perfect approach for labor productivity nor a sustainable source to increase productivity.

Japan can provide lessons with reference meanings in this respect, since it has experienced the "Lost Thirty Years." Starting from 1990, Japan's dependency ratio of population started to rise, meaning that the demographic dividend was disappearing rapidly. The Japanese economy's response to this was just the various ways we have discussed to increase physical capital, namely to increase capital-labor ratio. As a result, among Japanese economy's average labor productivity improvement, capital deepening's contribution rate increased significantly from 51% (during the period from 1985 to 1991) to 94% (during the period from 1991 to 2000), while during the same period the contribution rate of total factor productivity dropped straight from 37% to −15% .[8] Many research findings also show that poor performance of total factor productivity is an important reason for the economic stagnation in Japan.

In fact, in the studies about Chinese economy, there is no lack of convincing examples in this aspect. As is well-known to all, the financing conditions for the state-owned economies have great superiorities over those of the non-state-owned. And this kind of differential treatment for financing causes sustainability differences of productivity improvement. According to an econometric analysis,[9] during the period from 1978 to 2007, among the improvement of China's labor productivity (output per labor), the contribution rates of capital-labor ratio (capital per labor) and total factor productivity were respectively 26% and 74% in non-state-owned economies while things were just opposite in state-owned economies, with these numbers being 74% and 26% respectively.

These research findings' direct revelations are that, under the condition that capital-labor ratio contributes a lot for improving labor productivity and is growing rapidly, it often leads to total factor productivity's corresponding contribution's decline. In other words, now total factor productivity is the most sustainable productivity and thus the source of economic growth, yet excessive increase of capital-labor ratio will hinder the performance of total factor productivity in the overall economy. Therefore, once the capital deepening, which intends to increase labor productivity and even sustain economic growth, goes beyond a reasonable boundary, its effect might be completely opposite for the former and might be more haste, less speed for the latter.

6.4   Total factor productivity

The reason why many people believe that a country's economy presents the trend of capital-labor ratio increasing on the whole along with the improvement of the economic development level, is related to the spread of a so-called "Hoffmann's

Law." In the early 1930s, according to observations on early and middle periods of industrialization, German economist W. G. Hoffmann found that, along with the advancement of industrialization, sectors producing capital goods (heavy industry) tended to grow faster and faster compared with sectors producing consumer goods (light industry). The result was naturally that the whole economy's capital intensity became higher and higher.

This "law" is also consistent with early economic growth theory. For example, the famous "Harold-Thomas Model" assumes that the accumulation of physical capital is the only engine of economic growth. The Solow growth model gives the same reasoning. Interpretations of different economic growth performance in different countries based on this theory will come to this conclusion: those countries with insufficient capital accumulation will eventually lag behind the countries with faster capital accumulation. Therefore, in developed countries, due to labor shortage, the result of capital accumulation will surely become an increase in capital-labor ratio. Or we may see from the result that countries with better growth performance will have a higher capital-labor ratio.

According to this logic, the traditional growth theory will have an implied policy recommendation for catch-up countries, which is that the state should spare no effort to help society achieve a capital accumulation rate of critical minimum level, then use it as a material basis to improve labor productivity along with economic take-off and society's constant improvement of capital-labor ratio by itself.

However, there are a lot of classic cases in economic history rejecting the Harold-Thomas theoretical hypothesis and Hoffmann's empirical evidence. For example, the Soviet Union during the period of planned economy as well as China and India, which started industrialization in the 1950s were all countries clearly putting forward the implementation of heavy industry's prior development strategy. However, the results of this industrialization strategy's implementation all contradicted this policy's original purpose. Until these three countries began a series of system reform, India was characterized by industrial development badly lagging behind, while the Soviet Union and China manifested as having an abnormally high proportion of heavy industry with serious imbalance of industrial structure.

Robert Solow, the representative of the neoclassical growth theory, started from the law of diminishing returns on capital and found that the only source of long-term economic growth was an element in economic growth which could not be explained by regular input of factors of production, namely the total factor productivity. However, this factor of productivity came from a series of improvements such as technological progress, resource allocation and system innovation. In the mainstream neoclassical growth studies, a large number of literature concludes from the empirical perspective that total factor productivity can explain the difference of countries' growth performances to a large extent.

Economic developments of the Soviet Union before economic transformation and China before reform and opening-up were not successful. For instance, total factor productivities of the Soviet Union after the 1970s and China during the whole period from 1957 to 1978 grew negatively. Research shows that during the period from 1958 to 1978 China's GDP annual growth rate was 3.9%, among which capital and labor's contributions were 2.3% and 2.1% respectively, while total factor productivity offset inputs' contributions with its contribution rate for economic growth being –0.6%.[10]

In fact, not only the failure of the planned economies and developing countries have proved that it is productivity rather than the accumulation of capital that is an inexhaustible source of economic growth, since developed countries also have rich positive and negative materials in this regard.

A negative material is the Japanese economy after 1990. Japanese economist Fumio Hayashi and American economist Prescott found in their research of Japan's first "lost decade" that the reason for Japan's economic stagnation was neither enterprises' incapacity to get capital nor the problems of the financial system but was in the end total factor productivity's poor performance. Yet the reason for total factor productivity' poor performance was that government subsidized enterprises of low efficiency and industries in decline, resulting in the output share of low-efficiency enterprises being too high while investments conducive to improving productivity were reduced.[11]

While Singapore is a positive case, we have discussed the famous case initiated by Krugman questioning the economic growth sustainability of Singapore. In economic researche, empirical research findings for this debate are quite different, so people once suspected whether the concept of total factor productivity could become an empirically confirmable standard. However, this debate also enabled Singapore leaders to understand this pretty academic economics concept and its significance for economic growth sustainability, so they set a national goal of a 2% increase in total factor productivity per year.[12] Perhaps because of this the economic growth performance of Singapore is still eye-catching; it becomes an innovation-driven model. Various indices of Singapore such as global competitiveness and global innovation index are leading in the world, far ahead of the most developed country in Asia, Japan.

It is interesting that both Solow and Lewis's articles were published in the 1950s, and the former's theory has gained lasting fame, being the mainstream growth theory by far, while the latter's theory seems to be a flash in the pan, already losing the mainstream status.[13] However, neoclassical growth theory has not become the one and only way to prevent the mistakes of economic policies. Except that policy choices have been influenced by many factors of time and place, the failure of neoclassical growth theory also lies in its theoretical model's characteristic of being not open.

Worldwide economic growth experience shows that the manifestation and realization form of total factor productivity in different countries are ultimately related to development stage, resource allocation mechanism and economic policy, while in neoclassical growth theory many such important factors are processed to exogenous variables. The more inadequate, mainstream growth theory neglects dual economy characteristics of developing countries, while the unlimited labor supply characteristic may break up the law of diminishing returns on capital exactly, and productivity may be improved through reallocation of labor.

Hence, the theory more suitable for the actual situation of developing countries did not generate a positive policy impact effect in the past decades. Perhaps the initiator of neoclassical growth theory thought that increase in productivity should be done by enterprises; economists should provide the most explanatory framework for reality, without the intention to guide policymaking and implementation.

This thinking has its rationality. Total factor productivity is a residual in statistics, which generally puts together growth sources which cannot be explained by factor inputs. Therefore just understanding this theory does not make people know how to improve total factor productivity, especially that this productivity improvement is actually the result of thousands of producers' competitions and mechanism for the survival of the fittest. No matter how keen the government is to promote economic development, after all it cannot offer any help.

Even so, if the mainstream theorists of growth could have given Lewis's theory more respect and concern and make their own theories more open and inclusive, they could have formed a growth theory analytical framework with more explanatory power. Using the characteristics of dual economic development and its transformation into market economy to enrich and replenish neoclassical growth theory, thus forming a more consistent analytical framework, can not only help us to better understand the evolution the Chinese economy has experienced and challenges it faces so as to avoid policy mistakes but also can make contributions to mainstream growth theories with China's experiences and theories.

China's economic development so far can be seen as both a unique and successful experience and an important component of the Asian miracle. Other Asian countries and regions' economic development provide not only experiences of the few countries that have successfully stepped across the middle-income stage and become high-income economies in the world, but also negative examples of countries falling into the middle-income trap. In addition, there are warnings and lessons of high-income countries falling into economic stagnation.

A recently-developed advantage catch-up countries have in economic development is that they have quite a lot of successful experience and failure lessons to refer to. Openly using all kinds of economic theories, dialectically summarizing various economic policies' advantages and disadvantages and profoundly understanding the Chinese economy's particularity can help us to start the new engine of the Chinese economy's sustainable growth on the changed stage of development. The 19th National Congress of CPC Report puts forward a clear requirement to increase total factor productivity. Writing this academic term in a political report of the ruling party at National Congress means that the Party Central Committee grasps the future growth driver of China's economy and how to start it very accurately.

Notes

1 Miyazaki Isamu. (2009). *Memoir of Witnesses of Japanese Economic Policies* (pp. 188–189). Beijing: CITIC Press.
2 Arthur Lewis. (1954). Economic Development with Unlimited Supply of Labor. *The Manchester School*, 22.

3 Bai Chongen, Chang-Tai Hsieh, and Qian Yingyin. (2006). The Return to Capital in China. *NBER Working Paper*, w12755, Cambridge, MA.

4 Cai Fang and Wen Zhao. (2012). When Demographic Dividend Disappears: Growth Sustainability of China. In Masahiko Aoki and Jinglian Wu (Eds.), *The Chinese Economy: A New Transition*. Basingstoke: Palgrave Macmillan.

5 Bai Chongen and Zhang Qiong. (2014). Rate of Return to Capital in China and the Influencing Factors. *The Journal of World Economy, 10*, 3–30.

6 Cai Fang and Li Yang. (2013). Population Change and Resulting Slowdown in Potential GDP Growth in China. *China & World Economy, 21*(2), 1–14.

7 Wu Xiaoying. (2012). Get Rid of Speed Complex, Offer Space for Reform: Enlightenment of Growth Speed and its Impact on Structural Adjustment and Efficiency Improvement by Comparing China with East Asian Economies. *China Economic Observation·Global Vision and Decision-Making Reference, 12*.

8 Asian Productivity Organization. (2008). *APO Productivity Databook 2008* (p. 23). Tokyo: The Asian Productivity Organization.

9 Loren Brandt and Xiaodong Zhu. (2010, February). Accounting for China's Growth. *Working Paper*, 395, Department of Economics, University of Toronto.

10 Dwight Perkins. (2005). Looking at China's Economic Growth from a Historical and International Perspective. *China Economic, 4*(4).

11 Fumio Hayashi and Edward C. Prescott. (2002). The 1990s in Japan: A Lost Decade. *Review of Economic Dynamics, 5*(1), 206–235.

12 Jesus Felipe. (1997). Total Factor Productivity Growth in East Asia: A Critical Survey. In Asian Development Bank. *EDRC Report Series*, No.65 (p. 27). Manila, Philippines.

13 Gustav Ranis. (2004). *Arthur Lewis' Contribution to Development Thinking and Policy* (No.891). New Haven, CT: Yale University, Economic Growth Center.

7   Beyond the demographic dividend

Demographic dividend comes from the special properties of population structure, especially the age structure. These kinds of properties can earn some additional advantages for economic growth and support higher potential growth rate. Once conditions are ready, such potential growth capacity may be turned into actual high speed growth. In the case of being simplified, we can see that the growth rate of the working-age population – or another manifestation, dependency ratio – may be a highly generalized index; its special attributes may be reflected in the advantages or disadvantages of labor supply, human capital accumulation, savings rate, rate of return on investment, productivity etc. Therefore, we take the peak of the working-age population – or the turning point of dependency ratio of population from declining to growing – as a symbol of demographic dividend's disappearance.

It is true that we need to realize, as an inevitable result of demographic transition rules, that demographic dividend will eventually disappear, and long-term economic growth will need to find a more sustainable growth source in the end. However, if we can make an issue on tapping labor potential and changing the component factors of dependency ratio of population, namely to make the reduced number of working-age population more productive through a higher rate of employment, reallocation of labor and better human capital accumulation or, in the long run, to slow down the aging process by regulating the family planning policy some time in the future, we are undoubtedly making useful attempts to continue the demographic dividend. Since such opportunities of tapping potentials rely on reform; these corresponding practices may be regarded as surpassing demographic dividend or opening reform dividend rather than continuing demographic dividend.

7.1   Future challenges of employment

For many years, annual economic growth rate's "protection of eight," namely the GDP growth rate set by the government being not lower than 8% seemed to be a permanent rule. China suffered the strike of the Asian financial crisis in 1998. Prime Minister Zhu Rongji at that time required the government to implement the necessary policies to ensure a growth rate of no less than 8%. In 2009, in the face of global financial crisis's strike on China's real economy, Wen Jiabao, Prime

Minister of the State Council at that time, also put forward the requirement of "protection of eight." The information Premier Wen got from relevant departments was that 24 million non-farm employments needed to be created every year to avoid serious unemployment problems.

A phenomenon worthy to be noted is, since China entered the Tenth Five-year Plan Period (2001–2005), economic growth rate expected by all previous Five-year Plans were not high, for example, the "Tenth Five-year plan" around 7%, "Eleventh Five-year Plan" at 7.5%, "Twelfth Five-year Plan" at 7% and "Thirteenth Five-year Plan" no less than 6.5%. However, according to the implementation processes of the Tenth and Eleventh Five-year Plans, the government still wanted to exceed this expected goal, which was reflected in the requirement of "protection of eight" specially put forward in certain years. However, growth rate expected in the "Twelfth Five-year Plan" was set according to a lower goal, and there was no hard-and-fast rule for "protection of eight" when encountering difficulties. For example, the annual growth rate target in 2012 was 7.5%. And in fact, after the actual annual growth rate dropped to 7.7% in 2012, the GDP growth rate went down every year.

We should say that the central government's expectation for growth rate change is in accordance with economic laws, namely, one of the performance characteristics of economic development in new normality is the downward trend of economic growth. Before the "Twelfth Five-year Plan" period, China always had a higher potential growth rate, which was on the whole higher than the planned growth rate target. However, during the "Eleventh Five-year Plan" period, the trend of actual growth rate exceeding potential growth rate had showed up, while at the same time, starting from the "Twelfth Five-year Plan" period, potential growth rate had declined significantly. If economic growth continued at the previous actual growth rate, it would undoubtedly cause a big gap of negative growth. In other words, the economic growth target before that period still had room to approach potential growth ability, while the growth rate target after that period had already been quite close to the latter (see Figure 5.4).

Although the expected target growth rate in the "Twelfth Five-year Plan" was 7%, actually, the government still hoped to exceed this target during implementation. According to our calculations, the predicted value of the average potential growth rate in these five years was 7.55%, therefore, the ultimately achieved actual growth rate of 7.8% was still higher than the potential growth rate, and thus cyclical unemployment would not be caused. In fact, the urban registered unemployment rate and investigated unemployment rate both remained stable in these years; the ratio of jobs to applicants (also called opening-to-application ratio) on the urban public employment service market exceeded 1 as shown by the data, and in uptrend the minimum wage standard was increased greatly in most provinces, municipalities directly under the Central Government and autonomous regions in China. This trend has lasted to the "Thirteenth Five-Year Plan" and up to the present.

Change having more turning nature was that according to the demographic data, the 15–59-year-old working-age population peaked in 2010 and entered a negative growth period thereafter; absolute reduction was millions per year, and the predicted reduction of the population will be 29.34 million in the period from 2010 to 2020. Even considering labor participation rate, the economically active population of the same year (working-age population multiplied by labor participation rate) also peaked in 2017, then turned to negative growth; this means absolute reduction of China's labor supply.

At the same time, the medium-to-high speed of economic growth, especially the expansion of urban non-agricultural industries, still created a strong demand for labor. For example, the total urban employment scale increased from 347 million in 2010 to 414 million in 2016; the mean annual increase was 3%. If we regard this quantity and its change as the labor demand factor and regard the change of the working-age population or economically active population as the labor supply factor, huge change, in other words, fundamental reversing has occurred in the relation between labor supply and demand.

For a long time, we constantly remind ourselves or inform others, tremendous total population and labor force was China's biggest national condition, and China's labor market will be in the state of supply greater than demand for a long time. Such logic and policy inclination still continue, without due adjustment based on realistic changes to a large extent. To a certain extent, this emphasis is meant to remind the government and society not to ignore the prioritized status of employment. Within a certain period of time, in order to prevent the appearance of neglect of employment problems, denying the change of supply and demand in the labor market seems to be a white lie. However this protracted national condition and state changed fundamentally with the Lewis turning point in 2004 and the demographic dividend turning point in 2010; it was not influenced by people's will. Admission of such change, on the one hand, does not mean no worry of employment problems in China, and on the other hand, it's more helpful for us to identify and welcome new labor market challenges.

We only need to look at a simple phenomenon to find that this thinking related previously with policy does not make sense logically. That is, oral or documented policy priority does not necessarily guarantee actual policy effect. For a long time, employment was a much higher government policy priority in developed countries of the market economy (which are in a normal state of labor shortage) than in China (which has an infinite labor supply). For example, for quite a long time, central banks of Western countries mostly put "high employment" first among basic goals of monetary policy, while other goals were economic growth, price, interest rate, financial market and foreign exchange market stabilities. However, for a long time, employment was not reflected in China's macroeconomic policy goals.

For a long time, the mature market economy's macroeconomic policy goals had long been fixed on employment, while developing countries focused on promoting economic growth, thus bringing more employment opportunities through creating more job positions. However, due to the decline of Keynesianism and the rise of monetarism, over the past decades, no matter whether in developed countries or in developing countries, this macroeconomic policy tradition has undergone a huge change, becoming more and more simply focused on price stability, while some countries even have accepted inflation targeting. This is taken as a principle of the "Washington Consensus" in many countries having encountered debt crisis, which is embodied in the conditions for getting loans from the International Monetary Fund and World Bank.

This policy goals' deviation is based on assumptions that as long as price stability is achieved economic growth and full employment will naturally be reached as results. However, this single macroeconomic policy goal is proved to be based on a false assumption, when in fact full employment and economic growth will not be reached automatically after price reaches stability. Developed countries and developing countries' experiences show that such a policy shift has led to bad consequences, whose harm to developing countries is especially obvious.[1]

Since entering the 21st century, China's concern with macroeconomic policies for employment is opposite of many Western countries. In order to deal with the serious situation of employment in the late 1990s and safeguard people's basic livelihood, the Chinese government started to implement a proactive employment policy and launch a series of policy measures promoting employment and re-employment. In 2002, the 16th CPC National Congress Report put forward to implement long-term strategies and policies to promote employment and listed promoting economic growth, increasing employment, stabilizing prices and maintaining balance of international payments as the main targets of macroeconomic regulation and control. The central government's statement for employment has been gradually improved from the demand that expanding employment expansion be put onto a more prominent status in economic and social development and active employment policy to the implementation of developing an employment first strategy.

It is with this proactive employment policy, which pays great attentions to employment, especially the development of the labor market, promoting urban and rural employment expansion and labor resource reallocation under this policy framework, that China can give play to comparative advantage and realize high speed economic growth, successively pass the Lewis turning point and the turning point of demographic dividend's disappearance in a relatively short period of time and realize the transcendence of economic development stages.

However, we should see that in different economic development stages employment problems do not have the same nature, thus the type of policy should also change. The solution to structural employment conflicts was emphasized in the Report of the 19th National Congress of the CPC. China's economy started to change gradually from a typical dual economic development process to the neoclassical growth stage after transcending the Lewis turning point and losing the demographic dividend. Accordingly, the labor market began to experience an accelerated transition from dual structure to neoclassicism, and the employment contradictions it faced became more and more structural and frictional rather than on the whole.

That is to say, it has become more and more the focus of employment policy to respond to structural unemployment problems produced by the mismatch between the industrial structure change and laborers' skills as well as laborers' frictional unemployment problems during the period when laborers are looking for jobs on the job market, while also maintaining moderate economic growth to create job positions. China's employment problems mainly focus on three groups, which are given universal attention by the Chinese society: migrant workers, urban workers with employment difficulties and college graduates. We can see the structural and frictional employment difficulty and natural unemployment problems from these three groups.

At present, although official urban employment statistics mainly cover the employment of the urban population and include the employment of the rural labor force in urban areas gradually, a large part of peasant workers are still omitted by urban employment statistics. If we process the data and include migrant workers into them, then the total urban employment population in 2015 was 424 million; this number was higher than the number in the Statistical Yearbook, 39.7% of whom were migrant workers having entered town for more than six months. That is to say, migrant workers had been the main part of urban employment; their increment alleviates the negative urban employment growth actually incurred.

Seen from the survey in 2011, migrant workers' average years of education was 9.6 years. This human capital situation makes them properly adapt to labor-intensive jobs in the secondary industry (which requires the laborer to have 9.1 years of education), as well as in the tertiary industry (which requires 9.6 years of education). However, the trend of China's future economy is slowdown of economic growth and acceleration of industrial structure adjustment. According to positions' requirements for human capital, which are 10.4 years in the secondary industry capital-intensive jobs and 13.3 years in the tertiary industry technology-intensive jobs, migrant workers' levels of education are not enough to support them changing to the new jobs.

After experiencing the Lewis turning point and labor shortage phenomenon, under the condition of ordinary workers' salaries increasing very quickly, it seems that the new generation of migrant workers who were born after the 1980s do not understand the difficulty of employment and are more and more unwilling to enter high school after graduating from junior middle school, while their high job-hopping rate means that they have given up a lot of on-the-job training opportunities. More seriously, many rural adolescents are even eager to go out to work before completing compulsory education. However, this golden period of the labor market will not be sustained for a long time. Those migrant workers, whose human capital cannot satisfy the future labor market's demand for skills, will encounter the perplexity of structural unemployment.

Traditionally, "Come and Go" or migratory bird type labor migration mode is a means of solving peasant workers' unemployment problems. However, with the revolution of the agricultural production mode, labor-saving agricultural mechanization is quickened, and increase in labor productivity is accelerated correspondingly; agriculture can no longer play the role of surplus labor reservoir, labor migration becomes more and more one-way, thus this means it will no longer work in the future. The new generation of migrant workers born after the 1980s have become the dominant peasant workers; according to the survey in 2010, 33% of them have lived in towns at all levels rather than in rural areas before the age of 16 and 38% went to primary schools in towns at all levels. We can say that most of them never have farming experience, not to mention the intention to return to the rural area to be a farmer. Besides, change in the manner of agricultural production depends more and more on labor-saving technical change, thus agriculture is no longer the reservoir for labor force surplus.

We can see that the fundamental way to prevent migrant workers from facing employment risk is to improve their human capital and enable them to have skill updates corresponding to the industry structure optimization and upgrading. On the one hand, since migrant workers are a group who are updated constantly by new growing labor forces so far, creating good system conditions and making new growing laborers receive ordinary education and vocational education as much as possible before entering the labor market should be the key point of policy response. On the other hand, according to the requirements at the 19th National Congress of the CPC, the more fundamental approach is to break down institutional and mechanism disadvantages that hinder social mobility of labor force and talents, promote citizenization for the transferred rural labor force and realize equal access to basic public services including human capital training.

Contrary to the situation of migrant workers, urban laborers having permanent urban residential registration has shown a well-established aging trend. In fact, if there is no mass flow-in of rural laborers, not only could urban demand for labor not be met, but urban labor forces' ages would also be much older than actually shown. According to the data of the sixth census, for example, among the urban permanent working age population aged 15 to 59 in 2010, for the proportion of the age group from 20 to 29, foreign population accounted for 35.0%, while local registered population accounted for 21.6%; for the proportion of age group from 50 to 59, foreign population accounted for 7.2%, while local registered population accounted for 19.3% (see Figure 7.1).

Therefore, among labor forces with urban registered permanent residence, there is a larger proportion of population whose human capital accumulations are obviously insufficient, represented as the age being higher and level of education being lower; thus it is difficult for them to adapt to the industrial structure adjustment's higher demand for skills, nor can they adapt to the postponed retirement requirements in the future. Some of these laborers are recognized by the government as urban labors having employment difficulty, being taken as the targeted population for key support. In fact, this demographic composition feature of urban workers determines that there is always a relatively stable group, who are often in the state of structural and frictional unemployment, forming a typical natural unemployment. What's more, with the increasing population aging, the proportion of this group might increase.

Estimates show that since 2000 China's urban natural unemployment rate has been about 4.0% to 4.1%, which is in accordance with the registered urban unemployment rate over the years; we may see the changes of various unemployment rates and their relationships in Figure 7.2. As is well-known to all, the statistical object of the registered urban unemployment rate is only urban residents with

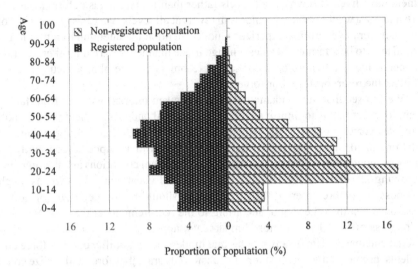

Figure 7.1 Age Composition of Urban Permanent Working Age Population

Source: Census Data in 2010, edited by Census Office of the State Council and Population and Employment Statistics Division of National Bureau of Statistics, China Statistical Publishing House, 2012

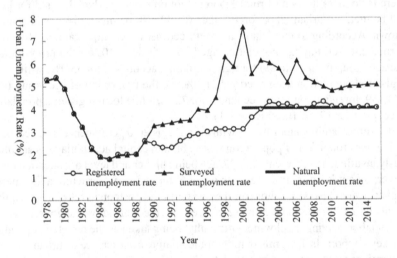

Figure 7.2 Changes of Urban Unemployment Rate in China

Source: National Bureau of Statistics: *China Statistical Yearbook 2012*; Du Yang and Lu Yang: China's Level of Natural Unemployment Rate and Its Meaning, *World Economy, 2011*, (4); relevant media reports

urban registered permanent residence, excluding peasant workers, that is to say, local workers with urban registered permanent residence are regularly employed, as seen from this characteristic of unemployment rate they only bear the structural and frictional natural unemployment. However, from the change trend of the surveyed unemployment rate in Figure 7.2, in fact, cyclical unemployment still happens from time to time, so obviously migrant workers become the only bearers of cyclical unemployment. Along with the macro economy's cyclical fluctuations, the phenomenon of migrant workers returning home and shortage of migrant workers appearing alternately and repeatedly can prove this conclusion.

Speaking of natural unemployment risk faced by urban workers, we have to mention a feature of this group's human capital composition. Due to the significant achievements of China's education development since the 1990s, which have abnormally and rapidly added to the new growing labor forces' years of education, China's working-age population's human capital distribution characteristic is that the older, the fewer years of education. Since urban laborers' ages are older, the group having insufficient human capital also accounts for a bigger proportion. Under the condition of industrial structure changing very rapidly, quite a large proportion of laborers have difficulties meeting the labor market's requirement for skills, thus easily falling into the state of structural unemployment. This is also a very realistic reason why this group is reluctant to accept the policy of extending retirement age.

University graduates' employment difficulty along with their wages' convergence to low-end laborers has more and more become a phenomenon attracting a wide range of social concern and become the basis for some skeptics to criticize enrollment expansion of colleges and universities. We should say that changes happening after the enrollment expansion of colleges and universities are dramatic and fundamental – making people fail to fully understand and properly respond – and are also inevitable. This fundamental change is that China has entered the stage of higher education popularization in a very short time.

Early in 1973, an American scholar Martin Trow proposed the theory of higher education popularization, pointing out that higher education gross enrollment rate within 15% was the stage of elite education; from 15% to 50% was the stage of higher education popularization; more than 50% was the stage of mass popularization of higher education. According to this theory, in 2002, the third year of enrollment expansion, China entered the stage of higher education popularization. After higher education entered the popularization stage, some regularities for university graduates' employment were gradually revealed. Public opinions and policies will be misled if these regularities are not recognized.

Labor economics research shows that the higher level of education degree, especially after receiving the education of bachelor's degree or above, the longer it will take for job seekers to realize their match with the labor market. That is to say, if university graduates want to find ideal jobs, they need to spend more time in job-seeking and conversion. Therefore, judging simply using university graduates' employment rate after a few months of their graduation as well as their starting salary level does not get the correct conclusion about this group's human capital advantage or usefulness.

What's more, as far as real labor market behavior is concerned, after experiencing a long time of job-seeking and realizing employment for the first time, laborers with a high degree of education will get career advancement faster or still be in the process of job-seeking. In addition, superior human capital conditions also give them more opportunities for career development and they have better career development through accumulation of time or rotation of jobs, thus eventually they are at an advantageous position in the labor market.

People will ask what labor market and government's active employment policies can really do for the employment of college graduates. It is undoubted that labor market signals are very important for leading the behaviors of each party concerned. Imagine if the phenomenon of unemployment and lay-offs didn't appear in the late 1990s, which motivated laborers to change employment expectations and skills and realize employment and re-employment through the labor market; the allocation of urban labor resources would not be established on the basis of market mechanism till now. The employment of college graduates is the same: a certain degree of structural unemployment is necessary for this laborer group's adjustments of expectation and job-seeking behavior.

In recent years, the labor market's supply and demand condition shows a seemingly contradictory phenomenon. On the one hand, laborers having college and university degrees are often not as popular as laborers having degrees of vocational high school, technical training school and high school. In fact, the condition of college graduates' employment is worse than that of junior high school graduates. On the other hand, the labor market has a very strong demand for laborers holding senior professional qualification certificates or senior professional technical positions, while laborers only holding junior vocational qualification certificates or junior professional technical positions are relatively unpopular.

This undoubtedly means that laborers' human capital is not useless, the question is what the labor market or employer uses to judge human capital. There is a "sheepskin effect" in labor economics. Which means that the employer cares whether job seekers are matched with their jobs but does not care about their educational background actually, yet when there is no other objective standard for judging ability of the job seekers in advance, educational background (sheepskin was used to make diploma in ancient Europe) is regarded as a substitution standard. If performance of the educational attainment represented by educational background is not as good as the skill level and competent degree represented by vocational qualification or professional technical title in real life or educational background is not converted to the employability skills required by the labor market, employers will attach more importance to qualifications rather than educational background.

This kind of signal is the information transferred by the labor market; on the one hand, it puts forward a proposition of how to align educational background with skills for teachers and students and proposes topics for the reform and adjustment of higher education system, on the other hand, it's a necessary pilot signal for government functioning and enriches the connotations of active employment policy implemented by government. Structural employment difficulties faced by college graduates indeed need the help from labor market functions and employment policies, but problems such as improper major and curriculum setup, being out of step with market demand and low teaching quality may also exacerbate structural employment difficulties faced by college graduates, putting forward many research topics for reforming and adjusting the higher education system. All of these put forward new challenges for the government's active employment policies.

However, no matter the phenomenon of university graduates' employment difficulty or the signals for this community's employment conditions released by the labor market, obviously neither of them can become the reason for slowing down the development of higher education. Experiences and lessons from each country's economic development cannot support the statement that education may be excessive; on the contrary, in almost all circumstances human capital is a magic weapon to overcome structural and frictional employment difficulties and help entrepreneurship and employment.

7.2 Will education be excessive?

Since the 1980s, China's education development has realized remarkable achievements, having not only consolidated previous education achievements but also realized education's great leap through popularization of nine-year compulsory education and expansion of higher education enrollment. In 2016, three-year preschool gross kindergarten enrollment rate was 77.4%, net enrollment rate of primary school was 99.9%, gross enrollment rate of junior high school was 104.0%; nine-year compulsory education consolidation rate was 93.4%, gross enrollment rate of senior high school was 87.5% and gross enrollment rate of higher education was 42.7%, overall indicators of educational development exceeding the average level of upper middle-income countries. This achievement of educational development has been converted to the increasing labor human capital through reform and opening-up, becoming an important contributing factor to the miracle of China's economic growth.

We can roughly regard teenagers graduating from schools at all levels who would not continue their education as the new growing labor force of that education level. New human capital per year depends on two factors, namely, educational development and population increment. Among the new growing labor forces, the proportion of teenagers only having primary school education dropped significantly after the mid-1980s; accordingly, the proportion of junior high school graduates was greatly improved, especially after 1990s; yet since the first decade of the 21st century the proportion of college graduates has increased rapidly, thus the proportion of high school graduates has also improved.

However, after entering the second decade of the 21st Century and further predicted to 2020 (Figure 7.3), we may see a slowing trend of human capital improvement. This change is first the consequence of demographic transition. Since educational attainment of the new growing workforce is higher than the workforce inventory, improvement of China's human capital has been made by the continuous entering of a new growing workforce to a great degree for a long time. Therefore, with working-age population entering the negative growth stage, the new growing workforce decreases year after year; the negative effect of new growing human capital caused by quantity factor starts to exceed the positive effect of

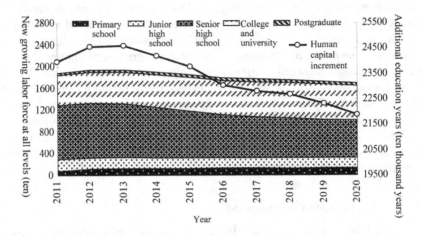

Figure 7.3 Changes in the Human Capital Composition of New Growing Labor Force

Source: calculated according to the *China Statistical Yearbook* issued by the National Bureau of Statistics of China in corresponding years

new growing workforce due to higher years of education, so new growing human capital decreases progressively.

Looking further ahead, the good trend of China's education development and human capital accumulation will not necessarily and naturally continue. Education development is mainly benefited by two prominent policy effects till today, namely the positive effects of popularizing 9 years of compulsory education and expanding enrollment of higher learning institutions. However, the unsustainability of education development is presented as new challenges faced by these two policies themselves on the one hand and policy consensus on how to realize the new breakthrough of education development that should be reached but has not yet been made on the other hand.

Government efforts to popularize compulsory education were officially launched in 1985. Although due to some negative factors, such as excessive rural debt caused in order to meet targets, debates between different views once appeared, in the end, this policy was proved to be far-sighted, which had a significantly positive effect on China's human capital accumulation. However, since elementary school and junior high school enrollment rates are already very high at present, the trend of diminishing policy effect has been shown, which means compulsory education can no longer make great contributions for significantly improving the population's years of education on the whole.

College expansion began in 1999, whose original intention was delaying teenagers' time until entering the labor market, thus alleviating employment pressure at that time. An unexpected effect was that China's higher education entered into the stage of popularization since then. The number of college graduates within a year jumped from 0.85 million in 1999 to 6.8 million in 2012. Enrollment expansion of colleges and universities also has a predictable side effect, which is driving the improvement of the high school enrollment rate, which together with the former has increased the new growing labor force's years of education.

As appeared in many other countries and regions, higher education popularization is often accompanied by phenomena such as graduates' employment difficulty and relatively decreased wages, which have also happened in China. This leads to the formation of a criticism wave assuming that the expansion has some blindness. Although such criticism has not been officially recognized, policies for it have begun to become cautious, and enrollment growth after 2008 has slowed down. For example, growth rate of ordinary university undergraduate and college enrollment decreased from 7.4% in 2008 to 3.5% in 2010 and then decreased to 1.5% in 2016. Of course, this downtrend does not exclude the impact of demographic changes.

In the condition that diminishing marginal effect of those policies mentioned previously has appeared, people will hope the state's financial spending on education will increase significantly. The target that the state's financial education spending should reach a share of 4% of GDP put forward by "China's Education Reform and Development Outline" and enacted early in 1993 was not finally realized until 2012. However, is this number enough to solve the problem of Chinese education's sustainable development? To answer this question, we need first to clarify which factors have already emerged and may hinder Chinese education's further development.

The concern that education may develop excessively exists in many people's minds. Of course, it is due to the appearance of university graduates' employment difficulty in the labor market that people make this speculation: should we not expand higher education in such a large scale? From the perspective of economics, determining whether the enrollment expansion of colleges and universities is blind or answering the question of whether the mass popularization process over the past 10 or more years leads to higher education's excessive problem according to human capital return rate is simple and straightforward. In this aspect, whether using data before or after the enrollment expansion, econometric studies all have shown that higher education has a higher return rate than the lower education stage.

In these studies, the conclusions using data after enrollment expansion is more meaningful. This is because before enrollment expansion, the proportion of university graduates was very low and "scarcity is precious," thus it was reasonable that they got higher returns in the labor market, and if higher education still gets a higher return rate after the enrollment expansion, it means that this expansion conforms to labor market demand. For example, Li Hongbin found that after college expansion in 1999, the scale average wage of employees having a junior college diploma or above was higher than high school graduate employees, and this continues to improve, reaching the height of 49% in 2009.[2]

It is also necessary for us to jump out of this utilitarian consideration of immediate return rate and answer this question from a longer perspective: why do we need higher education's rapid development? The former British Prime Minister Margaret Thatcher once said: we don't need to worry about China, because it is a country that can only produce washing machines and refrigerators, but cannot create ideas. For some people's wide quotation of these words, others disagree and think this statement does not conform to the reality that China has splendid cultural heritage and continuously makes prosperous achievements in culture during the period of reform and opening-up.

Indeed, we should never take a self-humiliated or nihilistic attitude toward achievements made by ourselves and cultural heritage created by our ancestors and the great leaps of Chinese people from standing up to becoming rich then to becoming strong. Besides, the quantitative and qualitative rise of Chinese scientific papers, the top ranking of the number of registered patents in the world, the rapid catching up of R&D investment scale, the excellent performance of Chinese high school students in International Student Assessment, Nobel Prize winners such as scientist Tu Youyou and writer Mo Yan – all these performances only show a drop in the ocean of the Chinese nation's creativity, which is certainly worth being proud of. However, we might as well consider what kind of attitude we should adopt to treat criticisms as Ms. Thatcher's from the following perspectives.

The Chinese proverb "hear all parties" should also include foreigners. Besides, in terms of international comparison, foreigners' impressions are also a frame of reference, even when they are superficial. Being contemptuous of anything from foreign countries does not conform to the mentality China should have as a big power. Singapore is a small country. When 20 years ago some famous economists criticized together its economic growth model, assuming that its rapid economic growth was only the result of factors of production's accumulation, while the improvement of total factor productivity driven by technological progress was lacking, Singaporean leaders also felt that they were losing face. However, they still adopted the attitude of "rather believing it" and set up national goals for the improvement of total factor productivity. Over the years, Singapore has been among the first several countries in the ranking of global competitiveness index, whose ranking rises year after year, which should be related to this attitude of hearing all parties.

The famous "Asking of Qian Xuesen" shows that lack of creativity due to institutional constraints is indeed China's reality. Famous scientist Qian Xuesen as still thinking on his sickbed until he passed away about why our universities couldn't be run according to the mode of cultivating talents of scientific and technological inventions, why we didn't have our own unique innovations and why we couldn't cultivate out outstanding talents. People of vision attempt to give their answers to the "Asking of Qian Xuesen" and hit the mark from different angles. At least there is one reason: Chinese universities have not formed a creative market.

Market here represents a stage or platform on which idea or creativity is bred, born, fed, motivated and grown. A famous university president in Chinese history, Mei Yi-chi, once said that great university here meant not a university with the greatest and most magnificent buildings. . . . However, nobody can talk of a university without "campus." That is to say, just as the core of the market is not its place but the transaction and flow of goods, the core of a university is not its hardware but its atmosphere to arouse creative ideas and exchange creative ideas. Therefore obviously, universities' healthy and rapid development is the premise to produce such a creative market. China's university system has many problems that need to be solved through reforms but fear of risks should never be the reason for giving up this system.

Preparedness ensures success. One good way to promote the true achievement of higher education's success is to gradually make families share more university education spending from now on. The reason why we invest in human capital or education lies in the return brought by such investment. And this return may be divided into private return and social return. The former embodies final market return to the families and individuals who invest in human capital through employment and entrepreneurship, the latter is exactly the so-called positive externality of education, i.e., the return on human capital that is not obtained by families and individuals is manifested as an increase of overall social efficiency, reduction of transaction cost, improvement of investment and educational environment.

An important finding in education economics is, if we rank educations' social returns from high to low, they are successively pre-school education, basic education, general education on the higher stage, vocational education and training. Accordingly, the private rate of return on education should have the reverse order. Obviously, in fields where private return is high, family and personal investments should be more guided, while in fields where social return is high, government payment is more suitable.

Speaking of government payment, the problem we are facing is how public education investment should be allocated to achieve the highest efficiency when it reaches a large proportion of GDP, under the condition of a large scale of public education investment.

Let's first look at a possible unreasonable situation. The Chinese government puts forward that government fiscal spending on education must reach 4% of GDP starting from 2012. Imagine that; what does it mean if this proportion of public spending on education is copied mechanically on each level of government? Compare Xicheng District in Beijing (where headquarters of many big banks and other financial institutions are located, thus having gathered a large proportion of China's national GDP) with Liupanshui (the poorest city in less developed Guizhou province) – for per capita public education spending enjoyed by permanent residents, the former is at least a dozen times of the latter. Whether such public investment differences can be both fair and efficient should be self-evident.

Let's see the situations at different stages of education. According to statistical data of the Ministry of Education, in 2016 enrollment of preschool education was 19.22 million, and 5.61 million had no opportunity of enrollment; enrollment of compulsory education was 140 million, assuming all the right-age population was in school (not exactly so in fact); enrollment at the senior high school stage was 28.87 million, and 4.12 million had not entered this stage; the number of students in universities and colleges was 32.80 million, and 44.02 million had not been enrolled by universities. Obviously, the proportion of investment in public education at different stages has an entirely different social return effect.

In addition, in 2016, 590 million people lived in rural areas of China, 790 million people were defined as urban resident population; the latter included approximately 169 million rural workers in urban areas, i.e., peasant workers. Most children of peasant workers were at a stage of compulsory education; they became left-behind children or migrant children. How do rural children, including left-behind children, the accompanying children of peasant workers in urban areas and the children with urban registered permanent residence, enjoy this public education expenditure equivalent to 4% of total GDP?

Let's go back to the basic theories in economics. An inexhaustible source of economic growth is the improvement of productivity, and an important means to improve productivity is allocating resources in the most efficient way. Winner of the Nobel Prize in Economics James Heckman pointed out in 2003 that there were imbalance problems in China's investment on education between physical capital and human capital, as well as between different regions, which lacks fairness and does not conform to the principle of efficiency.[3] Therefore, while increasing the investment of public resources in educational development, equal access and equalization principles should be followed to improve the allocation pattern of educational resources, so as to enhance education fairness, increase the service efficiency of funds and other resources notably and create new larger space for educational development.

As we have discussed, after demographic dividend disappears, infinite labor supply is no longer the characteristic of China's economic development. Accordingly, the phenomenon of diminishing returns on capital has intensified. The good news is that return on material capital diminishes; at the same time, human capital has shown more and more an increasing trend on its return. And, the increase of human capital is also a prerequisite for improving total factor productivity. Therefore, social resources transfer more from the field of material investment to human capital investment, inevitably bringing huge resource allocation efficiency and supporting the Chinese economy's sustainable growth.

Seen from a long-term point of view, investment in human capital has the characteristic of diminishing returns; however, there also exist differences of efficiency on how to allocate limited education resources here and now among various levels, areas and regions. For example, an equal amount of public spending on education has significantly less investment efficiency in Beijing Xicheng District than if it was allocated to Liupanshui. Therefore, according to the basic principles of resource allocation and starting from the problems faced by educations of all types and at all levels, we put forward the following policy suggestions for the development of Chinese education.

First of all, compulsory education is the key stage to laying a solid foundation for lifelong learning and forming an equal starting line between urban and rural areas and between children from families of different incomes, thus it is the government that should give full inputs of public resources. It is worth noting that, since preschool education has the highest social returns, and the decisive cognitive ability and non-cognitive ability at this stage of education is of extraordinary significance for coping with the challenges of artificial intelligence to employment, which means government payment for it is in accordance with the law of education and the principle of benefiting the whole society, it should be gradually incorporated into compulsory education.

Since China stepped across the Lewis turning point, job positions have increased that have more robust demand for low-skilled labors. The phenomenon so quite serious that children from some families, especially those from poor rural families, drop out from junior high school. Seen from the short-term interests of the family, this seems to be a rational choice; however, human capital losses will eventually be shared by society and family. Therefore, the government should practically reduce the proportion of family spending in the compulsory education stage and consolidate and improve the completion rate of compulsory education. Besides, through putting preschool education into compulsory education to make sure rural and poor children do not lose at the starting line also greatly helps to improve their completion rate in elementary school and junior high school stage and increases their equal opportunities to continue education.

Second, greatly improve the level of high school enrolment and promote the popularization rate of higher education. High school enrolment and university enrolment promote each other, being cause and effect at the same time. When high school popularization rate is high, the size of population having the desire to go to universities is big, while more chances of entering universities also pose a greater incentive for students to enter high school. At present, government spending within the budget is low for high school education, and the burden of family spending is too heavy. In addition to factors such as high opportunity cost and low success rate of entering university through examinations, this education stage becomes the "bottleneck" of future education development. Therefore, starting from continuously and rapidly advancing higher education popularization, the government should promote high school education free of charge as soon as possible. Relatively, higher education should further motivate society's enthusiasm for running non-government schools and the family's enthusiasm for more input.

Finally, through the guidance of the labor market, vigorously develop vocational education. China needs a group of teams formed by workers with high skills, which need to be cultivated by secondary and higher vocational educations. In all occident countries, especially Germany and Switzerland, the proportion of school-age students receiving vocational education is significantly higher than that of China. Based on the transformation and upgrading of the manufacturing industry, China should undoubtedly intensify vocational education and vocational training starting from its long-term development's requirement for laborers' quality. However, as the trend of an increasing proportion of ordinary senior high school students and a decreasing proportion of professional education students also appears in education at the senior high school stage in many other countries, the meaning behind it is also worth thinking about.

This probably means that, with the speedup of industry structure optimization and upgrading, the substitution of artificial intelligence for worker skills and other human capital deepens increasingly, meaning that the skills learned in costly professional education might become out of date very quickly, becoming "the skilled-art of slaughtering dragons – useless skill." Two proactive methods may be used for this. First, cultivation of generic competency should not be neglected for the students even in professional education; the channels between high school vocational education and vocational higher education and general higher education should be set up and reforms of the education system, teaching mode and teaching content should be sped up, so that students can have more choices to realize well-rounded development. Second, since this education category has a high private rate of return, the labor market incentives are relatively sufficient, so the investment enthusiasm of households and enterprises should be more relied on, and government investment should be lower than that of ordinary senior high school.

7.3   Dealing with "getting old before getting rich"

In the 40 years since China's reform, it has not only experienced the fastest economic growth in the world but also completed the transformation of population type from "high fertility rate, low mortality rate and high growth rate" to "low fertility rate, low mortality rate and low growth rate" with a speed faster than other countries and regions in the world. As early as the early 1990s, China's total fertility rate dropped below the replacement level of 2.1. According to the United Nations' estimation, in 2006 China's total fertility rate dropped to 1.4 and remained so later; this level is not only lower than developing countries' average and the world's average but also lower than the average level of developed countries.

As an inevitable outcome of demographic transition whose main power is the decline of birth rate, population aging degree will deepen, and for China, which has experienced the fastest demographic transition process, its aging speed is more outstanding. According to the data of the United Nations, the proportion of the population over 60 years old to the total rapidly increased from 7.2% in 1980 to 8.2% in 1990, 9.9% in 2000, 12.4% in 2010 and 15.2% in 2015.

However, only observing longitudinally from the time series is not enough to reveal the severity and particularity of China's aging process. If we compare China's aging degree with its economic development level, we can see a prominent characteristic that China has achieved a high aging degree on a lower income level, in other words, China has a higher aging degree than other countries at similar economic development level, i.e., forming the so-called getting old before getting rich characteristic. In 2015, the Chinese population over 60 years old accounted for 15.2% of the whole population, the population aged over 65 for 9.6%, while mean values of these two proportions in upper middle-income countries excluding China were only 10.9% and 7.3% respectively (see Figure 7.4).

Population aging is an irreversible process that will not be transferred by people's wills. In today's world, most developed countries have entered the high aging stage. The methods to deal with aging are often accompanied by the level of economic development. High-income countries in Europe and North America often have the following conditions to cope with the impact of aging. By contrast, China's conditions in relevant aspects have not been fully formed yet, thus relevant works should be quickened, and preparations should also be made to live with "getting old before getting rich" within a certain time.

First of all, in developed countries, a series of systems for coping with aging have been matured to some corresponding extent, including a retirement pension

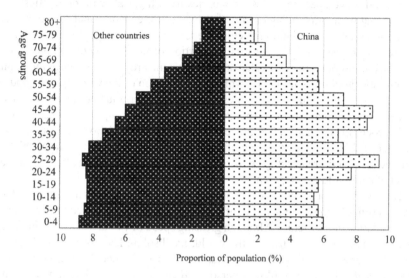

Figure 7.4 Population Age Structure in China and Other Upper Middle-Income Countries

Sources: United Nations, Department of Economic and Social Affairs, Population Division, *World Population Prospects*: The 2015 Revision, DVD Edition, 2015

system, medical system and other social welfare systems. These systems are sufficient for providing services needed by the elderly, such as support, care, medical treatment and even spiritual comfort etc. Developed countries have also encountered the retirement pension system's sustainability problems, thus they have tried corresponding reforms, guaranteeing the elderly to be basically satisfied on the whole in these countries.

Due to the fact that China is still at a lower stage of economic development with its social security system starting relatively late, although development speed is unprecedented its current social security is still not enough to cope with the challenge of population aging. In aspect of coverage, in 2015, 260 million urban employees participated in basic pension insurance, which accounted for 64.9% of urban employment, and 290 million urban employees participated in basic medical insurance for urban employees, which accounted for 71.5% of urban employment. However, for labor force transferred from rural areas working in cities, their proportions of participating in these two insurances are only 16.4% and 18.2% in 2014 respectively. Besides, since China's pension insurance for urban workers still practices the "pay-as-you-go" system, lack of capital accumulation function, with urban workers' individual accounts not being filled while dependency ratio of the population rises rapidly, China's recessive debt problem and institutional sustainability problem should be worried about. In addition, although basic pension insurance and basic medical insurance systems have been established gradually for urban and rural residents, coverage rate is not high, and security level is still very low.

Second, developed countries' economies have high labor productivities. The reason that population aging constructs a burden for economy and society is that, with the aging of population structure, dependency ratio of population becomes higher and higher, which means the proportion of the dependent population not involved in production process becomes bigger; the proportion of the aging population especially becomes larger, while the proportion of the working age population engaged in productive activities becomes smaller, thus producing negative impacts on economic growth from aspects such as labor supply, savings rate etc. This process is unchangeable; however, improvement of labor productivity can just offset this population ageing effect. Fortunately, for most countries, higher productivity and greater degree of population ageing are the results of a higher level of economic development.

However, China is still at low economic development stage, and labor productivity has not been so improved to offset the negative effect caused by the change of population age structure. Although growing speed of China's labor productivity is faster than other countries in the world, its absolute level is still much lower than developed countries so far. For example, the Conference Board uses the GDP that is created by each employed person and calculated according to purchasing power parity to measure labor productivity and make international comparison. According to the data, the labor productivity of China in 2017 was only equivalent to 21.3% of the United States, 28.3% of Germany, 29.8% of Britain and 32.8% of Japan. Compared with some emerging economies, it is equivalent to 45.5% of Russia, 61.0% of South Africa, 85.4% of Brazil and 151.7% of India.[4] If we calculate GDP according to the exchange rate method we are used to, China's labor productivity level will be lower compared with developed countries.

Third, laborers in developed countries have higher human capital. One of the challenges of population aging is labor shortage; therefore, improving labor participation rate through adjusting labor market policies, for example, extending retirement age, is naturally an appropriate means to deal with population aging. In developed countries, human capital accumulation has been long; relatively elderly workers also have more years of education, which are enough for them to increase employment time and expand labor supply.

But for China, whose education is developing very quickly but started relatively late, the educational level of the working-age population shows such a feature: the older a person is, the lower his educational attainment might be (Figure 7.5); at the same time new growing laborers' education level is increasing rapidly, human capital improvement of the workforce inventory is relatively slow, especially manifested as a very low education level of the elderly labor group. Lower educational attainment means that, with gradual substitution of old skills, such workers lack the ability to study new skills. Therefore, even under the condition of labor shortage, it is difficult for this group who will soon retire to provide effective labor supply.

Generally speaking, if a man travelling light needs to leave his necessary baggage behind in order to cross a fast-flowing river, he will ultimately turn back to build the bridge and road to achieve the aim of crossing the river with his baggage. Just like him, the "getting old before getting rich" China, which does not have the

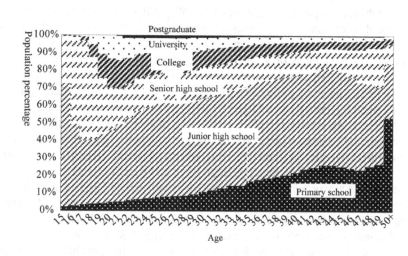

Figure 7.5 Education Composition of Age-Specific Population

Source: calculated according to the data on the website of the National Bureau of Statistics of China: www/stats.gov.cn/tjsj/pcsj/6rp/indexch.htm, downloaded on Dec. 30, 2017

condition to cope with the challenge of population aging, must learn lessons in system construction, productivity improvement and human capital accumulation to reach the other shore of well-off society under population ageing condition; there are almost no other shortcuts besides this one.

However, if we explore the factors which have caused China's "getting old before getting rich" phenomenon, we may still find some windows of opportunity uniquely owned by China, which can also be counted as better late than never. Apparently, the birth control policy that has been implemented for several decades, especially the One Child Policy implemented since 1980, enabled, more or less, the demographic transition in China to be faster than other countries, thus the aging of population came earlier. So, while people are still willing to have more children, the birth control policy should be adjusted as early as possible to create a more balanced demographic structure in the future effectively.

Since it was symbolized by an Open Letter of CPC Central Committee to All Members of the Party and the Communist Youth League concerning the Control of Population Growth in China in 1980, the "One Child Policy" has been implemented for nearly 40 years. However, it is not accurate to understand the family planning policy implemented in China for over 30 years simply as a "One Child Policy." In fact, when evolved to about 2010, China's family planning policy had roughly developed the following patterns: (1) one child policy. Including nationwide urban residents and rural residents in 6 provinces, covering 35.9% of total the population. (2) one-and-a-half child policy. Rural couples are allowed a second child if their first is a girl. Including rural residents in 19 provinces, covering 52.9% of the total population. (3) two-child policy. Rural residents are generally allowed to have two children, including rural residents in 5 provinces, covering

9.6% of the total population. (4) three-child policy. Minority farmers and herdsmen in some districts may have three children, covering 1.6% of total population. In addition, Tibetan urban residents in the Tibet Autonomous Region may have two children, and the number of children is not restricted for those of Tibetan nationality and the underpopulated minority farmers and herdsmen.

The family planning policy has not been implemented strictly all along. First, family planning policy started together with the reform oriented to establish the market economic system; therefore, on the basis of unchanged policy and an established population control target, the family planning policy is combined more and more with economic development, rural poverty alleviation, family construction, an integrated approach to the population issue and benefit orientation. Next, for a long time many provinces allowed couples in which both husband and wife are the only child in their respective families to have two children and allowed peasant couples in whom one spouse is the only child to have two children successively. Finally, nationwide more fundamental and significant policy adjustment started from 2014; all couples in China in whom one spouse is the only child are allowed to have a second child, and since 2016 any couple in China may have two children.

Just as in many other countries and regions, the determinants influencing China's demographic transition are not merely family planning policy but also attributable to the high speed economic growth and social development promoted by reform in the same period. According to research, in the first decade of reform and opening-up, family planning policy, level of GDP per capita and level of human capital evidently attributed to the sharp decline of fertility the rate. However, in the following decade, the marginal effect of the family planning policy on fertility decline almost disappeared, while the role of the other two variables still existed.[5]

Frankly, at least to a considerable degree, it was fast economic and social development that enabled China's fertility rate to drop below the replacement level at the beginning of the 1990s, and it continued to decrease significantly thereafter; rapid growth of population was controlled. Up to this point, China followed the general rule of demographic transition. But what's unusual is that China completed the transition process from high birth rate to low birth rate in about 30 years, which was doubled in developed countries and in some cases took even more than a century. Compared with developing countries of equivalent income level, China completed demographic transition at an earlier stage, thus it formed a unique feature of getting old before getting rich.

After the adjustments of the family planning policy in 2014 and 2016, a nationwide survey reflected that young couples were still entangled with being unwilling or daring not to have children even after permitted by policy. Studies at home and abroad show that social gender equality, educational development, women's labor force participation, social norms and values, urbanization and population mobility, housing, income etc. will influence reproductive decisions and reproductive behavior. Now these act almost in the same direction, affecting women postponing reproduction and waiving the birth of the second child jointly; their comprehensive resistance is far greater than the relaxation of family planning policy.

For many years, the actual birth rate in China was always lower than the birth rate expected by people. Therefore, there is a space and possibility to increase birth rate, but external support is required to relieve the pressures caused by reproduction on households, especially on women; the core is to solve the conflict of women and couples between working and parenting, for example, policies related to parental leave and women's employment protection, generally available child-care services and universal preschool education. Some European countries gradually adopt a series of effective child-friendly policies, break away from the long-term down-trend of fertility rate and keep an appropriate level of women's LFPR.

However, in order to maintain the long-term sustainable development of China's economy and complete its transition to a high-income stage, eventually we cannot count on the reversal of the demographic transition process; therefore, to solve the problem of getting old before getting rich, we need to rely on the transformation of economic development pattern, on reforms to develop system dividend to change the driver of economic growth and on exploring new growth sources so as to cross over the middle-income stage as fast as possible. In later chapters, we will have an in-depth discussion on this.

Notes

1 Deepak Nayyar. (2011). Rethinking Macroeconomic Policies for Development. *Brazilian Journal of Political Economy*, *31*(3), 339–351.
2 Li Hongbin. (2012, October 18). Return on Education in China. *The Wall Street Journal's Chinese Website*. Retrieved from Social Sciences in China Website www.cssn.cn/news/564656.htm
3 James J. Heckman. (2003). *Policies for Increasing Investment in Human Capital*. Shanghai: Fudan University Press.
4 Official Website Database of the Conference Board. Retrieved December 30, 2017, from www.conference-board.org/retrievefile.cfm?filename=TED_1_NOV20171.xlsx&type=subsite
5 Du Yang. (2014). Labor Market Changes and New Sources of Economic Growth. *China Opening Herald*, *3*, 31–35.

8 Achieving balanced development

Passing necessary turning points of economic development such as the Lewis turning point is not bound to conclude in healthy and sustainable economic growth, yet it does mean that the traditional growth is coming to an end. To maintain long-term sustainable growth, not only should potential of traditional economic growth be exploited through reform and new increased sources like human capital, total factor productivity etc. be dug out, but a more balanced growth model should be developed. The latter emphasizes promoting the transition to economic growth mode, i.e., to raise the economic growth on the basis of providing the most equal opportunities for labor force participation, promoting the integration of urban and rural economic and social development and enhancing the coordination between industries. Meanwhile, such balanced development is consistent with shared development to narrow the regional gap, improve income distribution and achieve equal access to basic public services.

8.1 To improve Labor Force Participation Rate (LFPR)

Since 2011, negative growth in the working-age population has begun; this does not mean negative growth of labor supply correspondingly. Because quantity of the labor force (i.e., economically active population with employment willingness) is the product of the working-age population and labor participation rate, the prediction based on possible increase in the labor participation rate of each age group is that the economically active population will start negative growth approximately 7 years later than working-age population. However, on the one hand, labor participation rate might not increase, on the other hand, even if increased somewhat it will decrease eventually, therefore an absolute reduction of labor supply quantity will occur sooner or later.

In any case, if we want to avoid excessive decrease of labor force, the only way is to increase the labor force participation rate (hereinafter referred to as LFPR). Generally speaking, the LFPR in China is much higher than that in other places around the world. However, the agriculture labor force in China accounts for a very high proportion, which results from the fact that the household contract system protects arable land for every farmer. That is, the comparatively high LFPR is actually generated from the special nature of agriculture. Once the agriculture factor is excluded, the situation will be somewhat different.

China's sixth census data in 2010 shows that the LFPR of people over 16 years old is 70.8%, and that of people between 16 and 64 is 77.3%. If classified by the region type, the LFPRs of people over 16 years old in cities, towns and villages are respectively 62.2%, 67.3% and 77.6%; for people between 16 and 64, the rates are respectively 68.2%, 73.3% and 84.9%. However, if we just take the non-agriculture labor participation rate into account, the rates will fall considerably. Take people at the age of 20 to 25 for example; the LFPR is 72.6% when applying for total labor, yet it declines significantly to only 62.8% once the agriculture labor is eliminated (see Figure 8.1a).

According to the data from the International Labor Organization, during the year of 1990 to 2011 the LFPR of people over 15 years old declined from 78.7% to 74.1%. This change, however, is mainly the effect of education deepening, i.e., the improvement of compulsory education penetration, the increase of high school enrollment rate and the continuous enrollment expansion of college have led to the

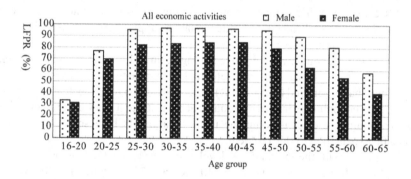

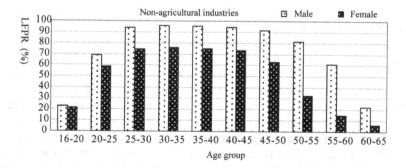

Figure 8.1a LFPR in China as per Scope, Age Group and Gender

Source: calculated by the author with 1% data sample from the sixth census

teenage school time extension, which naturally resulted in the LFPR decrease of this age group. For example, the LFPR of the age groups 15–19 and 20–24 have fallen from 64.8% and 91.2% in 1990 to 36.2% and 83.9% in 2011. Overall, in 2011, the LFPR in China was 74.1%, which was 10% higher than the world average of 64.1%, 14.1% higher than the developed countries' average of 60.0% and much higher than other places outside East Asia.

According to the 1% population sample survey data in 2015, the labor participation rate of each age group decreased. Gross enrollment rate of schools at all levels still increased in this period, for example, the proportion of junior high school to senior high school and the proportion of senior high school to university increased 6.2 percentage points and 11.2 percentage points respectively from 2010 to 2016. Therefore, the effect of educational deepening on the decrease of LFPR still applies, at least for the population of education age. However, it cannot give an adequate explanation of why labor participation rate of the population at other ages decreased.

Nevertheless, such a situation itself does not change our analysis, thinking and conclusion; it only intensifies the urgency to increase LFPR. That is to say, although we do not hope to block out the educational deepening process and hope to still strengthen human capital accumulation unswervingly, for the decrease of LFPR caused by other factors we should still make policy-oriented adjustments according to general rules that influence labor supply factors so as to increase LFPR to the maximum extent.

Once talking about how to improve non-agriculture LFPR, there are two potential pathways people would usually refer to, i.e., to raise female labor participation rate (hereinafter referred to as FLFPR) and to extend the retirement age. Globally, the idea is undoubtedly in the right course and has its target as well. However, it is not that simple when considering the actual situation of China, so below is a more specific explanation to this problem.

Compared with the international level, the FLFPR in China is comparatively high. In 2011, the above-15-year-old FLFPR was 67.7%, higher than the world's average of 51.1% and the developed countries' average of 52.8% and much higher than other developing countries' average. The LFPR of male and female is higher in its equality than the average of the world and the developed countries and is much higher than that of other developing countries.

However, the tendency in China is that the LFPR of females declines faster than that of males, according to the data from the International Labor Organization. Besides, to take both gender and age into consideration, there appears an unfavorable trend for females in the labor market. For instance, according to the 2010 census data in Figure 7.1, the LFPR of females over 40 years old dropped significantly faster than that of males. Recently, the new female entrants to the labor market suffer increasing discrimination in job hunting, which may cause FLFPR to decrease further in the future. Therefore, to maintain the LFPR in China, we should strictly implement the relevant labor laws and regulations and try our best to eliminate the gender discrimination.

The unique retirement ages in China have been developed historically. China's labor market has a long history of institution segmentation. One is the segmentation of labor market between urban and rural areas, that is, farmers cannot receive relevant employment benefits as the urban employees do, not to mention retired or not retired; the other is the segmentation in the urban labor market, including different retirement ages for cadres and workers and different retirement ages for men and women.

At present, the existing legal bases of retirement age are *State Council on the Placement of the Sick and Elderly Cadres Interim Measures* and *State Council on the Workers Retirement or Resign Interim Measures*, which are both issued in 1978 yet apply respectively for cadres and workers. More specifically, for males, no matter whether cadres or workers, the retirement age is 60 years old; for females the situation differs, because those with cadre identity are supposed to retire at the age of 55, while those with worker identity have reached the retiring age when they are 50. Besides, the actual execution may deviate from the above rule because of the person's occupation, cadre ranking and physical condition.

Therefore, considering the current legal retirement age of employees in China and also the disparity between females and males, it seems logical to boost the LFPR through raising the retirement age and meanwhile eliminating the gender difference. In addition, owing to the economic and social development, and improvement of life quality, the life expectancy of the population in China has increased from 67.8 in 1982 to 74.8 in 2010, for males from 66.3 up to 72.4 and for female from 69.3 up to 77.4. Under the conditions of extended healthy life and improved human capital, healthy elderly people become a valuable human resource.

In most developed countries, one of the policy instruments used to explore the labor supply potential is to raise retirement age, i.e., to enhance the elderly people's LFPR. For instance, above half of the countries in the Organization for Economic Cooperation and Development (OECD), which mostly comprises high-income market economy countries, have raised or are planning to raise their legal retirement age. In 2016, based on start of work at age 20, the average normal retirement age of males in OECD countries was 64.3 years old; that of female was 63.4 years old. In 2016, for workers in these countries, the average normal retirement age of males increased to 65.8 years old; that of females was 65.5 years old; the retirement age in Denmark, Netherlands and Italy exceeded 70 years old. On average, male retirement age in OECD countries will increase approximately 1.5 years; female retirement age will increase approximately 2.1 years on the basis of 2016 .[1]

Despite the fact above, it is not without argument to raise legal retirement age in these countries; moreover, situations can be much more complicated in the actual policy implementation than in the original intention. Events that have happened in Europe in recent years have shown that the public in some countries opposes the government's attempt to raise retirement age. The reason for this conflict between popular will and policy intention may be seen from different arguments of workers and policymakers on the motives to adjust retirement age.

The public who object to the retirement age adjustment policy believe that the government is motivated to raise the retirement age in order to reduce the burden of pension payments. However, the explanation from the government side is that the laborers have been so long indulged in the over-generous pension insurance system that they are unwilling to lose the vested interest. With the accelerated process of population aging, the pension gap increasingly becomes a real or potential problem indeed. Especially the pay-as-you-go mode, which was formed when the working-age population was still high, will eventually trap us in straitened circumstances once the population age structure changes. As a result, the government really needs to consider the policy adjustment of raising retirement age from the aspect of how to sustain the pension insurance system. This conflict between understanding and interest inevitably makes the retirement age adjustment a political policy, which is constrained by factors other than population aging.

There is also another official explanation that the purpose to postpone the retiring age is to improve the LFPR so as to tackle the insufficiency of labor force supply brought by the population aging. However, this explanation cannot be widely acknowledged by the public in many European countries. Nevertheless, in order to deal with the possible severe shortage of labor force supply resulting from the group retirement of the population born from 1947 to 1949, Japan commenced to implement the *Adjustment Law of Elder People's Employment and Settlement*, which legally requires enterprises to postpone the elderly's working days. This practice significantly improved the employment environment of people between 60 and 64 while increasing labor supply; this also increased their average income level and promoted the expansion of the domestic consumption demand in Japan accordingly.[2]

Yet a crucial problem worth consideration is that even though the retirement age can be legally raised, it does not mean the elder workers will, as a result, get employed. Even in developed countries, age discrimination in labor markets still exists, which naturally leads to the employment difficulty of elder people. What's more, a number of countries suffer from the pressure of high youth unemployment, so their governments even introduce some policies to encourage early retirement in order to make room for young people. The implementation of these policies has partly achieved the decrease of elder people's LFPR, but it hasn't contributed anything to reduce the youth unemployment.[3] It shows that the implementation effect of one policy depends on whether the remedy suits the situation, rather than what its original intention is.

The situation of China differs prominently from those of the developed countries in the two important conditions, which decline postponing the retirement age as an option in the near future. The difference mostly stands in the overall characteristic of labor force, which is mainly measured with the benchmark of human capital. In China, the labor force community currently approaching retirement is the transition generation. For historical reasons, their human capital endowments put them at a competitive disadvantage in labor markets.

The feasibility of postponing retirement age to increase labor force supply is dependent on that the elder workers do not differ that much from young workers in education levels, and that, in addition to their working experience, they are very competitive in the labor market. This is a fact in developed countries. For example, among the working-age population in America, people of 20 years have education years of 12.6, while those of 60 years have more than 13.7. However, the situation differs in China. At present, among the working-age population in China, the education level gets lower with age. For instance, people at 20 years old have 9 education years, but those at 60 years old just have 6 years, which widens the education level gap between China and America from 29% at 20 years old to 56% at 60 years old.[4] Although this is an earlier research finding, the situation has not been changed thus far (see Figure 7.5).

Under this circumstance, once the retirement age is raised the elderly workers will be put at a disadvantage. In Western countries, the labor markets need an additional labor supply, so to extend the statutory retirement age can provide greater incentives for workers; however, in China, these kind of policies only mean to narrow down the choices of laborers and even put part of the elderly workers in a very fragile situation: they cannot get employed and cannot get pension at the moment either.

At the coming of the Lewis turning point, labor shortage occurs continuously, and the stress of employment amount has been obviously reduced, but the employment structural contradiction in labor supply stands out; i.e., the structural unemployment and frictional unemployment related to the laborer's professional skills and adaptabilities become increasingly prominent. Data shows that currently the demand for the elderly workers in the labor market hasn't increased with the arrival of the Lewis turning point. What's truly meaningful is actual retirement age, rather than legal retirement age. Labor participation rate decreases with the increase of age; this means that actual retirement age is much lower than legal retirement age; increase of the latter will only enlarge this gap.

As revealed by the sixth population census (Figure 7.1), the labor participation rate of the working-age population in non-agricultural industries peaks at the age of 30–35, then drops year after year with age. For example, it drops from 86.0% at age 30–35 to 57.0% at age 50–54 and then down to 37.6% at age 55–60 and 13.8% at age 60–65. The labor participation rate of females decreases more seriously. The reason why the LFPR declined with age is obviously that the elderly workers lacked competitiveness in the labor markets.

It's thus clear that, at least in the current situations of China, to simply extend the retirement age is not a feasible method to increase the LFPR of elderly people. Perhaps we should not, in order to enlarge the overall size of the labor force and reduce the burden of supporting the elderly people, make an issue of the population currently approaching retirement age, but we should create conditions to cultivate the young generation today into workers with sufficient human capital, flexible adaptability to the industry structure adjustment and great capacity to extend their working days in the future. Therefore, extension of retirement age is certainly the ultimate way, yet its pushing strategy should be progressive.

China should start to design a retirement age policy with differences and freedom of choice; on the one hand, it should focus on raising actual retirement age rather than statutory retirement age; on the other hand, it should form a necessary reward and punishment mechanism to encourage voluntary delay of retirement. The framework of this policy should include the following contents: developing education and training through legislation and strict enforcement and gradually advancing the broad labor market system and social insurance system arrangement.

The non-agriculture LFPR of great potential and with Chinese characteristics should be improved by the development of peasant workers' labor supply. The suppressed LFPR is manifested in two aspects: first, peasant workers are usually shocked by the periodic unemployment as the fluctuation of the macro-economy, and then many of them have to go back to their hometowns. Actually, every peasant worker will re-make his/her decision during the spring festival about whether to leave their homes again. If he/she is still young and welcomed to the labor market, the decision is obvious. However, if the labor markets suffer the strikes like financial crisis, the elderly peasant workers would probably decide not to go out any more.

Second, peasant workers have no urban registered permanent residence, cannot enjoy relevant social insurance and social assistance and especially cannot expect to live an easy life at an old age in cities, so they have retreated from urban labor markets when they are still at a comparatively young age, thus exited high-productivity employment. Therefore, from a lifetime perspective, their non-agriculture LFPR is low. And this decreases the overall non-agriculture LFPR of the working-age population.

Restricted by the household registration system, the non-agriculture LFPR of peasant workers has been artificially depressed; this must be solved by promoting citizenization-centered urbanization so as to stabilize the labor supply of peasant workers, relieve the pressure of labor shortage, keep reallocation of labor force between regions and between industries and achieve the active effect of increasing potential growth rate.

8.2   The nature of urbanization

A picture once circulated on the Internet, the night light distribution effect on Earth, which was taken and released by the National Aeronautics and Space Administration (NASA). It shows that, in outer space, lighting intensity varies in different countries and regions in the world. People explained one after another that such a situation reflected population intensity or, more precisely speaking, that lighting intensity was closely related to a broadly defined urbanization level. Looking at this picture (Figure 8.1b, the author downloaded this picture in 2012), people might notice that, at that time, China was of very low brightness, and you can hardly even see whether China is actually brighter than India. Of course, China's urbanization was further promoted thereafter, also reflected in the improvement of nighttime lighting intensity.

This light distribution picture on Earth, in addition to being closer to a direct reflection of urbanization level, is also often used as a metaphor in which the light intensity stands for the economic development level or the brightness closely related to the per capita GDP. In fact, this is not merely a metaphor. Economists did identify the intensity of economic activities on the Earth according to the NASA lighting map – and thus regional distribution of economic development level.[5]

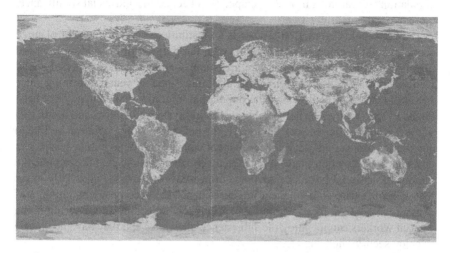

Figure 8.1b The Night Light Distribution on Earth

Source: www.thetimes.co.uk/tto/multimedia/archive/00363/VIDEO_EARTH_AT_NIGH_363137a.jpg

Now let's use obvious or hidden meanings of this distribution map to inspect the level and characteristics of urbanization in China.

It has been a long time since people pictured the urbanization where rural residents migrate to urban areas as a process of chasing "the light of cities." The so-called light of cities represents not only the colorful cultural life in cities but also more opportunities for employment and business establishment and even the better and more sufficient fundamental public services. In 2016, the urbanization ratio, i.e., the percentage that the people living in cities for more than 6 months make in the overall population of China, had reached 57.4%. This number, however, contains complicated meanings and needs further analysis.

The official statistics of the urbanization ratio are derived according to the permanent resident population, that is, the population living in cities for over 6 months. This statistical caliber can easily make us think of the statistics concept – peasant worker or migrant worker, i.e., people who are out of their hometown for over 6 months. At present, there are 169 million migrant workers in China, most of who have entered cities at all levels. It is clear that the urban population, which represents 57.4% of people in China, actually includes peasant workers.

However, the peasant workers who are classified as the urban permanent population do not actually have a registered urban permanent residence. If counted according to the traditional statistical caliber, that is, the urban permanent residents with non-agricultural household registration, the urban permanent population in 2016 makes up only 41.2% of the population in China. Then what is the essential difference between the urbanization measured with the percentage of registered urban permanent residence and that measured with the urban permanent population? Apparently, from the perspective of economic and social significance, these two vary greatly.

The household registration system is an institutional arrangement of planned economy, which emerged in the 1950s with the purpose of preventing the rural population from migrating to urban areas and segmenting the supply of social welfare in urban and rural areas. Now after more than 30 years' reforming since 1980s, the labor force flow and the population migration have already not been bound by this policy. The household registration system still exists and is still tied with series of public services. Therefore, the peasant workers, who can be free to enter cities and get employed there, cannot equally enjoy the public services in cities because they don't have a registered permanent residence; for example, the various basic social insurance coverage of peasant workers is significantly lower than that of registered permanent urban residents, the accompanying children of peasant workers are faced with difficulty in receiving compulsory education, the peasant workers cannot enjoy the subsistence allowance and they have no chance to enjoy security housing etc.

Basic social insurance programs, such as social pension insurance, work-related injury insurance, basic medical insurance and unemployment insurance specified in relevant laws and regulations should be covered based on the employment identity rather than the registered permanent residence, but the household registration system determines the very strong mobility of peasant workers and also provides an institutional basis for employers to treat them discriminatorily, hence it still hinders the peasant workers from receiving sufficient social insurance coverage. In 2015, 60.3% of migrant rural workers did not sign a labor contract with their employers; basic social insurance specified in the Labor Contract Law cannot cover these peasant workers without a labor contract. Due to the insufficiency of enjoying basic public services, the peasant workers cannot fully and completely play their roles as consumers and laborers.

First of all, the peasant workers cannot become regular consumers as can other urban permanent residents, and their consumption is incomplete because they are full of worries, worries of their old age livings, sickness, unemployment, the education of their children and their unsteady income. Overall statistics shows that, compared with urban residents spending 74.3% of income on consumption, they only spend 32.9% of their income on consumption. Some investigations show that the peasant workers would send back about 1/4 of their income to their rural home as a personal guarantee to balance their consumption. First, since wage income accounts for a larger and larger part in the income of peasant households, such remittance is an important part of expanded household consumption. Second, due to the lack of basic social insurance, precautionary savings is an inevitable choice of self-protection. Third, since the outgoing work time of peasant workers is shortened greatly, this remittance also serves as personal savings to smooth lifetime consumption.

Second, the peasant workers haven't become actual citizens and they are just migrant workers who will come and go, which prevents them from fully functioning as an important labor force supply. On the one hand, peasant workers are frequently impacted by the periodical unemployment due to the macro-economy fluctuation, and the urban policy environment will also change periodically for peasant workers; many of them have to return to their hometowns. On the other hand, they will voluntarily withdraw from the urban labor force market when they are still at a comparatively young age, for they cannot enjoy the related social insurance and social assistance, they are especially not expected to live out their lives in cities; plus there are institutional barriers for household relocation.

According to estimates, in 2014, of all the employees in urban areas, peasant workers accounted for about 38%. That is to say, though the peasant workers do not have a registered permanent urban residence, and they cannot equally enjoy the relevant basic public services, they have already become the main part of urban employment. However, not being registered as permanent residents disables them to light themselves up. The number of urban permanent residents has increased to169 million because of peasant workers, but these new migrants still live in construction sites, crowded dormitories or their working places, so they cannot add the lights of cities. We could say this is the reason why cities in China do not really light up.

A new phenomenon may be seen from demographic data: rural population aged 16–19 peaked in 2014; the absolute number has decreased since then. What does this mean? Sometimes, peasant workers are also called agricultural transfer population in official documents. This name seems unlike "rural migrant worker," which is somewhat discriminatory, yet its connotation is not so accurate. Because the large scale agricultural labor force has been transferred up to the present, peasant workers are far from surplus labor transferred out of agriculture. Of the new peasant workers every year, almost all of them are new graduates of rural junior high schools and senior high schools, i.e., the population of 16–19 years old.

Therefore, decrease of this population group inevitably leads to the decrease of rural migrant worker increment, thus the total number changes little and even becomes stagnant. In fact, the growth rate of peasant workers decreased from an average of 4% in the period of 2005–2010 to only 0.3% in 2016. That is to say, the total number of peasant workers has really tended to be stable in recent years. Meanwhile, age structure also changed, i.e., the number of the youngest group decreased, whose proportion in total number of peasant workers decreased (Figure 8.2). Which factors kept the total scale of peasant workers constant, and how did these factors maintain a balanced level of total number of peasant workers?

It is no doubt that the 16–19-year-old rural population has decreased progressively year after year since 2014, yet it still keeps a large absolute scale. For example, from population forecasts, population of this age group will decrease from over 35 million to 30 million in the period of 2014–2020. A considerable part of over 30 million population at this age go to urban areas for work every year; they become a gross increment in the statistical number of peasant workers. Meanwhile, the group above 40 years old in peasant workers has greater willingness to return to their hometowns; they form a specific probability of returning to one's hometown. Now that the gross increment of going to urban areas is an established number, the willingness to return to one's hometown of the peasant workers above

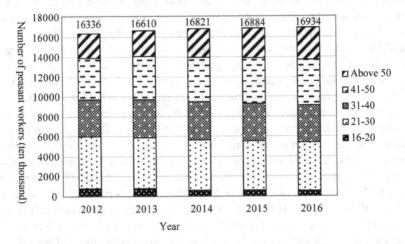

Figure 8.2 Total Number and Age Composition of Peasant Workers

Source: 2016 Migrant Workers Monitoring Survey Report released by the National Bureau of Statistics of China, official website of the National Bureau of Statistis of China: www.stats.gov.cn/tjsj/zxfb/201704/t20170428_1489334.html, download on May 7, 2017

40 years old becomes the determinant of net increment and thus the total number of peasant workers. Accordingly, how policy treats peasant workers, friendly or exclusively, determines whether labor mobility moves forward from rural to urban, or backward from urban to rural.

Why os labor mobility differentiated as forward and backward; what's their respective meaning? Nobel Prize-winning economist, Simon Kuznets, regarded labor transfer from agriculture to non-agricultural industries as a process to improve productivity; therefore, we may regard the reallocation process of labor force from the low productivity sector to the high productivity sector as the Kuznets process.

In the period of 1978–2015, overall labor productivity increased 16.7 times in China. It may be broken down by statistical means, wherein 56% was the combined contribution of the increase in labor productivity in three industries, while the remaining 44% came from reallocation of labor force among three industries according to the direction of increase in productivity, i.e., the contribution made by the Kuznets process. It may be seen that, if labor mobility is inversed to be backward, i.e., the inverse Kuznets process, labor productivity will decrease.

With demographic change, China's urbanization slows down inherently, although slowdown is not evident from the increased amplitude of resident population urbanization rate in recent years. Yet we may see through further observation that the composition that pushes urbanization has changed.

We may break down the additional urban population (urbanization increment) according to the demographic data in 2010. The result shows that the contribution rate of natural growth of the urban population is 16%; the contribution rate of population growth whose registered permanent residence was moved from rural areas to urban areas is 3%; the contribution rate of population growth that entered urban sectors for residence without moving their registered permanent residence (i.e., peasant workers) is 26%, while the contribution rate of local transfer population is 53%. That is to say, the main contribution that maintains the current urbanization speed comes from the change in urban and rural population division scope, for example, county upgraded to city, township upgraded to town (neighborhood) and changing village to residential community (neighborhood committee). Such local transition of registered permanent residence is not accompanied with changes in type of employment and place of residence and does not generate general the effect of urbanization.

Correspondingly, the contribution of peasant workers residing in urban areas (residing for 6 months and above) to resident population urbanization decreased from 39.1% in 2004 and 26.8% in 2011 to 2.9% in 2015 and 2.3% in 2016. The contribution of this part of peasant workers in urbanization increment is a productivity increase factor, or the expected effect of urbanization or the Kuznets process in a true sense, because the supporting factor behind it is reallocation of labor force.

It may be seen that unfriendly policy attitudes of the municipal government toward peasant workers will intensify the reverse willingness of peasant workers and lead to the macroeconomic result of decreased productivity. On the contrary, the urbanization whose connotation is to realize citizenization of peasant workers is a typical window of opportunity in which institutional reform promotes economic growth. What is more, both positive policy and negative policy with respect to the direction of labor mobility will achieve immediate effect.

Economists accept that reform may bring dividends to promote economic growth, yet they generally think sufficient time is required to obtain reform dividends. For example, Homi Kharas, the world bank economist who initially put forward the concept of the "Middle-Income Trap," points out that it will take at least 10 years or more to see the reforming effects of developing capital markets, accelerating the innovation and development of high level education, improving the city management, building up a livable city and forming agglomeration effect, effective government by law, decentralization of authority, anti-corruption etc.[6]

Nevertheless, to view things from the national circumstances of China, there are indeed some revolution areas that, if substantially carried forward, will receive the immediate effect of boosting economic growth. The household registration system revolution is among these areas. To be specific, pushing forward the citizenization of peasant workers by the household registration system revolution can achieve the effect of hitting three birds with one stone, i.e., increase potential growth rate from supply side by increasing labor supply and keeping resource reallocation and promote the balance and sustainability of demand factors that fuel economic growth from the demand side by expanding consumer groups.

Nowadays, the economic growth in China is in the slowdown stage. The potential growth rate, measured with the supply of production factors like capital, labor force etc. and the increasing speed of production rate, tends to decline. The laws of economics and the international experience both show that the right policy response to deal with economic growth slowdown is not to surmount the potential growth rate by stimulating the demand but to improve the potential growth rate by digging out the institution potential. The household registration system revolution and the citizenization of peasant workers can not only help truly realize the urbanization in China by changing the requirements of the economic development mode but also produce prominent results of increasing the potential economic growth capacity.

As elaborated, promoting the further migration of rural labor force can improve the potential growth rate by increasing labor force supply and creating the efficiency improvement of resources reallocation, and it can also enlarge the peasant workers' consumption level by increasing the social insurance coverage. If the household registration system is reformed, a large portion of peasant workers' social insurance coverage rate will achieve the citizens' level. In that case, even if their income is not raised, their consumption budget will increase by at least 1/3. It is predictable that the process of citizenization will inevitably further enhance the migrant workers' income stability, increase their LFPR and, as a natural result, improve their income, which will significantly expand the residents' consumption demand.

Let's see what consumption demand can be created by the demand income effect brought by the citizenization of peasant workers. If peasant workers can make their budget for revenues and expenditures like residents with the urban household registration, they can save 1/4 of the income that they previously sent back home, and the disposable income can be increased by 33.3%. Looking at it from a different perspective, gross payroll of 169 million peasant workers calculated according to an average annual wage in 2016 will reach 6.64 trillion Yuan, equivalent to 24.8% of the national total consumer spending of 26.77 trillion Yuan in this year. In other words, if peasant workers spend this 1/4 of wages in consumption, they may increase urban household consumption expenditure by about 6%.

What's more, according to the input-output table of China, about 73.1% of final consumption expenditure of China in 2016 is urban household consumption expenditure, and 26.9% is government consumption expenditure. The latter refers to the consumption expenditure that the government spends in providing public services to the whole society and the net expenditure that the government uses to cover the free-of-charge or lower-price goods and services provided to the residents. The urbanization cored with citizenization of peasant workers can, on the one hand, significantly improve the household consumption level, for it provides more stable employment opportunities and more equal basic public services for the migrant workers; on the other, it can reasonably enlarge the government consumption scale, because it strengthens the government responsibility of providing equal basic public services. These two effects will further manifest in the enlarging of national consumption demand, which will help stimulate the economic growth rebalance.

8.3 Agriculture should be self-supporting

The ownership of arable land per capita in China is enormously lower than the world average, so many will think that the agriculture in China innately lacks comparative advantage, and some studies even estimate that the gap between the sown area of farm crops and the actual needs in China has reached 600 million *mu* (a unit of area; one *mu* is equal to 666.67 square meters), which accounts for 20% of the whole sown area. In consideration of this, some believe that to import more agricultural products, especially food, is a strategy to make best use of the advantages and bypass the disadvantages. However, even though we can actually and reasonably lower the self-supporting level of agricultural products, we should not choose to weaken the self-supporting ability and over rely on the import; we should do it under the condition of self-sufficiency and utilize the comparative advantage strategy.

On the other hand, food security is ultimately the guarantee of production capacity. Starting from this, China will eventually demand an agricultural production mode that can be self-reliant and also has market competitiveness. So to speak, all the possibilities of sustainable economic growth in future China are based on the agricultural modernization.

Since entering the 21st century, agricultural policies in China have tended to be preferential for agriculture, achieving commendable effects in agricultural production increase and peasant income increase. However, we cannot help asking whether it can, by continuing this policy tendency, maintain the agricultural development and further realize the agricultural modernization along with industrialization, informatization and urbanization. To answer this question, we need to divide the agriculture in China into three phases and examine what has been achieved and what challenges we are still faced with according to the tasks that need to be fulfilled in every phase.

In the first phase of the agriculture in China, its mission is to solve the food supply problem. This problem has run through the past, present and future and became prominent in 1980s and 1990s. In this phase, the core task is to increase the supply of agricultural products, especially the food supply, by improving the incentive mechanism and the market environment and enhancing the productivity of scarce production factors. And this mission has been achieved since the rural economy reform in early 1980s.

For instance, during 1978 to 2014, the agricultural output per capita increased: the food output per capita improved by 40.2%, the cotton output per capita by 95.7%, the oil plants by 3.74 times, the red meat by 4.79 times, the aquatic products by 8.9 times and the milk by 29.0 times. This group of figures shows not only the achievement of food supply but also the prominent effects in improving agricultural labor productivity successively by technical advance of efficient land use and labor-saving.

Looking into the process of agricultural mechanization, we can see the agricultural technology advance and its mode alteration, and we can also observe the sensitive response of agriculture development to the change of production factors' scarcity. That is, in the time shortly after the reform and opening-up, abundant surplus labor accumulated in agriculture; the focus of technological progress was not saving labor but saving land, reflected by the slow growth of small farm implements. Until recently, the labor shortage in agriculture had become prominent, thus the large-scale agricultural machinery started to develop rapidly, which shows the labor-saving characteristics of this technological change.

During 1979 to 1995, the average annual growth rate of total power of large and medium tractors was 0.84%, while the growth rate of associated farm implements was −1.7%; average annual growth rate of total power of small tractors was up to 11.2%, and growth rate of associated farm implements was 10.5% in the same period. Thereafter, with large scale transfer of the agricultural labor force, relative scarcity of the factors of production changed, i.e., a labor shortage occurred in agriculture; the direction of technical change was reversed. In the period of 1996–2012, average annual growth rate of the total power of large and medium tractors was 11.8%; growth rate of associated farm implements was 13.2%, while average annual growth rate of the total power of small tractors decreased to 4.7%, and the growth rate of associated farm implements was 6.7%.

Then, in the second phase of agriculture in China, the mission was to deal with the rural income problem. This mission runs through time and it is not bound to a specific period either. Since the reform and opening-up, the peasants' income has improved rapidly and significantly. However, there were twists and turns. In 1980s, rural income rose comparatively fast, because the initial reform began in agriculture. Then along with the overall implementation of economy reform, the rural income growth lingered compared to the urban income. After entering the 21st century, the central government has put forward the policies of industry re-feeding agriculture, urban areas supporting rural areas, providing more and taking less from agriculture or providing more and taking none from agriculture, so the peasant income again increased significantly and the urban-rural income gap has tended to narrow down.

The growth of rural income is mainly contributed to by the prices of agricultural products rising, the surplus rural laborers turning to the wage income employment and the increasing of government investment on issues of agriculture, farmers and rural areas. In 2016, the peasant worker population, which has been stably transferred from agriculture to non-agriculture, had reached 280 million, of whom 169 million had realized offsite migration, and most of them entered cities at all levels; the actual wage level of peasant workers has increased by 2.5 times compared to that in 2003. Since 2002, China has implemented subsidy policies for agricultural production successively, including subsidies for growing superior grain cultivators, direct subsidies to grain producers, general subsidies for agricultural production supplies and direct subsidies for the purchase of agricultural machinery; the total expenditure in 2013 was over 160 billion Yuan.

Accordingly, the urban-rural income gap has been narrowed obviously. The press circle and even the academic circle generally believe that the current urban-rural income gap, i.e., urban and rural income ratio based on peasant household income 1, is still as high as 2.73. Yet this result has not been adjusted according to different price changes in urban and rural areas. If calculated according to constant prices, the ratio of the urban residents' income to the peasants' income in 1978 was 2.57; the ratio in 2009 became 2.32, reaching the peak, and it decreased to 1.91 in 2016.

However, peasant income growth and the narrowing of the urban-rural income gap rely less and less on agricultural income itself. Especially in the case of large scale labor transfer and facing the Lewis turning point, non-agricultural business and wage incomes have become the uppermost components in peasant household income. For example, in 2014, 63% of cash disposable income of peasant households was irrelevant to agricultural business, while in the income growth of that year, the contribution of non-agricultural income was up to 75%. This reality raised thought-provoking agricultural development issues, which should be considered at the third stage of agricultural development.

Then the mission in the third phase of agriculture in China is to settle the food security problem. As time goes by, it becomes an increasingly prominent mission to establish agricultural production conditions and methods to secure the food supply by providing adequate incentive mechanisms and incentive intensity, and it is, as well, an inevitable issue after the first two phases. To maintain the necessary self-sufficiency of food is undoubtedly an important part of food security strategy for China, a country with a large population, and the core requirement of food security strategy should be a sustainable agricultural production mode with a solid foundation and complete incentives, in which the productivity can be continually promoted with the technology advance.

One prolonged discussion topic of the development of economics is how a country can improve its agricultural productivity with the times after it has just gone through the Lewis turning point of labor shortage. The essence of dual economy is the surplus laborers in agriculture, thus the marginal productivity of agricultural labor is extremely low, near zero. At this time, the surplus rural laborers transferring from agriculture to meet the increasing labor demand in non-agriculture would not impact the agricultural output level. Generally, the first two phases of agriculture in China are overall correspondent to the typical development period of the dual economics.

Once the Lewis turning point is surpassed, it means that the marginal productivity of agricultural labor is still low, but it is above zero. At this point, if the productivity is not rising, the agriculture will be adversely affected by the continuous labor transfer. As such, some development economists give the Lewis turning point another name – the food shortage point, i.e., if the productivity cannot be improved to adapt to the economic development phases, there would be problems like inflation caused by food shortage.[7] China finished its Lewis turning period in 2004, and it has entered the third phase of agriculture development in the post Lewis turning point time and started to face brand new and severe challenges.

In the whole process of economy reform marked by agriculture, the productivity of agriculture in China, including the labor productivity, the land productivity or the total factor productivity, has improved prominently. However, in some specific historical periods, for example, when China reached the Lewis turning point, if comparing its agricultural labor productivity and land productivity with that of other countries or areas around the world, there was still huge gap to fill and great potential for improvement (see Figure 8.3).

For example, we may learn from previous research literature that Japan approximately in 1960 and South Korea and China's Taiwan Region approximately at the beginning of the 1970s reached their Lewis turning point respectively, while

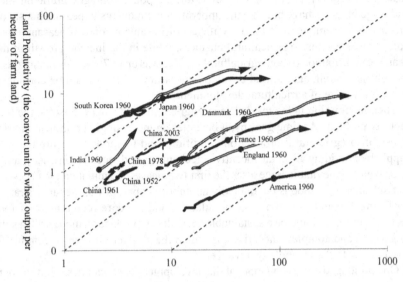

Labor Productivity (the convert unit of wheat output per male laborer)

Figure 8.3 The Historical Comparison of Agricultural Productivity

Source: Zhao Wen. *China Agricultural Development under the New Pattern.* Economy & Management Publishing House. 2012: 145

Mainland China reached this turning point in 2004. In Figure 8.3, compared with these East Asian economies, the land productivity gap of Mainland China was still wide in 2003. While compared with the level of developed countries in 1960, the agricultural labor productivity gap of China is more evident. A policy implication derived from this is that China needs to face new challenges at the third stage of agricultural development as soon as possible.

In the phase of agricultural development focusing mainly on resolving the peasant income problem, it is necessary and effective to implement industry nurturing agriculture and an urban supporting rural policy. Viewed from the perspective of peasant income increasing, rural poverty alleviation and food security, if the government did not significantly raise the expenditure, the long-term liabilities on agricultural productivity condition from the planned economy period would not be compensated; the majority of peasants would be unable to get rid of poverty and thus it would be difficult to establish a base for the current agricultural development and the rural development. However, viewed from long-term agricultural development, it cannot form a self-supporting agricultural production mode merely by compensation.

There is a long-lasting and far-reaching theory tendency, and the theory regards that agriculture is an innately weak industry, which cannot, like other industries, grow by itself in the market-oriented economy and that the price mechanism cannot produce enough agricultural production incentives. According to this logic, a good policy to deal with issues of agriculture, farmers and the rural area is to do our best to increase the governmental expenditure of agriculture. However, different ways that the government adopts to increase the agricultural input will produce different effects; what's more, it is not active enough to rely only on the government.

It is ubiquitous in the developed countries for their governments to compensate agriculture, but the real sustainable and competitive agriculture should be established based on its own self-supporting ability. Indeed, China on the present developing stage still needs the policy of urban areas supporting rural areas and industry re-feeding agriculture. However, it becomes increasingly urgent to build up a production mode base for the future of modern agriculture.

Agriculture, as an industry, has its vulnerability because the natural risks it is faced with and the long production cycle make it special in regard to the industrial insurance and the production fund raising. Nonetheless, the practice of the agricultural development in developed countries has shown that by reasonably combining the government and the market the previously mentioned specialties of agriculture would not prevent it from becoming a competitive and self-supporting industry.

Actually, the most prominent characteristic of agriculture is the continuous decline tendency in its share of the national economy. In China, the significant manifestation of this characteristic is that the value share of agricultural production declines faster than the labor share, which results in the comparative productivity of agriculture being remarkably lower than that of non-agriculture. Well, the resolution is ready-made, that is, to realize the complete migration of agricultural labor and the rural population according to the law of economic development and, meanwhile, to create a self-contained market mechanism and adequate price incentives.

First of all, compensations will never create necessary incentives. Take the currently most popular direct subsidy for planting grain as an example. This subsidy form cannot produce the initiative of planting grain. Under the framework of the WTO, it is prohibited to use government expenditure to impact the grain output, for it is a subsidy leading to unfair competition. In other words, the subsidy complying with the WTO cannot stimulate the increase of grain output.

Of course, this policy does not have other special distortion effects only in this way. In fact, under the condition of contracted land circulation, the direct subsidy of planting grain is received by the contracted right owners rather than the actual cultivators. However, if there is no successive subsidy to stimulate the productive effects, the administration costs will increase and the rent-seeking behavior will emerge. In addition, to prevent low grain price from hurting the farmers, the country implements the policy of purchasing the bulk farm products at the lowest price. Under the circumstance of comparatively low and steady prices, presently the bulk farm products like cotton, grain etc. are all purchased at the lowest prices, which means the market mechanism is marginalized greatly in agriculture.

Second, it is not enough to forge a modernized agricultural production mode only by the government. The Eighteenth National Congress of the Communist Party of China proposed to facilitate the synchronous development of industrialization, informatization, urbanization and modernization of agriculture, which is summed up as the Four Synchronous Modernizations. The precedent condition of realizing the Four Synchronous Modernizations is to implement industrialization, informatization, urbanization and modernization of agriculture with the same incentive mechanism and intensity. When Thodore W. Schults criticizes the thoughts that the peasants are irrational and that agriculture is born a weak industry, he emphasizes the key to transform the traditional agriculture as such: the peasant will be able to turn stone into gold by touch if given enough incentives.

Entering the WTO means that we should take into consideration of the agricultural markets and prices both in and outside China. The national and international interaction brings about challenges and opportunities. On one hand, the international agricultural products market sets an upper limit for the national agricultural product price. The WTO forbids the long-time trading protection and maintaining the price of national agriculture higher than the international level, which will actually torment the price signal. On the other, the price fluctuation in the international market can affect the stability of the national market, and it can also be used as a price incentive to promote the peasants' income.

The key to making use of this incentive mechanism lies in conforming to the times, rather than going against the current. China used to passively respond to the fluctuation of the international agricultural products market. When the agricultural product price of the international market was higher than that of the country, the government would always closely restrain the agricultural output, thus the peasants never had a chance to make a profit from the international price rising. While the price in the international market is comparatively low, to increase import and reduce the export would suppress the domestic agricultural price, thus would make the peasants the final victims. However, these problems can be resolved in the modern market system by mechanism design and innovation.

Third, other institutional arrangements related to the issues of agriculture, farmers and rural areas are inadequate to support the forming of a modern agricultural production mode. For instance, there is a policy tendency opposite to the thought regarding agriculture as an innately weak industry and it expects to maintain a migrant bird mode of the labor flow and population migration attributed to the worries that the agriculture is declining and the rural economy and society are withering. This should be the policy root reason why no realization of urbanization cored with citizenization has been achieved.

Actually, a bashful urbanization cannot build a modern agricultural production mode on the base of price incentives and scale operation. Under the circumstance of lacking stable settlement, the peasants going out for work dare not transfer the management right of the contracted land, and they are not willing to abandon the spare homestead, so, even under the most strict land management system, the utilization rates of productive land and living land have both gone down.

For example, the total number of peasant workers in 2014 was 274 million, of which 106 million worked in their hometowns on non-agriculture. To view this from the nature of employment, these laborers had undoubtedly left the land; however, most of them were still managing agriculture at the same time, so the contracted land and the homestead were retained beyond doubt. In the same year, the peasant workers, i.e., the peasants who had left their hometowns for over 6 months, had reached 168 million, of which 132 million were members of families which belonged to the registered permanent rural residents who did not have time to work on agricultural production, but they would not abandon their contracted land and homestead. Except that, there are 35.78 million peasants who migrate from rural areas and totally separate themselves from rural life and agricultural production. However, in most cases, they do not abandon the contracted land and homestead under their names. Some of them transfer their contracted land to others yet still enjoy the governmental subsidy of planting grain.

Thus it can be seen that the rural households or the households that engage in full-time or part-time work on agriculture production or actually own the management right of the contracted land do not materially decrease along with the reduction of agricultural labor. This would result in the fact that the agricultural operation scale cannot be enlarged in concert with the agricultural employment decrease, which hinders the improvement of agricultural labor productivity. The American writer Thoreau depicted a self-sufficient agricultural production mode in his *Walden:* to live a simple life, only eat the grain harvested by himself, a man just needs to cultivate several square rods (one square rod is roughly equal to 25.3 m²) of land, and it is much cheaper to use a shovel than farm cattle.

The average land scale of Chinese peasant households is not only far less than European and American developed countries, Eastern European countries, Latin American countries and African countries; it is even significantly less than its Asian neighbors. The World Bank calls the situation of average cultivated land per household less than two hectares a "small land operator"; China's average scale of 0.67 hectares per household is only 1/3 of this standard and may be called an ultra small peasant household. Since the land of each peasant household in China scatters in a number of different locations, each peasant household has average five, six and even more dispersed lands (Gao et al., 2012), almost no different from the situation depicted by Thoreau.

If such a land operation situation is not changed fundamentally when the total amount of labor force decreases, it is not only unfavorable to mechanized farming, land boundaries and ridges but also waste land. In addition, an ultra small operation scale not only hinders producers to respond actively to price incentive, which is unfavorable to forming specialized and professional operation, it also leads to diminishing marginal returns of agricultural material and capital inputs. For example, compared with that at the early stage of reform, currently marginal productivity of labor in food crop production has increased tens of times, meanwhile, marginal productivity of capital has decreased by half.

A picture downloaded from "Google Earth" (Figure 8.4) gives a sharp contrast of two cultivated land areas on Chongming Island, Shanghai City, in which a certain operation scale has been developed for the land on the top left corner through centralization, and there are field ridges, less but more efficient kennels and less housing occupation. The other land on the bottom right corner is typical scattered and small-scale operation. Apart from the economic principles related to scale

Figure 8.4 Comparison of Land Centralization and Decentralization on Chongming Island,
Shanghai City

Source: https://maps.google.com/maps?11=31.641353,121.566156&t=k, downloaded on Jul. 15, 2013

economy and other factors, one can tell the low efficiency of the land occupied by
housing, ridges and kennels as well.

On the tendency that many economists blindly emphasize the importance of the
agricultural operation scale, the Nobel economics laureate Theodore W. Schults
points out that there exists fake inseparability of production factors in agriculture,
thus the land operation scale is not as important as people may consider.[8] The fake
inseparability of production factors refers to the usage of tractors, which should
match the land operation scale. Assume that a set of joint harvesting equipment
works on a small plot of land; apparently it cannot be efficient. Therefore, the
fake inseparability means the tractors can be large-scale or small-scale, and it
can change according to the land scale. Furthermore, every operation unit, for
example a household, owns a limited area of land, or we can purchase mechanization services, rather than purchase a whole set of cultivation machinery, to settle
the limited land problem.

This theory of Schults' fits for and thus would help the agriculture in China for
a long period of time. The economists and the rural policy researchers of China do
not advocate over stress on scale operation for two reasons. One is that they worry
the scale operation will provide excuses for local carders and village collectives to
sway the agricultural basic operation system of household management and would
hurt the incentive mechanism of agricultural production. Another worry lies in the
possible phenomenon that some laborers may have no land to cultivate due to the
enlarging of operation scale under the condition of surplus laborers.

So far, the agriculture development in China indeed verifies the hypothesis of
fake inseparability of production factors. As previously mentioned, in the early

stage, the small-size agricultural machinery increased rapidly, which is correspondent to the household operation conditions of small-scale land and surplus laborers; then in the next stage, large-scale agricultural machinery mushroomed, and this is the mechanization way of labor-saving to suit the conditions of land scale enlarging, laborer shortage emerging and household purchasing machinery services.

Ultimately, the small average household scale and decentralized plot distribution increase the negotiation cost of peasant households for collaborative purchase of farm machinery services and restrict use of large-scale farm machinery services; scale economy also exists in the activities of peasants to purchase means of production and related services before, during and after production; the bargaining, information collection, result evaluation and other transaction costs are too high for peasants due to insufficient scale. In the case of a small operation scale, it is difficult for producers to respond effectively to market signals, and they can hardly develop effective induction mechanisms of technological change.

When the agricultural development enters a new phase, it becomes increasingly urgent to enlarge the land scale and it is now on the agenda, and it gets more and more important to improve agricultural productivity by the technology of saving land and labor because of the large amount of rural laborers and migrant population from agriculture to cities at all levels. Based on the basic operation system of household management, we could explore a special way of land concentration to realize the agricultural modernization by further guaranteeing peasants' utilizing right and transferring right of contracted land, respecting their originality and innovating a new system.

Notes

1 Organization for Economic Co-Operation and Development. (2017). *Pensions at a Glance 2017: OECD and G20 Indicators*. Paris: OECD. Retrieved January 1, 2018, from http://dx.doi.org/10.1787/pension_glance-2017-en
2 Bank of Tokyo-Mitsubishi UFJ (BTMU). (2012). Japan's Mass Generation Aging Impact: On Adjustment Law of Elder People's Employment and Settlement. *BTMU Japan Economy Watch, 22*.
3 George Magnus. (2009). *The Age of Aging: How Demographics Are Changing the Global Economy and Our World* (p. 108). Singapore: John Wiley and Sons.
4 Wang Guangzhou and Niu Jianlin. (2009). The Structure Status Quo, Problems and Development Forecast of Education Aggregate in China. In Cai Fang (Ed.), *The Green Paper on Population and Labor No.9*. Beijing: Social Sciences Academic Press.
5 J. Vernon Henderson, Tim L. Squires, Adam Storeygard, and David N. Weil. (2016). The Global Spatial Distribution of Economic Activity: Nature, History, and the Role of Trade. *NBER Working Paper*, 22145.
6 Homi Kharas. (2011). China's Transition to a High Income Economy: Escaping the Middle Income Trap. In Edwin Lim and Michael Spence (Eds.), *Medium and Long Term Development and Transformation of the Chinese Economy: An International Perspective* (pp. 470–501). Beijing: China Citic Press.
7 Refer to Gustav Ranis and John C. H. Fei. (1961). A Theory of Economic Development. *The American Economic Review, 51*(4), 533–565.
8 Theodore W. Schults. (1987). *Transforming Traditional Agriculture* (pp. 92–94). Beijing: Commercial Press.

9 Redefinition of government functions

Transiting from dual economic development with demographic dividend to economic development with more and more neoclassic growth features, economic deceleration is quite natural, because in the latter period economic growth is increasingly driven by technological advancement and productivity improvement. Thus, creating a series of necessary institutional conditions that haven't existed yet and promoting innovations by competition are urgent tasks at the development transition. However, the Chinese economy hasn't developed into a pure neoclassical growth pattern after all, which means there are still many traditional growth potentials to dig out.

Both discovering new growth sources and digging out the potential of traditional growth sources require more deepened reforms; they are the reform dividends that must be obtained from China's economic growth in the future. According to China's previous experience and lectures, the core of economic system reform is to redefine the functional boundaries between government and market and between society and enterprise and to promote creative destruction by building a good policy environment so as to realize the transformation of an economic development pattern, industrial restructuring and growth-driven conversion.

9.1 Breaking government paradox

Nobel Economic Prize winner Arthur Lewis was confused about the fact that "a government failed maybe because it did too little or it did too much,"[1] which is regarded as the "Lewis Paradox." This theoretical paradox of economics of development looks like a curse of economic development practices, limiting the reasonable boundary of the economic function of Chinese and foreign governments at all times.

The earlier industrialized developed countries have been unable to break this Lewis Paradox all along. Since the birth of modern economics, the argument that the government is just a "night-watcher" has been generally accepted. Adam Smith says the government should keep away from economic activities and the market as far as possible except for the engagement in basic functions involving national security and order.

But it should be noted that many people do remember his "night-watcher" but ignore his "basic functions involving national security and order." The latter includes protecting the society from the violence and aggression of other independent societies and protecting social individuals from bullies and attacks of other individuals as well as establishing and maintaining some public works or public institutions as well. Since a long time ago, the dominant conception of Western countries has been that the government should stay away from economic activities as far as possible: the smaller the government, the fewer functions and actions, the better the government.

However, the world economic history also indicates that there are at least two common issues that cannot be solved without government. One is that not everybody, not every group, could gain equal benefits from the economic development; the other is that economic growth cannot automatically or perfectly regulate itself, so economic crises and periodic disturbance repeat.

In fact, varieties of economic crises repeat periodically and develop into global economic crises when the globalization is deepened. Usually it first breaks out in developed countries that adore the free market economy where most ordinary labors undertake the consequences, and then it spreads to the world and harms the poor in developing countries. In addition, no matter whether in developing countries or developed countries, even in fast growing economies, poverty is like a ghost, haunting forever. Some international organizations and internationally active economists also promoted neoliberal economics, but propagation of the latter did not eliminate the Matthew effect: the rich get richer and the poor get poorer. Independent of man's will, these facts prove that a government is not better because it does less.

Since British economist Keynes' theory of government intervention dominated Western economics, market economy countries have accepted the concept that a government should influence economic activities in a necessary range. Some countries even have been inclined to emphasize planning and regulation and industrial intervention policies and frequently introduce macro-economic policies and establish high welfare institutions. Typical cases include "Roosevelt's New Deal" featuring large-scale investment in the USA, Keynesian-dominating macro-economic policies in Western countries and the economic plans of a high ratio of state-owned economy in France and other countries.

Nevertheless, the enhancement of government intervention in economy neither eliminates the periodic economic phenomenon of developed countries nor wipes out poverty but exacerbates economic fluctuation instead, for example, the States suffered from stagflation where economic recession and inflation coexisted, and European countries found it difficult to sustain high welfare policies due to planning failure and market failure. Thus, the theory of the neo-liberalist economy that advocates a free market economy and opposes government intervention re-emerges and wins the wide market. Developed state governments such as the Reagan administration in the States and the Thatcher administration in the United Kingdom put this theory into practice through series of policies like privatization and developed into the so-called Washington consensus, integrating the theory and the polices before outputting to developing countries and transition countries.

Developing countries fail to escape the curse of Lewis paradox also. The structure of the early development economics asserted active government intervention, dominated in the world from the 1950s to 1960s and had material influence on policymaking of developing countries. But, as a result of government distortion, developing countries didn't surpass their objectives as wished, and the neoclassical and neoliberal economics concerning economic functions of government revived and dominated 1970s instead. The opinion denying the positive influence of government made a great clamor. But when economists attempted to illustrate the experience of later industrial economies, the theory turned to a new trend where the positive influence of government was valued again.

For example, many Latin American countries successively exerted two different development strategies. The first time they were affected by the local theory of aggressive development economics and began to exclude trade and market and overemphasized on the role of government; the second time they were affected by the thought of neo-liberal economics imported by the "Chicago Boys" and turned to overdependence on trade and foreign capital, promoting the market mechanism and limiting the role of government. The two development strategies theoretically and practically are totally opposite, but in many cases their consequences are quite similar in that neither achieves favorable economic outcomes and results in the so-called Latin American Trap or middle-income trap.

The rise of the Asian economy is concluded by Western scholars at first as the successful influence of the free market; even later it's taken as a good story for the verification of the "Washington consensus" focusing on trade liberalization, market-oriented price and privatization. On the other hand, when performing more studies on the experience of Asian economic development, many Western scholars notice the unique role of the governments of Asian countries and regions and conclude that it is a "developmental state." From the same case, opposite theories are summarized. It means the theoretical arguments on economic functions of government still do nothing help to crack the Lewis paradox.

In China, "decentralization-centralization" has been repeated for a long time between the central government and local governments, between government and enterprises and between the market and the society; the vicious cycle or the deadlock seems to be impossible to break the cycle in which "delegating powers to lower levels causes chaos but getting powers back results in zombie economy." Under the planned economic conditions before the reform and opening-up, this "decentralization-centralization" cycle usually happened between the central government and the local governments and between administrative departments, but since the 1980s when the reform was oriented by the market, the "decentralization-centralization" cycle has happened more between government and enterprises and between the market and the society.

Previous experience indicates that repeated decentralization and centralization hasn't touched the substantial relation of government and market. Foreign observers usually conclude China's reform to be the central government delegating powers to the local governments and believe the decentralization intensifies fiscal encouragement for the local governments; plus the political objective assessment mechanism for officials enhances the motivation of the local governments to push up the local economy, so China's rapid economic growth is promoted through the competition of local economies. This explanation does make sense to some degree, but it should be noted that the decentralization doesn't solve the problems between government and market. Local governments intervene in economic activities too much and sometimes run local economies like enterprises. It's imaginable that the sustainability of such an economic development mode is of great concern.

In the dual economic development period with the special growth source – demographic dividend – the economic growth is mainly driven by the inputs of capital, labor, land and resources. As the sources of economic growth are analyzed in Chapter Two (refer to Figure 2.2), the capital accumulation contributes to 70% economic growth. During this period, the government plays a positive role in attracting foreign businesses and investments and mobilizing land resources; it can affect investments and even make direct investments by leveraging the industrial policies and the regional development strategies to promote large-scale projects.

Since demographic dividend disappeared in 2010, labor supply and the population dependency ratio have been more unfavorable to economic growth; capital return has been decreased more and more; contributions of capital accumulation have inevitably declined; the economic development mode overdepending on the inputs of production factors are difficult to sustain. Therefore, the source of long-term sustainable growth only comes from more efficient resource allocation and innovation-oriented technological advancement.

In this brand-new economic development period, if the government continues to make too much intervention in economic activities as before, it's bad for us to gain these new growth sources. There is a perception that after the economic development stage changes and the traditional comparative advantages disappear, a state is needed to prospect the dynamic comparative advantages in the long term and from a more macro perspective, to utilize subsidies to encourage investors to enter into industries with potential comparative advantages, to make accessibility polices to prevent investors from entering into industries without potential comparative advantages or to directly promote the applications of new technologies as a supplier of public goods.

However, the good expectations of government can hardly come true. First, the government uses large-scale projects to intervene in economic growth and inclines the allocation of limited resources to a few industries and enterprises, which reduces the efficiency of resource allocation. Second, the government cannot always be confident about the direction of technological innovations or substitute the innovations of thousands of enterprises. Last and most importantly, the exploration of dynamic comparative advantages and technological innovations relies on competition pressure and the creative destruction mechanism where enterprises have innovation impetus only when they are under survival pressure and are liable to afford potential failures during their innovative activities; the final overall success is based on plenty of individual failures.

The greatest danger of government intervention in economic activities, especially intervention in investing activities in the form of industrial policy, is that it refuses to undertake risks or afford failures. When risks and failures come, the government is inclined to safeguard the existing resource allocation pattern, even prevent the exit of inefficient enterprises in the form of incentives and protection, and it actually deepens the inefficiency of resource allocation; finally it increases leverage ratio and inevitably accumulates high government debt, even resulting in zombie enterprises.

The previous analysis shows that the exploration of a correct answer to the relation of government and market is far from a conclusion, but, from an internationally comparative perspective as well as the experience and lessons from exploration in China, we have recognized a government's economic functions: its realization paths and practices should be diversified and it's impossible to have an universally applicable pattern or consensus.

An icon of Western mainstream economics and in some degree a traitor, Nobel Economic Prize winner Stiglitz pinpointed: "there won't be another consensus, but the Washington Consensus provides no answers to such a question of which strategy has the greatest possibility of promoting the development of impoverished countries.[2]" Every country has different social institutions, historical backgrounds, realistic problems and direct restrictions; in one country, its different periods and development stages have different institutional requirements, so the government must have different functions and roles.

At least we have found a helpful theoretical starting point where we give up struggling with the Lewis paradox about "how much a government should do" and focus on a better definition about "what should a government do and undo." When this fundamental issue is clear, we move on to the secondary issue about "how to do." Combining various theories of economics, a great variety of exceptional economic practices in all countries and the outstanding issues about the functions of Chinese government, we have made conclusions about how the government affects economic development, what measures the government shouldn't take in conventional economic activities, and what the government should do to make a difference in the fields that need intervention.

First, the economic function that the government should fulfill is to provide public goods. The government should prevent various monopolistic conducts and protect fairness and adequacy of market competitions by laws and necessary economic regulations, and establish a social security system and labor market system to provide social protection for the vulnerable groups in economic development. Even in the fields that provide basic public services, the government should explore its and its social organizations' specialization and avoid doing everything by itself and explore and form a new growth engine in case development stage changes. China's economy has an increasing demand for a policy environment adaptive to creative destruction, which should increase productivity from resource reallocation and provide social policy support for workers.

Second, as to direct economic activities, the government should use fiscal and monetary policy means to regulate macro economy and implement industrial and regional policies to explore dynamic comparative advantages and balanced economic development. But, when performing these functions, the government should minimize its direct engagement in economy, stop distortion of the prices of production factors and avoid discriminatory treatment to different business operators. After economic development in China enters new normality, a series of supply side factors related to the disappearance of demographic dividend gradually lead to the regression of the economic growth rate to the mean. Here, most important of all is to differentiate the long-term factors and short-term cyclical factors of economic growth accurately and avoid changing macroeconomic policy instruments for solving short-term fluctuations into long-term and normalized instruments.

At last, in order to have a good relation between government and market, more respect for laws of the market and to better play the role of government, a series of reforms in important fields should be pushed, including streamlining administrative institutions and establishing a serviceable, efficient and honest government; reforming and improving the basic social insurance system to achieve equilibrium of basic public services; establishing law, regulation and public service platforms to create a policy environment favorable to innovations and talents; eliminating institutional obstacles impeding smooth transfer of production factors like labor and capital among departments, regions, urban and rural areas and enterprises; implementing necessary redistribution policy and narrowing the long-standing income gaps between urban and rural areas, between regions, between sectors and between different groups. These reforms involve government itself and require greater political will, courage and wisdom.

9.2 Removing allocation obstacles

Suppose neighboring farmland A and B have the same productivity and are close to an irrigation pond; irrigated farmland increases its output, so we suppose water is an important production factor determining the production output, and this pond is just enough for two farmlands. If this pond is exclusive to farmland A, it's well or even over irrigated, consequently its marginal output decreases; meanwhile farm B has a seriously inhibited output capability due to shortage of irrigation. Under such a circumstance, farmland A and B differ in productivity and the efficiency of resource allocation is greatly reduced. Suppose farmland B is much better and outputs more than farmland A if they have same irrigation, so if farmland B is poorly irrigated compared to farmland A, the efficiency of resource allocation is further reduced. Once the water is allowed to flow to farmland B and the two farmlands are both well irrigated, the efficiency of resource allocation is tremendously improved, and the total outputs are substantially increased.

Applying this metaphor of two farmlands into industries, sectors and enterprises and observing the allocation situations of all production factors like labor, capital and land, conclusions are easily made: if institutional inequality and reallocation obstacles of resource allocation exist, productivity disparity continues and the efficiency of resource allocation hardly reaches its high point; if institutional obstacles impeding resource allocation are removed, the efficiency of resource reallocation is gained; the latter is essential to TFP.

The concept of total factor productivity is often misread; even eager positive government cannot find a grip on immediate effect. If total factor productivity is understood ultimately as resource reallocation efficiency, it's favorable to answer the question of what government could do to increase this productivity. First, total factor productivity originated directly from the Kuznets effect. Nobel Prize-winning economist Kuznets attributed the power and result of industrial structural change to reallocation of resources or factors of production between industries, which increased the productivity. Next, total factor productivity originated directly from theSchumpeter effect, i.e., mobility and reallocation effects of resources or factors of production between businesses under creative destruction conditions. Finally, although technology application and other innovation factors are important sources of productivity, technological advance is not a homogeneous process; productivity may be finally increased only if those earliest and most successful innovators could obtain and use more factors and resources.

During the whole reform and opening-up, the biggest change of the industrial structure referred to the resource reallocation that the ratio of agricultural laborers rapidly decreased and the ratio of non-agricultural employment rapidly increased. During the planned economy, untransferable production factors, especially laborers, accumulated surplus labor on a substantial scale in agriculture, which was the pool of surplus laborers and had a low marginal productivity of labor like in most developing countries. A major achievement of economic reform is creating significant improvement of resource allocation.

This effect is released under reform conditions where abundant labor supply is an endowment condition, plus the institutional legacy of distorted distribution of labor force in a planned economic system. Specifically, once institutional constraints are eliminated, rural surplus labor and redundant staff in state-owned enterprises will move between urban and rural areas, between regions, between industries and between enterprises as guided by the principle of productivity; become main components of total factor productivity and thus labor productivity and make significant contributions to economic growth.

Research shows that, in the period between 1978–2015, labor productivity (GDP per labor force participant) in China actually increased 16.7 times, of which primary industry increased 5.5 times, secondary industry increased 13.5 times and tertiary industry increased 5.2 times. In overall labor productivity increase, the total contribution of all industries to labor productivity increase was 56%, in which contribution of secondary industry was the highest. However, this contribution from the simple sum of productivity increase in three industries cannot explain all sources of increase in labor productivity. That is to say, the contribution of industrial structural change manifested as reallocation of labor to increase in labor productivity was 44%. In which, the static shift effect, i.e., the contribution of labor shift to the industry of high labor productivity in the initial year, was 5 percentage points; the dynamic shift effect, i.e., the contribution of labor shift to the industry of faster increase in labor productivity, was 39 percentage points (Figure 9.1).

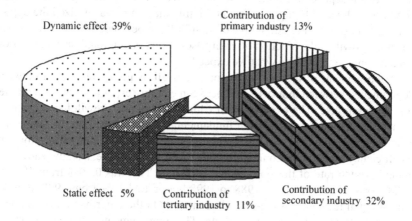

Figure 9.1 Contributions of Sectors and Structures to Labor Productivity Growth

Source: Analysis of China's Economic Reform Effect – From the Perspective of Reallocation of Labor by Cai Fang, Economic Research Journal, 7th issue, 2017

With the large scale of transfer and movement of laborers, the proportion of agricultural laborers decreases significantly; surplus rural laborers also tend to decrease. Due to the negative growth of the new workforce, the space to achieve resource reallocation efficiency and thus support TFP improvement in China will become more and more narrow. However, when only the resource allocation efficiency is concerned, TFP improvement potential is not completely developed yet. The resource allocation efficiency mentioned earlier is only explained by applying the example of two farmlands into primary, secondary and tertiary industries; if the metaphor is applied into the inter-industry or inter-enterprise, it can be imagined there is still huge potential for resource allocation. Now, we cite two independent but logically identical study results to explain the existence of the potential efficiency.

The first study tells us in matured market economies like the United States access, exit, growth and extinction of enterprises constitute a creative destruction and create the resource reallocation efficiency, which improves TFP productivity accounting for 30%–50% total productivity.[3]

The other study involves China. Economists discovered that China's enterprises within the industrial sector differ much in their productivity. The productivity disparity is much higher than that in the United States no matter by what index it is measured. It's beyond doubt that enterprises with low productivity are not eliminated, and enterprises with high productivity don't expand themselves. It's thus deduced and quantitatively confirmed that if the law of the fittest to survive prevails, production factors will be better allocated, and the productivity disparity among enterprises will decrease to the level in the United States; finally, China's industrial TFP will increase 30%–50%.[4]

The two independent studies mentioned previously coincide to get the identical conclusion about TFP improvement and imply that China has utilized the opportunities to improve TFP. The source of high TFP can be expected from the life and death or growth and extinction of enterprises. What institutional obstacles do we need to remove to achieve what we expect?

The movement of production factors, after all, is not quite smooth between departments, between industries and between enterprises; as a result, the completion is incomplete. The experience of Chinese economic growth has repeatedly shown that the competition is the fundamental driving force and the source for efficiency improvement. On one hand, the state-owned economy has improved its efficiency under more competition pressures. For example, a study[5] shows the annual growth rate of the state-owned economic TFP was 0.70% from 1978 to 1988, down to –0.05% from 1988 to 1998 but up to 4.19% from 1998 to 2007, almost equal to the non-state-owned economy. On the other hand, the competitive non-state-owned economy has faster TFP improvement than the state-owned economy during the whole reform period. The annual growth rate of TFP was 1.36% in state-owned departments but 4.74% in non-state-owned departments from 1978 to 2007. The former accounts for only 28.7% of the latter.

The same study also shows that, excluding infrastructure factors, the state-owned economy has a higher capital to labor ratio, lower capital return rate and worse TFP performance than the non-state-owned economy. For example, from 1978 to 2007, compared with the non-state-owned economy, the growth rate of capital per labor of the state-owned economy was 270% and the growth rate of production per labor was 95%, but the TFP growth rate was only 1/3. This comparison implies resources are not allocated into departments with higher productivity.

But if we not just focus on the average numbers from 1978 to 2007 but observe and compare the state-owned and the non-state-owned economies in different periods, we can see from 1998 to 2007, when the state-owned enterprises kept dropping their proportion in total industrial output, their fixed asset ratio and employment ratio after the deepened reform, both state-owned and non-state-owned economies were under greater competition pressure and their increased speeds of capital per labor, output per labor and TFP were quite similar. As it is, the reform is not about which types of enterprise business ownership should exit the market but to create favorable conditions for free access and exit of competitive industries. Only competition encourages innovation and achieves optimized resource allocation.

It may be seen that, with total factor productivity as resource reallocation efficiency letting us understand the things to be done by a positive government for this issue, it is not to exceed its own duties and meddle in others' affairs to select which industry or business has the potential to increase productivity and hence initiate intervention by means of industrial policy but to build a creative destruction environment by developing factors of the production market and maintaining market competition. Because of this, if the concept of industrial policy must be used, what should be done is not to pick winners artificially but to grasp some bottleneck industries, find out existing institutional mechanism issues in these industries and strive to eliminate existing institutional barriers. The effect will certainly promote reasonable mobility of resources between industries, trades, regions and businesses and increase the allocation efficiency of factors of production.

9.3 Fear for poverty and unequal distribution

Strictly speaking, when Confucius says "don't worry about poverty but rather about the unequal distribution of wealth," he doesn't intend to emphasize "don't worry about poverty" but "about the unequal distribution of wealth." This philosophy doesn't contradict our philosophy of making a big cake and distributing the cake equally. In fact, Chinese and foreign history experience and lectures tell us making a big cake is undoubtedly the necessary condition for distributing the cake equally, although not the sufficient condition. For example, in the first decade of the 21st century, some Latin American countries like Brazil had good performance in economic growth and correspondingly dropped their Gini coefficients substantially. The United States since 1970s has slowed down its economic development and made some preferential policies, so poverty incidence has increased significantly, income and wealth have become clearly polarized, and it has become a developed country that has the most unequal income distribution and the biggest Gini coefficient.

In contemporary China, people's income level has risen significantly; meanwhile, a wide income gap and polarization of wealth also appear. In the policy research field, academic circle and press circle, people are keen on discussing income distribution reality and generally recognize that the income distribution is closely correlated with the government's preferential policies, so discussion on equity and efficiency last forever. When time changes and the income distribution situations change, reagrdless of the discussion from a theoretical point of view or making a voice for vital interests, opinions fight against each other tit for tat.

Fairness and efficiency become a widely discussed proposition that at first target equalitarianism and absence of incentive mechanisms during the planned economy. The "Communal Dining System" prevailed in that period, and the way to wealth was legally and practically blocked. To solve these problems, Deng Xiaoping proposed an objective in the middle of the 1980s that allowed some people to get rich first, and thus all people would be well-off together. Consequently an official theory was developed that involved "giving priority to efficiency with due consideration to fairness." Since its proposal at the Third Plenary Session of the 14th CPC Central Committee in 1993, this statement, for a very long time, has been the most widely accepted consensus, which criticizes the malpractices of traditional equalitarianism and the prevailing communal dining system, emphasizes giving priority to efficiency, strives to establish incentive mechanisms and has positive influence on the mobilization of the initiatives of laborers and entrepreneurs.

When the market mechanism of production factors gradually becomes the basic mode of resource allocation and income distribution and the income gap between regions, the urban and the rural, departments and the social members tends to expand, people start to value the fairness of income distribution. Especially when some institutional factors result in an unreasonable income gap and even wealth disparity, most people suggest policies should turn more to fairness. These new recognitions are also reflected in the official statements on fairness and efficiency.

For example, the report of the 16th CPC National Congress made a new statement that "in primary distribution, we should pay more attention to efficiency; in redistribution, we should pay more attention to fairness," strengthening the function of the government in regulating income distribution and making the solemn promise to narrow the gap if it is too wide. After the 17th CPC National Congress, official expressions gave consideration to both fairness and efficiency more clearly. For example, in the 18th CPC National Congress Report: "a proper balance should be struck between efficiency and fairness in both primary and secondary distribution, with particular emphasis on fairness in secondary distribution." It was required more clearly in the 19th CPC National Congress Report: "We will see that government plays its function of adjusting redistribution, move faster to ensure equitable access to basic public services and narrow the gaps in incomes."

In common discussions, most people more or less take efficiency and fairness as two opposite concepts and believe their relationship more like "you can't have your cake and eat it too". In fact, this theory comes from Okun's *Equality and Efficiency: The Big Tradeoff*, published in 1975. The Chinese versions don't mistranslate the subtitle of this masterpiece but more or less deviate from its original meaning and mislead people. Most versions translate "the Big Tradeoff" into "big choice," but actually it means "accepting or refusing," either this or that, only one may be chosen, implying that "you can't have your cake and eat it too."

Since politicians and policymakers cannot say determinedly "I prefer fairness" or "I would rather have efficiency" in most cases, the cognition of taking fairness and efficiency as opposite and not being able to have both may cause misunderstanding and cause policies to be constantly changed; either let it develop to be out of control regardless of deteriorating income distribution or result in extreme distribution policies. It goes against the roles of primary distribution and redistribution mechanisms or substitutes populism policies for social distribution policies. Some countries even have catastrophic outcomes, and their policy intentions and effects are least aligned.

Efficiency and fairness are both objectives of development. Efficiency is the key to mobilize the initiatives of economic development participants and the core to establish effective incentive mechanisms, while fairness is the ultimate objective of economic development and also the benchmark to measure efficiency. Efficiency and fairness are essentially not contradictory. On the premise that efficiency is ensured, making a big cake is the material base for equal distribution, and then the economic development achievements can be shared. Only when equal distribution is ensured will efficiency be attained and find its own destiny. But efficiency and fairness have different emphases and won't be balanced automatically.

Unified consideration of both efficiency and fairness requires a people-centered development thinking, not only should their overall balance be realized, but the choices also have to be made in their priority order and policy preference according to different principal contradictions in different periods or development stages. Then, what's the most outstanding issue facing China in income distribution at present? What are the difficulties to reform the income distribution system? What's the breakthrough to propel the reform and gain material achievements? Now we are going to combine the general rules of income distribution with China's exceptional contradictions together to discuss the above issues.

Nobel Economic Prize winner Simon Kuznets had a famous observation that as an economy develops the economic inequality at first increases and then decreases after it reached a certain turning point. This natural cycle is called the "Kuznets inverted U-curve." As there is much empirical research proving and denying this observation to date, the relation between economic development and income distribution advanced by Kuznets is viewed at most as a hypothesis. It must be admitted there are a variety of factors affecting income distribution, and the dominant factors vary according to the economic system, development stage and preferential policies of a country. Even if there is a changing trend similar to Kuznets' observation, it must be complicatedly embodied.

For this fact observed by Kuznets and its generalization, whether followers or questioners, their starting point was mostly whether the inverted U-shaped curve existed. In the direction of such a discussion, once the long-term dynamics of capital accumulation and subsequent yawning income gap trend revealed by Piketty in his *Capital in the Twenty-First Century* were widely accepted, Kuznets' theory seemed to be over, any argument around it became unnecessary. However, if we turn from argument to trial answering: which policy efforts should be made – which institutional conditions should be ready and created to meet the Kuznets turning point of income gap from top to bottom – then we may continue our research on income distribution issues and obtain helpful policy implications.

Along with different development stages of China's economy, income distribution pattern also experienced corresponding changes. Generally speaking, the change of income distribution is mainly influenced by three factors, and the income gap may be widened or narrowed. The relative effects of three factors vary in different periods, so their comprehensive effect results in the specific track of the changes of income distribution.

With gradual development of the labor market, laborers have both a population difference and individual difference in labor capital, so the income splits and even the income gap widen. In a sense, this effect helps improve labor enthusiasm and education incentives. The reform and opening-up to promote economic growth is not nationally widely carried out and advanced at the same time, so economic development opportunities are not equally distributed among regions and population. Income increases happen one after another. Even when the opportunities are identical, laborers hardly simultaneously take the opportunities to increase income and get rich due to different family status, ages, genders and education levels.

We may take an example of the economists' most quotable rate of return to education. Generally speaking, return to education may be observed from two points of view. First, from the point of view of overall economic growth, the increase in average years of education of workers promotes output growth with a certain contribution portion. This return to education always exists, even if the labor market development level is low. Next, from the point of view of individual workers, high educational attainment generally represents high human capital endowment of workers, also greater contribution to enterprise output, therefore, the human capital reward of an enterprise is to pay higher wages to these persons. This is the so-called private return to education.

Under the traditional system a lack of incentive mechanism, "getting an equal share regardless of the work done," means that human capital of staff and their contributions to the enterprise are generally not embodied in wage levels. This is the so-called the same no matter whether doing more or less and the same no matter whether working well or poorly. With the advance of reform, enterprises face increasing competition, and the labor market development level increases gradually. Human capital of workers is more and more recognized and embodied in wage difference.

For example, some Chinese scholars use micro data to get the conclusions that the rate of private return to education increased from 1.2% in 1989 to 2.2% in 1993, 3.8% in 2000 and 8.9% in 2006.[6] In fact, it doesn't mean the rate of return to human capital increases per year, but, in the contribution of human capital to enterprise output, the part obtained by individuals has been recognized gradually and embodied in wages. Although this result generated by development of the labor market widens the income gap between laborers, generally it has positive incentive effects.

However, the increased rate of private return to education may have unfavorable effects on widening the income gap. Some scholars discover that the RRE of high-income groups is way higher than that of low-income groups. The former has natural institutional advantages in getting education opportunities. For example, as the public education resources are distributed unequally, big cities have more education opportunities and better education quality than small and medium cities and the rural areas. The high-income groups have more social connections and even privileges to make their children enjoy better education resources. The income gap caused by education resources is morally unfair; it's inefficient for education investment and development and causes inter-generational poverty.

With the expanding scope of employment of urban and rural residents, especially as the rural laborers have more opportunities for non-agricultural employment, the income gap between the urban and the rural is narrowed, and the total income distribution is improved. The earlier employment and development opportunities are accessible to the groups with competitive human capital, but increased employment opportunities will benefit more and more labor groups. This is the so-called trickle-down effect.

During the whole reform and opening-up, China was generally at the dual economic development stage, where a plenty of surplus laborers transfer from the agriculture to the non-agricultural industries, the labor participation rate increases, and more common households and labor groups share the economic growth achievements. The migrant workers get employment opportunities for salaries higher than the income of agricultural work, so the overall poverty level of the rural areas is reduced. Even if it doesn't narrow down the income gap between the urban and the rural, it does inhibit the widening income gap between the urban and the rural.

The household contract system based on the institutional feature of equal land distribution ensures laborers unrestrictedly mobilize in pursuit of a higher income and a better life. Even if the wage rate stayed consistent, the expanded scale of labor mobility would increase the income of farmer families substantially. The effects of labor mobility on increasing income of farmer families and narrowing the income gap between the urban and the rural can be observed from the following three aspects.

First we look at the poverty reduction effect of labor mobility. Except for those families with insufficient laborers or incompetent employability, insufficient employment is the biggest reason for poverty in most impoverished families. Previous studies show the non-agricultural employment opportunities are first accessible to the groups with skills or influential family background in rural areas, but when employment opportunities increase, the impoverished families begin to get benefits. Outside work means it's possible to get a higher income. Studies indicate that the impoverished families increase 8.5% to 13.1% net household income per capita by sending their laborers out to work in cities.[7]

Second we look at the contributions of wage income to the income increase of farmers. According to the National Bureau of Statistics, the net income of farmer families is divided into wage income, household business net income, property income and transfer income. Increased outside employment opportunities substantially increase wage income of farmer families and also the share of wage income in total family income. Wage income becomes the main source of increasing the income of farmers.

This effect may be seen clearly from the experience of China's economy before reaching the Lewis turning point. For example, in the period of 1997–2004, when wages of peasant workers did not increase substantially, since the scale of peasant workers increased from less than 40 million to above 100 million, the gross payroll of peasant workers increased at a mean rate of 14.9% per year, while the proportion of wage income of peasant households, even when underestimated, increased from 24.6% to 34.0% in net income of peasant households.[8]

Actually the current statistics system omits a large portion of working income. As the household survey of official statistics is conducted separately in the urban and the rural areas, whole families moving into cities and the rural family members going outside for work are excluded from the urban samples due to their difficult accessibility and are also excluded from the rural household samples because they are no longer permanent rural residents, so the working incomes of migrant workers are substantially underestimated. A local survey discovered that the disposable income of urban residents is overestimated by 13.6%, the net income of rural residents is underestimated by 13.3% and the income gap between the urban and the rural is overestimated by 31.2% due to the sampling and the definition of official resident survey statistics.[9]

Demographic transition and labor mobility eventually eliminate the infinite supply of laborers in the dual economic development stage. This symbolic turning point is the Lewis turning point, which doesn't mean absolute shortage of laborers but temporary shortage of laborers if the wage has no material increase. Once this

process begins, the wages of ordinary workers will continue to increase. Therefore, after the Lewis turning point, the growth of income of migrant workers and
farmer families is accelerated; consequently the income gap between the urban and
the rural is narrowed. The narrowed income gap between the urban and the rural
definitely reduces the inequality of overall income.

From the published official data of the National Bureau of Statistics, we select
the income gap between the urban and the rural and the Gini Coefficient of national
residents to describe the changing tendency of the income distribution pattern.
Generally, the income gap ascends for a long time, but when the Chinese economy
reached the Lewis turning point, the widening income gap was inhibited and narrowed gradually after it peaked around 2009 (Figure 9.2). In a less strict sense, we
may as well regard 2009 as a landmark time point of China's economy reaching
the Kuznets turning point.

Due to problems in the reform process, the widening or barely narrowing income
gap caused by the issues arising from the reform and opening-up or the periodic
phenomenon arising from the uncompleted reform should be finally solved by
deepening the reforms on economic institutions and adjusting social policies. In
order to improve the utilization of natural resources and stock assets of government and state-owned enterprises, during the institutional transition, some state-
owned assets are privatized, many mineral resources and other resources are used
by individuals or groups and the right to derive benefits from lands is owned by
individuals or enterprises. As a result, all sources and assets are divided and distributed; the nominal state ownership and the actual "no one to possess" turn into
individual or group ownership and then produce individual incomes in hard cash.

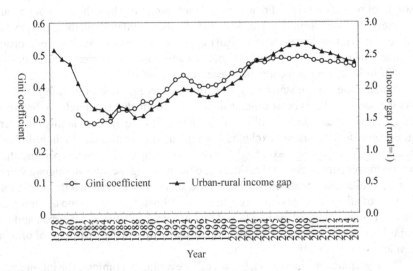

Figure 9.2 The Change Trend of the Resident Income Gap

Source: China Statistical Yearbook issued by National Bureau of Statistics of China in the past years;
www.stats.gov.cn/tjdt/gjtjjdt/t20130118_402867315.htm (downloaded on Nov. 5, 2016)

As the reallocation of resources and assets is unsupervised, many practices are not standardized or transparent; even violations of laws and regulations are frequent, so the subsequent benefits are usually gray incomes, which are distributed in an extremely unequal way and constitute the major factors that widen the income gap. Scholars estimate that all kinds of off-payroll incomes or gray incomes in 2008 were 2.19 times as much as the official disposable income per capita of urban residents, and 80% was concentrated in the 10% highest income group.[10]

Just because of this, Chinese society still pays close attention to income distribution and common people often have no obvious sense of the improvement of income distribution. To get an accurate recognition of the changing trend of actual income distribution, we could divide the present income gap into two levels: the income gap of labor market, i.e., difference between people's incomes obtained from employment and the social income gap, which is mainly caused by unfair distribution of factors other than labor. The previous description tells us the income gap of the labor market has inclined to decline, meeting the expectation of the Kuznets curve, but the social income gap has no fundamental reversal.

It may be seen that the problem lies in the difference between the concept connotations of two income gaps. Men of insight generally believe that unequal income distribution is one of the sources of potential social risks in the future. In fact, we may analyze the issues based on the trend shown in Figure 9.2 and propose important issues about the income distribution system.

We should see that the tendency in Figure 9.2 is concluded without the consideration of the distribution of gray incomes beyond the statistics. If it's considered, we can estimate that the fundamental reversal of the income distribution status has not come yet. This special source causing unequal income distribution implies the preferential fields of the reform. To solve the unequal income distribution, we can do something from three aspects including increment, stock and income stream.

If we solve the unequal income distribution from increment, we should strictly abide by laws and follow standardized procedures to institutionally stop the intervention of powers during the development of lands and mining resources. In order to prevent depriving farmers of benefits during the expropriation of rural collective lands and the change from rural residents to urban residents, it should accelerate affirming the rights of land contracts and homesteads and prohibit any infringement on the property rights of farmers. The state-owned economy continues to restructure. To prevent the state-owned assets from losing to individuals and groups, it should clearly and strictly define the property rights and standardize the change of the property rights. The more fundamental solution is to enhance the supervision of administrative officials who possess the power of resource distribution, intensify corruption fights and preventions and minimize leaders' and cadres' individual power of resource distribution.

In fact, with economic development in China entering new normality, the central government no longer puts forward binding requirements for local growth rate, and it even implements macroeconomic control policy to prevent systematic risks, suppressing infinite power of local government on resource allocation. The anti-corruption campaign has obtained an absolute effect; the punishments of grand corruption, petty corruption and micro corruption, banning illegal income, have held back the increase of corruption incomes significantly. Reform focuses on the decisive role of th market in resource allocation, and it is also favorable to prevent more incremental property income inequalities.

To solve the unreasonable stocks of individual or group assets and their income flows, we should focus on laws and taxations to regulate high incomes. At present, the Chinese taxation system featuring a high indirect tax ratio, low direct tax ratio and no progressive tax has little effect on income distribution regulation, so it should enact categories of taxes that regulate income distribution like legacy tax and estate tax as soon as possible. Meanwhile, it should encourage and promote the employee stock ownership plan, which has certain effects on asset equalization.

Expanding employment of urban and rural residents is an important motivation factor of narrowing the income gap. However, to date the narrowed income gap is still at its preliminary stage. Whether it becomes a stable tendency and evolves into the Kuznets turning point is up to the reform relevant to the income distribution system which states that the institutions effective for the long term should be constructed to create favorable conditions for the Kuznets turning point.

Just as the Kuznets turning point will not occur naturally, the material narrowing of the wage income gap depends on construction and improvement of such a series of labor market institutions (including labor laws) as minimum wage, labor unions and wage collective bargaining. The administrative policies on income distribution and people's livelihood improvement still have critical effects on narrowing the income gap. For example, more tolerant and equalized education is the fundamental method to narrow the income gap and prevent intergenerational poverty. Finally, the government should pay great efforts to improve income distribution with a view to the balance between economic growth and the redistribution policy.

Economic growth, technological change and globalization are undoubtedly helpful social progress processes, yet these processes will not generate the trickle-down effect automatically and could not ensure equal benefits of each group naturally. Therefore, the redistribution policy should be a policy orientation. In addition, with the increase of per capita income level, the role of government policy in income distribution pattern is enhanced; this is a policy evolution trend with regularity. For example, from the situation in 28 OECD countries of small income gap, through the redistribution policy the average Gini coefficient decreases from 0.47 after primary distribution to 0.30 after redistribution, that is to say redistribution decreases the average Gini coefficient of these countries by 17 percentage points.

9.4 Social protection is not a negative incentive

No matter whether in rich or impoverished countries, personal capabilities vary a lot, for example, high or low education; young, prime or senior age; healthy or sick, so some social memberships are relative or absolutely vulnerable after all; even if one person has advantages in these capabilities, he is still exposed to irresistible economic strikes like unemployment or bankruptcy and various natural risks and then falls into a difficult life. Therefore, people need social protection to prevent, respond to and overcome the vulnerabilities that reduce people's welfare.

Social protection refers to the system composed of a series of policies and programs including social insurance, social assistance and labor market institution. "Ensuring people's access to childcare, education, employment, medical services, elderly care, housing, and social assistance" mentioned at the 19th National Congress of CPC also refers to the life that the government expects all social members to enjoy through the basic public services it provides.

Social protection is a vogue word but has a long history of theory development and policy dispute. According to Malthus, the social protection we talk about today only exacerbates and does not alleviate human disasters and poverty. Under the hypothesis that food growth cannot satisfy the needs of population growth, he believes the root of poverty is population growth. Therefore, any efforts attempting to help the poor finally result in opposite consequences due to the increased birth rate. He not only fights against any theoretical conception on social protection but also proposes the policy to gradually abolish *the Act for the Relief of the Poor* in United Kingdom.[11]

Just as his poverty trap is broken after the Industrial Revolution, Malthus' opinion repelling all social protections based on his own "law of population" conflicts with his vague theory of "effective demand." In modern society, the root of poverty is no longer that absolute output is insufficient to meet people's needs for adequate food and clothing but institutional drawbacks and policy inclination that hinder vulnerable groups from accessing their own shares. In any time and any society, vulnerability is inevitable. In today's world, any opinions objecting to social protection for vulnerable groups cannot win over academic or moral alliance anymore.

Stuttgart Muller, a Malthus contemporary, warns that social assistance generates two outcomes: assistance itself and the dependency on assistance. No doubt the former is helpful but the latter is harmful to its most extent. The dangers of the latter may offset the positive effects of the former.[12] This "Muller Puzzle" of how to gain the balance between the mutual aid of social protection and the incentive of the labor market is much more disputable than Malthus' theory.

Now, China's institution and policy system that gives social protection full play comprises three parts. The first part refers to the basic social insurance system including social pension insurance, basic medical insurance, employment injury insurance, unemployment insurance and maternity insurance for urban employees and residents and new social pension insurance and new cooperative medical insurance for rural residents. The second part refers to the social assistance system including the subsistence allowance system for urban and rural residents, the medical assistance system and other compensation and relief payment system. The third part refers to the labor market system including the minimum wage system, wage collective bargaining system, labor contract system, labor dispute arbitration and conciliation system. Combining all these together, we try to give a Chinese answer to the "Muller Puzzle."

At a stage changing from high speed economic growth to drastic structural adjustment, Chinese society has increasing institutional demands on kinds of social insurances. When the potential growth rate is at a high level, restriction of the actual growth rate comes from the shocks of the demander. Overall increased employment coincides with periodic unemployment. During the biggest unemployment shock in the end of the 1990s, China established the social pension insurance and unemployment insurance systems in a short time. After that, when the potential growth rate decreases, the basic social insurance system will be improved continuously; the role of social insurance will be intensified rather than weakened.

As the industrial restructuring accelerates, laborers are more exposed to structural unemployment risks. Not only may the skills of migrant workers differ from the requirements of enterprises, but also new laborers with high education background may have difficulties in finding a job because of unmatched human capital. To solve the structural unemployment, the government should implement encouraging employment policies and also deliver the signals of skill requirements through the labor market so as to provide incentives for individuals to receive education, for schools to reform the education system and for the society to enhance employee training. The signal delivery means some of the labors will get laid off.

As for enterprise competition, the mechanism for the market to give its role full play is the creative destruction. On the labor market, competition pressure is necessary, but the "destructive" mechanism cannot be applied onto laborers. Therefore, it must have a safety net with wide coverage to give social protection to those laborers that are temporarily excluded from the market. It would be difficult for China to accomplish the tasks of economic transition and industrial upgrading without a solid social protection system and policy supporting thevulnerable groups.

In China's labor market, there is a contradictory phenomenon. On one hand, the industrial upgrading creates huge demands on labors with higher education; on the other hand, employment difficulty of college graduates is quite outstanding. To solve this contradiction, the competition mechanism of labor market and the social protection mechanism should be combined before their full utilization.

One important reason that college graduates struggle to find a job is that their employment scope is too narrow. China had only 10.1% employees with a college degree in 2010, 30 percent lower than 40.1% in the USA in 2006. Comparing the distribution of employees with a college degree in both countries, we find out Chinese college employees are over-concentrated in finance, information, education and health and public management industries, in other words, the ratio of college employees in these industries in China is extraordinarily high, even higher than the USA.

But in the directly productive industries, the proportion of higher education graduates in total employment is much lower in China than in the USA. For example, as to the ratio of college employees in agriculture, China has 0.6% while the USA has up to 24.6%; in the manufacturing industry, China has 10.3% while the USA has 30.0%; in traffic industry, China has 10.8% while the USA has 27.1%; in the business, trade, catering and tourism industries, China has 11% while the USA has 28.6% (Figure 9.3). To a certain degree, this is a realistic reason that the real economy in China is not strong enough and a manifestation of a real economy that is not strong.

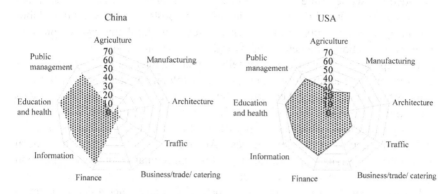

Figure 9.3 The Ratio of College Employees in Different Industries of China and the USA

Source: Hu Ruiwen et al., China's Education Structure and the Supply and Demand of Talents, research report, 2013

Laborers with higher education usually don't voluntarily turn from high-end service industries to traditionally low-end positions in manufacturing, even in agriculture industries. On one hand, the directly productive industries need to upgrade themselves before they increase their demands on high-end laborers; on the other hand, only leveraging the market and experiencing job hunting, employment pending, employment, unemployment and re-employment could provide a more balanced and diversified employment structure for college graduates. This transition is also the period when laborers encounter shocks, so it definitely needs the social insurance system to provide a safety shelter.

The labor market transitioning from overall oversupply to structural undersupply stimulates laborers' demands on the labor market system. Since the 21st century, labor disputes and even conflicts between employees and employers have rapidly increased. Medium coverage or gossips are not statistical evidence of some significant conclusion, but we can have certain judgment on China's labor relation from the increased recorded labor disputes.

The recorded labor disputes have two categories. One refers to the cases accepted by labor disputes arbitration institutions at all levels in China, and the other refers to the conciliation cases. Two categories were totaled 208,000 in 2000 and kept gradually increasing per year. In 8 years, from 1999 to 2007, the mean annual percentage increase was 14.3%. However, a great leap forward happened in 2008. Recorded cases in this year were 98.0% more than that in the previous year. The number of cases mediated increased by 56.2%. The number regressed to a steady increasing trend again after 2009; the number of two kinds of cases only increased at a mean annual speed of 2.3% in the period of 2008–2016.

The substantial increase of labor dispute cases in 2008 was a typical consequence of legislation. In that year, three laws related to labor employment were simultaneously carried out, including the Labor Contract Law, Employment Promotion Act and Law of Mediation and Arbitration of Labor Disputes. These laws extended the scope of the protection of rights and interests of labors, intensified the protection, reduced rights protection cost and prolonged the validity of labor dispute appeals. No doubt they had positive effects on stimulating rights protection awareness of laborers and encouraging rights protection activities.

The experience of many countries tells us that the intensified labor disputes or employment hospitality during the specific development stage are not the outcomes of worse employment conditions but the awakening consciousness of rights protection because laborers had more requirements regarding wage, workfare and working conditions, when the supply-demand relationship of laborers changes and employment opportunities increase. According to the economic and social development experience of the countries, this is a regular common phenomenon symbolizing that laborers have higher requirements on the labor market system.

European and American countries, Japan, Korea and other Asian economies have finally recognized the inevitability of such "problems incidental to growing up," have learned to conform to the rule of "growing pains" after paying heavy prices in the period of frequent labor and capital frictions and have established complete labor market systems, improved employment quality as a whole, formed institutional frameworks to solve employment disputes and opposition and maintained social stability. On the contrary, those countries falling into the middle-income trap suffer from social disharmony, even unrest, due to the failure to establish institutions actively or passively or the excessive promises that cannot be kept or inappropriate repressive policies.

Regarding whether China should make an active response to the desperate demands on the establishment of labor market systems, the academic circle, even the policy researchers, haven't reach a consensus. A lot of people are quite worried about the labor contract system, the wage collective bargaining system and even the minimum wage system and believe that these systems will result in increased labor cost, reduced competitive advantages of manufacturing products and, moreover, will encourage laborers to undertake rights protection activities and increase transaction cost in economic activities, even cause social instability.

Obviously, these viewpoints reverse the cause and effect. The rise in wage itself, and the accompanied changes of balance inclination in labor relations, are inevitable results of China's economy after the Lewis turning point; institutional improvement should be made to adapt to such changing trends. On the contrary, if social instability really occurs, it should not be attributed to the labor market system but the adverse consequence of lack of such an institutional arrangement.

A high-profile and influential economist Zhang Wuchang always disapproves of the establishment of labor market systems. When the NPC Standing Committee approved the Labor Contract Law, Professor Zhang Wuchang wrote a critical comment and was even impatient to attach this comment to his book as an "unpleasant postscript."[13] After that, he spared no efforts to persistently condemn this law both in speech and in writing. Although similar vocal criticism was not a common phenomenon, many other advocates thought this law and some changes in labor relations that occurred after its implementation should be responsible for the operation difficulties of manufacturing enterprises, the too fast rise of wages and the loss of comparative advantage.

Economists have always had different opinions on the role of the labor market system, and the author of this book has no intention or ability to put an end to this long-standing debate. However, the following considerations may help to illustrate the necessity of strengthening the institutional construction of the labor market at this stage of China's economic and social development.

Economists are always hardhearted and ice-cold when talking about competition and efficiency. Economics is about sense, so it has no ground to claim that economists are more rational than emotional. However, the difference between the labor market and the product market and other production factor market is that its trade entities and trade targets are living people. Marshall once said it mattered nothing for the supplier of bricks whether bricks were used to build sewers or palaces. But the seller of labor force – the laborer must care about how labor force will be used after the sale. Besides, asymmetric information exists in the employment relationship of the labor force, so the reasonable rights and interests of under-informed laborers are usually infringed on in the unruled market transactions and employment.

No one denies kinds of labor market systems intend to solve the vulnerability of entities of different labor markets, but their disagreement lies in whether the protection beyond the balanced supply and demand in labor markets becomes a negative incentive for hardworking employees and initiative employers. The international comparison indicates that the developed countries have established perfect labor market systems that have positive effects already, but many developing countries do have relevant systems that have no effects at all or generate negative incentives due to insufficient labor protection.

This means that social protection including the labor market system is a system phenomenon related to development stages. So there is eventually a turning point where, once stepped over by the economic development, the labor market systems will become indispensable. This turning point logically is closely correlated with the Lewis turning point that reflects the supply-demand relationship of laborers. When infinite labor supply turns into a shortage and the employment issue changes from total number to structural transition, China is more desperate for labor market systems. Economic theories and practices should advance with the times, so people like Professor Zhang Wuchang shouldn't take the alternative options at the specific development stage as eternities.

Therefore, in employment, to let employers and employees know how many and what laborers are needed in the labor market, the supply-demand signals should be delivered in the forms of wage level, unemployment rate or employment difficulties, even the competitive surviving in jobs, but giving the most basic social protection to market participants is an inescapable responsibility of the government. Those societies with more social cohesion anytime anywhere usually get profits from their perfect labor market systems.

Some scholars, with good intentions, i.e., disproving possible arguments over insufficient social protection to criticize the Chinese system, thought China no longer a low welfare country but among high welfare countries in the world based on the proportion of public expenditure on social security in GDP up to 10.5% in 2012.[14] As a varied result of development stage and as an important achievement of central government policy focused on people's livelihood, China has really achieved unprecedented results in the generalized social protection field. However, the clue implied in the previously mentioned conclusion that China relies on social protection does not tally with the facts.

Current strength and coverage of social protection in China is far from enough to make people dependent on it. The prolonged dispute about the "Muller Puzzle" may make some sense to the developed EU countries where contradictory cases coexist. For example, during the finance crisis and the debt crisis, social protection and economic performance conflicted with each other in Spain, Greece and Italy, and social protection and economic performance promoted each other as well in Sweden, Denmark and Finland. North European countries with typically high welfare had very healthy economic development during the European debt crisis or at least had enough outstanding achievements to defeat other countries in Europe.

Many researchers believe one of the important reasons that Latin American countries stay in the middle-income trap for so long is that these countries emphasize solely redistribution, neglect market mechanism and implement populist welfare catch up regardless of their own current development stages and fiscal capabilities.[15] Some Latin American countries did make too many promises on welfare but finally could hardly achieve equalization or even make material fulfillment. But it is at most one of the expressions of typical countries in the middle-income trap rather than the fundamental reason why they have fallen into the middle-income trap.

To a certain extent, the populist policy as a phenomenon of Latin America, especially excessive commitment to welfare, is rather the last option for some countries stuck in the middle-income trap for a long time due to economic stagnation. Many factors lead to slow economic growth, stagnation and even regression; when the cake is no longer bigger, not all commitments on social protection are kept if they are too many; they are even sometimes simply a means of political campaign, even just lip services.

Therefore, this dispute is of specific significance to China yet not so straightforward. General Secretary Xi Jinping pointed out that we should always proceed from the reality, increase income based on the increase in labor productivity, increase welfare level based on sustainable growth of economic and financial resources. Compared with European countries, even Latin American countries, China has a very low level of social protection by far. Those who are worried about too much social protection focus on the level of benefits and the relevant rules of social protection projects. However, it's quite obvious, and it must be recognized that China's social protection has not only a small coverage but also a very low absolute level.

Take the coverage of five types social protection projects for example. According to the peasant workers monitoring survey conducted by the National Bureau of Statistics of China, in 2014, compared with registered urban residents, the employment stability of the peasant workers employed locally and nonlocally was insufficient; only 38% of them signed labor contracts with employers; peasant workers could not fully and equally enjoy basic public services with respect to the proportion participating in basic social insurance, work-related injury insurance (26%), medical insurance (17.6%), pension insurance (16.7%) and unemployment insurance (only 10.5%). In fact, even urban employees with a local registered residence are far from being fully covered by the previously mentioned social insurance.

Take a look at the minimum wage level and its changes. From the collected data of hundreds of nationwide cities and minimum wages, we can see the efforts made to improve the minimum wage standard. More cities have strived to increase the average of their minimum wages in recent years, and their improvements are increased year after year (Figure 9.4). However, in the period from 1995 to 2013, the actual annual growth rate of average minimum wage was only 8%, lower than the GDP growth rate and the growth rate of average wages of urban employees in the same period. In 2013, minimum wage standards in 287 cities were selected; the average level was compared with average wage in urban units – it was only 19.2% that of state-owned units, 27.5% of collective units and 21.2% of other units. Not very high when compared with the international level.

The current coverage and protection of the minimum subsistence allowance system at present is far from enough to make people dependent on it. In 2016, after application and public notification procedures, 14.802 million urban people obtained minimum living standard security, accounting for only 1.9% of the urban resident population and 2.7% of the urban registered population. Calculated according to the year round total fiscal expenditure for the urban minimum

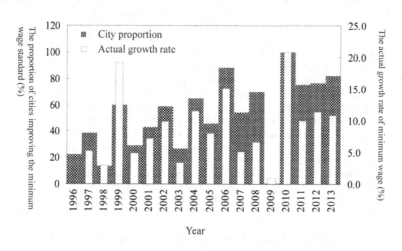

Figure 9.4 The Cities Improving the Minimum Wage Standard and the Average Increase

Source: the minimum wage database of the Institute of Population and Labor Economy of Chinese Academy of Social Sciences; the data in the database is collected and edited from the websites of human resources and social security departments of all concerning cities

living standard security at all levels (68.79 billion Yuan), the average subsidy obtained by low-income people was only 4,647 Yuan per capita per year; this subsidy level was only 13.8% of the per capita disposable income of urban residents in the same year. The number of rural residents who obtained minimum living standard security in the same year was 45.865 million, which accounted for approximately 7.8%, of the rural resident population, 5.5% of the rural registered population. Calculated according to the year round total fiscal expenditure for the rural minimum living standard security at all levels (101.45 billion Yuan), the average subsidy obtained by low-income people was 2,212 Yuan per capita per year, which accounted for 17.9% of rural per capita disposable income in the same year. The rural minimum living standard security standard is only slightly higher than the rural poverty alleviation standard, while the latter is only slightly higher than absolute poverty standard set by the World Bank (constant price 1.9 international dollars in 2011).

Notes

1 Author Lewis. (1994). *The Theory of Economic Growth* (Trans. by Liang Xiaoping). Shanghai: Shanghai Joint Publishing House, Shanghai People's Publishing House.
2 Joseph Stiglitz. (2005). Consensus on Post Washington Consensus. In Huang Ping and Cui Zhiyuan (Eds.), *China and Globalization: Washington Consensus or Beijing Consensus*. Beijing: Social Sciences Academic Press.
3 Lucia Foster, John Haltiwanger, and Chad Syvereson. (2008). Reallocation, Firm Turnover and Efficiency: Selection on Productivity or Profitability? *American Economic Review, 98*, 394–425.
4 Chang-Tai Hsieh and Peter J. Klenow. (2009). Misallocation and Manufacturing TFP in China and India. *The Quarterly Journal of Economics, 124*(4), 1403–1448.
5 Loren Brandt and Xiaodong Zhu. (2010, February). Accounting for China's Growth. *Working Paper*, 395. Department of Economics, University of Toronto.
6 Wang Zhong. *The Rate of Return to Human Capital, Salary Structure and Income Inequality: 1989–2006*. Retrieved from www.doc88.com/p-73547169251.html
7 Du Yang, Albert Park, and Wang Sangui. (2005). Migration and Rural Poverty in China. *Journal of Comparative Economics, 33*(4), 688–709.
8 Cai Fang, Du Yang, Gao Wenshu, and Wang Meiyan. (2009). *Labor Economics: Theory and Chinese Reality* (p. 220). Beijing: Beijing Normal University Press.
9 Gao Wenshu, Zhao Wen, and Cheng Jie. (2011). Effects of Rural Labor Mobility on the Statistics of Income Gap between the Urban and the Rural Residents. In Cai Fang (Ed.), *Reports on China's Population and Labor (No.12): Challenge during the 12th Five-Year Plan Period: Population, Employment and Income Distribution* (pp. 228–242). Beijing: Social Sciences Academic Press.
10 Wang Xiaolu. (2011). Gray Income and National Income Distribution. In Song Xiaowu, Li Shi, Shi Xiaoming, and Lai Desheng (Eds.), *China's Income Distribution: Discussion and Dispute*. Beijing: China Economic Publishing House.
11 Malthus. (2012). *An Essay on the Principle of Population*. Beijing: Huaxia Publishing House.
12 Quoted from John Hoddinott. (2010, March 22–24). Safety Nets and Social Protection: Opportunities for Mutual Learning between Asia and Latin America, a Background Paper for the IFPRI and Universidad del Pacifico Conference, *Fostering Growth and Reducing Poverty and Hunger in Asia and Latin America: Opportunities for Mutual Learning*. Lima, Peru.

13 Zhang Wuchang. (2009). *The Economic System of China*. Beijing: China CITIC Press.
14 Wang Shaoguang. (2013). Is China Still a Low-Welfare State? Social Protection "New Leap Forward" in China from the Comparative Viewpoint. *People's Tribune Academic Frontier, 3*. Retrieved January 10, 2018, from www.rmlt.com.cn/2013/1212/198102_7.shtml
15 Fang Gang and Zhang Xiaojing. (2008). "Welfare Catch-Up" and "Growth Trap": Lectures of Latin American Countries. *Management World, 9*.

10 Embracing the great rejuvenation

When the Chinese economy maintains rapid growth and China's comprehensive national power is increasingly enhanced, regaining the worldwide leading position of both material and cultural civilization is becoming the realistic dream of billions of Chinese. It's appropriately defined as the "Chinese Dream." China is the only country in human history that continues the ancient civilization and experiences rise and fall and then great rejuvenation. However, the past economic growth achievements cannot promise future high quality development; overall income increase doesn't mean the development is naturally tolerant and sharing; the task to step over from the middle-income phase to the high-income phase is even more difficult than getting rid of the poverty trap. Great efforts are needed to realize the great dream.

In the practice of socialism with Chinese characteristics, the Chinese Communists offer from new perspectives a deeper understanding of the laws of governance by the Communist Party, laws governing socialist construction and law of human society development, in which the law of human society development has more general meaning for developing countries. Although the Chinese do not output their development model, such understanding of laws, especially after extracted with Chinese wisdom, is nothing short of an optional Chinese solution and is an important Chinese approach to making new and greater contributions to human beings.

10.1 "Needham Thesis"

The Chinese people propose a grand target for themselves that by 2050, marking the 100th anniversary of the founding of the People's Republic of China, the great rejuvenation of the Chinese nation will be achieved. This "Chinese Dream" is elaborated as "rejuvenation" rather than "revitalization," because in history China was not always backward in science and technology development and economic prosperity, but outpaced the world for a long time.

Western economic historians deny so-called Eurocentrism and make a clear statement that the contemporary economy of Europe and its overseas immigration areas being in the absolute leading position of science and technology, economy and per capita income is not as it always was. Scholars' research indicates that around 1500 the world's wealth was concentrated in the East, where China occupied the most important position. After that Europe started to rise. In late 18th century the "Great Divergence" emerged between the East and the West.[1] During the same period, China began to fall behind the West in economy, science and technology and people's livelihood and gradually degenerated into a poor and weak country.

The prolonged academic curiosity of most subjects is to find out the explanations of the rise and fall of a nation. Economists persevere to develop kinds of theoretical frameworks with the hope of demystifying economic growth. What inspires scholars to take China, which has experienced rise and fall, as the main object of study is the so-called "Needham Thesis" named after the famous Chinese science historian Joseph Needham. This thesis attempts to answer why in pre-modern society Chinese science and technology was far ahead of other civilizations but lost its leading position in modern times.

For the Needham Thesis, the dominant explanation for a long time comes from the so-called high-level equilibrium trap theory. This theoretical assumption believes Chinese agricultural practices in history combined traditional technology and productive factors into such a perfect mix that a living standard much higher than the earlier European history was maintained, resulting in rapid population increase. Consequently excessive and cheap labor force left no room for labor-saving technologies to be useful.[2] According to this theory, only large-scale applications of capital-intensive or labor-saving technologies would complete the necessary technological change to avoid the Malthusian trap. But actually this assumption fails no matter whether reasoning the economic theoretical logic or observing the historical facts.

First of all, Europe did experience land cultivation and border exploration in the medieval period but had a tight human-land relation for most of its history. In other words, for such resource endowment, even some differences exist between China and the West; they are not big enough to cause radically different modernization power. The Malthusian equilibrium trap may always be explained.

Second of all, economic studies indicate that the agricultural technological advancement is caused by relatively scarce productive factors, that is to say, when labor shortage is more severe, labor-saving technology will be invented and used earliest; when land shortage is more severe, land-saving technology will be invented and used earlier; between the labor-saving technological change and the land-saving technological change, neither is superior to the other. Empirical studies demonstrate that, in fact, a country with a large population has more pressure and driving forces to achieve faster technological advancement and population growth due to the tight population-land relation.[3]

After all, either high-level equilibrium or low-level equilibrium is a specific reflection of the Malthusian trap. Any chance to increase food production is eventually a temporary disturbance factor. The resulting population growth will finally pull the productivity to the equilibrium level for subsistence.

Over the past 200 years, the Malthusian theory has been constantly criticized but still has an enduring influence in intellectual circles, because this theory does provide a logical explanation for thousands of years of human economic activities before the Industrial Revolution. As an economic pattern that exists for such a long period and across such wide territories, it of course won't be stereotyped. So, the Malthusian trap has both high-level and low-level equilibrium.

In fact, the "high-level equilibrium trap" can neither perfectly explain the "Needham Thesis" nor justify itself with the historical evidence. For example, according to Maddison's statistic data, in 1500, Italy, the richest country in Europe, had 143% per capita GDP higher than Finland, the poorest country; Britain, the birthplace of the Industrial Revolution, was 57.6% higher than Finland. The per capita GDP of 12 European countries was higher than China, 33% in 1500, 51.3% in 1600, 72.2% in 1700 and 110% in 1820.[4]

Economists attempt to explain or demystify the "Needham Thesis" with more rigorous theories. For example, Lin Yifu believes China's lead in technology in pre-modern society is because of more innovations created by a large population; the reason that later China's science and technology and even are economy falling behind the West is the failure to transform modern technological innovation modes based on large-scale experiments. He concludes that discouragement of technological innovations and the imperial examination system that focuses on repeating and explaining the "Four Books" and the "Five Classics" lead to the unsuccessful transformation of the science and technology innovation modes. No doubt this interpretation comes to the point that China's backwardness resulted from the failure of modern technological innovation. But what still needs to be explained is why China has such an unparalleled imperial examination system.

The usage of economic theories is their explanatory power, and the core is their logical consistence. Therefore, a theory to better demystify the "Needham Thesis" can explain both the history and the reality correlated to the history, without theoretical loops. In other words, it cannot change one proposition to another and then come to an end. Induced institutional change theory holds that an institutional form can be created and exists, inevitably for a specific purpose, and its long standing conditions lie in political gains to retain this system greater than the political costs to abolish this system as a whole. So we need to explain why China has developed and kept such an unparalleled imperial examination system.

For example, if the question of why China has such an unparalleled imperial examination system is not reasonably answered, the issue is actually not solved. Besides, if the "Needham Thesis" of why China lost its leading science position is proposed on the comparison between China and the West, then the theory should reveal the related material differences rather than paradoxical differences between China and the West.

In a typical society before the Industrial Revolution, the normal state of economic development is that the Malthusian vicious cycle of poverty or per capital income repeatedly falls down to the subsistence level (i.e., no development). But once opportunities for the Industrial Revolution, even the occasional opportunities, are coming, the accumulation of material capital, human capital and technology advancement to the minimum level for catching opportunities determines the breakthrough of the Industrial Revolution in a country. Therefore, we try to observe the differences between China and the West in the society prior to the Industrial Revolution from the macroscopic and long span perspectives in order to find out the reasonable explanations of the "Needham Thesis."

In the economy lingering over the subsistence level, the scales of thousands of agricultural families, even handicraft families are almost the same. All achievements of "potatoes" are eventually to maintain a high or low subsistence level, thus they are just production modes to constitute a high-level or low-level equilibrium trap. Individual economic units do not have the critical minimum efforts to break the low-level equilibrium trap. Whether capital accumulation and technological advancement are benefited by the functions of the economies more than families, like the feudal lord economy, village economy and national economy determine the outcomes of different economic developments. Exactly on this level, the West and China have great divergence.

During the process of development of the Western feudal system, the relation between the monarch and the local lords is typically feudal, the former enfeoffing lands to war heroes and the nobles, while the latter restricting their activities to the designated lands, setting up a separatist regime by force of arms and developing into self-sufficient closed economies. In return, the monarch requests the local lords and the nobles to render a service in wars, especially when permanent state armies are not established. The feudal lords providing military services as knights or leaders of armed forces and coming to serve as soon as called reflects the contractual relationship between the monarch and the feudal lords.

The mutual benefits of land-focused property and military service are implicitly or explicitly settled in the form of contracts and also confirm the validity of the monarchy. In other words, the validity of the monarchy is always vulnerable but generally guaranteed by the contractual relationship thanks to the reciprocity and mutual benefits. In other words, both parties of the relationship are still willing to make efforts to maintain and respect such a contractual relationship.

The feudal lords with enfeoffment resources also have valid property rights. The economic growth and resource appreciation arising from their enfeoffment are protected by the property rights. Therefore, the feudal lords are the hierarchy close to economic activities and gain direct benefits out of these activities. They are a stable stimulus to promote seignorial economic prosperity. Besides, even the unstable factors of property rights also stimulate the economy. In most cases, foreign invasion and neighboring lords' plunder are likely to cause property damage and even loss. Thus, building castles as strong as possible by maximum economic strength and technological capabilities is the only effective way to protect private properties. The capabilities either to protect homelands or seize territories are closely correlated with the economic development of the manors.

The church has many similarities with the feudal relationship mentioned above in aspects of economic activities. Priests diligently transcribe the religious classics and make incomparable contributions to preservation and transmission of classic sciences, culture and arts in that ancient time when printing business was underdeveloped and most people were illiterate. One special thing worthy of mention is the eternal dream of all local church leaders to construct magnificent and everlasting churches, which require accumulation of material capital and also recruitment, encouragement and cultivation of human capitals. Once a church is constructed, it means a new business center whose promotion to local commodity economy is much better than those profitable economic activities.

Under such an institutional framework, the elite class could enter into the governing class either by fighting for the king to get enfeoffment or by increasing their fortunes through becoming local economic organizers, even senior monks, or robberies or the nibbling of other manors' fortunes. This is objectively a strong stimulus to local economic development.

By far, the most important factor correlated with human capital accumulation has been revealed. The relationship between the king and the feudal lords is more like a reciprocal contract where the validity of the monarchy is rooted. It's unnecessary to have a system to bother feudal lords to express their loyalty. This is why the early Western society has no such system as the imperial examination system hindering human capital accumulation.

Once there are stimuli for economic development and prosperity within specific areas, the requisite institutional conditions, according to Douglass North, would develop into the trend where private benefit is closer to social benefit, and then the institutional environment supporting productive economic activities would be formed, so material capital and human capital required for the Industrial Revolution would be accumulated. In fact, in a specific period, they already exist; it just needs a little luck and the perfect timing.

Compared with the West, Chinese feudal society is atypical. In the very early period, the grand-unified Central Empire was established. As the emperor was too far away, the central government was not engaged in general productive activities, except mobilizing national power to construct necessary infrastructure like defensive great walls and large water conservancy facilities and organizing economic activities. Local governments, just as local agencies of the central government, were only responsible for the central government and had no direct interests in local economies. Therefore, the economic development was actually the mix of separate economic activities of households.

As this typical small-scale peasant economy (the landlord economy usually is expressed as individual tenant economy) was very flexible and vigorous, many systems like free trade of lands helped promote economic activities. But it lacked a middle class with direct interests and economy of scale to organize and encourage technological innovations, leading to impedance of material capital accumulation and the furthering of revolutionary breakthrough technological advancement.

More importantly, the imperial dynasty and local officials and squires were not typically contractual but authoritatively hierarchical. The validity of the imperial dynasty was not based on its reciprocity and mutual benefits with local officials and the nobility. Therefore, the fundamental and sole guarantee of the validity was to establish a feudal ideology and etiquette with the complements of the Divine Right of Kings and central military strength. Under such circumstances, the Confucianism advocating self-restraint and restoration of rites became the dominant ideology. After Dong Zhongshu "proscribed all non-Confucian schools of thought and espoused Confucianism as the orthodox state ideology" in the Western Han Dynasty, the imperial examination system, whose sole usage was to elaborate the ideology of the governing class and express loyalty, was established in the Sui and Tang Dynasties and well-reasoned to last for over 1,000 years.

This imperial examination system is an open official selection system, guiding all elites (also the potential troublemakers) to elbow through the single-log bridge of imperial examination to enter into the governing class. With such an elite selection system, the elites find the path to recognize the dominant ideology, verify the validity of the imperial dynasty, express their loyalty to this system and get themselves promoted, while science and technology and crafting skills are seen as clever tricks and wicked craft, a shame to speak of. Thus, the imperial examination system blocks the path of human capital accumulation beneficial to technological innovations.

It's true that kinds of technological innovations are created anytime in productive activities. In the country with an enormous population, there are plenty of such officials or squires and even normal craftsmen passionate for scientific exploration that have made tremendous contributions to human civilization accumulation. But these are not the mainstream inspirations of the intellectual. The creation of direct knowledge is random and the accumulation of indirect knowledge is discontinuous, not enough to reach the critical level of expediting science and technology revolution, so the industrial revolution cannot spontaneously burst at an appropriate time.

After the macroscopic comparison of the modes of material capital and human capital accumulation between China and the Europe before the Industrial Revolution, it's not difficult to uncover why China lost its leading position in economic prosperity and technological development in the earlier period and why China is not the hometown of the Industrial Revolution. When the world was in the Malthusian poverty trap, China was earlier to move into or always in the high-level trap. When Europe moved from the low-level trap to the high-level trap and accumulated necessary material capital and human capital for the Industrial Revolution, China didn't move into this stage and lost the choice to break out the industrial revolution.

The updated data of the World Bank complementary to Angus Maddison's history data show us the clear rises and falls of China's economic development in past thousands of years (Figure 10.1). During 1000–1600 AD, China's per capita income was on the average level of the world; as for the economic scale (GDP), China was ranked first in the world for a long time, even had 1/3 of the world's GDP in 1820. But, from that moment, China fell into a stagnated economy during the "Great Divergence" of the world economy. Its GDP-to-world ratio and per capita GDP-to-world ratio fell all the way down and pushed China to enduring impoverishment and long-standing debility gradually.

Before the founding of the People's Republic of China, China got trapped in deep distress, experienced domestic strife, foreign aggression and economic stagnation, and the people were living in misery under the heavy pressure of three mountains. From 1820 to 1952, the annual growth rate of GDP and per capita

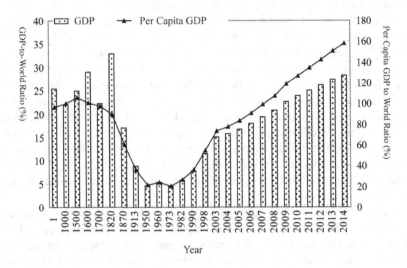

Figure 10.1 Changes of China-to-World Economic Ratios

Source: the data before 2003 come from Angus Maddison, *Contours of the World Economy, 1–2030AD, Essays in Macro-Economic History*, Oxford University Press, p. 379, Table A.4; p. 382, Table A.7; the data after 2004 are calculated according to relevant indices recorded in the World Bank's database (http://data.worldbank.org/)

GDP was 0.22% and –0.88% respectively, but during the same period Europe had 1.71% and 1.03% respectively. The position of the Chinese economy in the world fell to the nadir.

The economic growth in the first 30 years of the People's Republic of China was materially affected by the traditional planned economic system and the major policy faults. Rejection of the market system, over-high accumulation rate and industrial structural imbalance resulted in very low improvement on people's live-lihood. It failed to catch up and surpass the developed countries and emerging industrial economies; what's worse, its development gap was even widened. In the end China didn't hitchhike in the great convergence of the world economy after 1950 and lost a valuable 30 years to develop its economy. In 1978 there were still 2,500 million rural people without adequate food or clothing; year round living expenditure was less than 100 Yuan.

After the reform and opening-up, along with the removal of a series of insti-tutional barriers, huge physical capital and human capital were accumulated and reallocated effectively; the backwardness of China in the "Great Divergence" for centuries was finally changed to the "Great Convergence" toward the developed economies. China started the grand journey to the rejuvenation of the Chinese nation and has gained surprising economic and social development achievements, becoming the second economy in the world. As shown in Figure 10.1, the reform and opening-up is the turning point for the Chinese economy to rise from the valley; since entering the 21st century, especially since the 18th Party Congress,

China's GDP ratio and per capita GDP ratio keep sharply rising in the world. Just as mentioned in the 19th Party Congress Report, the Chinese nation, which since modern times began has endured so much for so long, has achieved a tremendous transformation: it has stood up, grown rich and is becoming strong; it has come to embrace the brilliant prospects of rejuvenation

10.2 The Two Centennial Goals

Witnessing the economic and social development achievements gained since the reform and opening-up, Chinese people are more confident. The great rejuvenation of the Chinese nation is neither a theory nor a motivational slogan; it will be definitely promoted steadily and quickly. Reviewing Deng Xiaoping's "three-step" strategy, the Party Central Committee's "goal of building a moderately prosperous society in all respects" and then the sublime Two Centennial Goals, it represents nothing but a history of Chinese economic development since the reform and opening-up. It also enhances the decision and confidence to attain the goals.

From the late 1970s to the late 1980s, Deng Xiaoping was repeatedly researching, consulting and pondering over the feasibility of attaining the goals including "quadrupling," "a moderately prosperous society" and "$800 per capita income." For example, after the Party and state leaders including Deng Xiaoping made a series of investigations of neighboring countries and regions, the goal to achieve four modernizations by the end of the 20th century was first modified as Chinese modernization in the practical and realistic way and then evolved into the concept of "a moderately prosperous society." The assumption to "quadruple" both the industry and the agriculture in 20 years, proposed by Hubei Province in 1980, was developed into the strategic conception of "quadrupling" gross industrial and agricultural output values in 20 years from 1981 to the end of the 20th century.

In 1983 when meeting the President of the World Bank, Alden Clausen, Deng Xiaoping introduced China's goal of "quadrupling" gross industrial and agricultural output values, and expected the World Bank to organize an economy survey tour to China, make some optional advices on the main issues facing China in next 20 years in order to attain the previously mentioned development goals, especially on the basis of the international experience, and make some feasible research on these goals.

Responding to Deng Xiaoping's proposal, the World Bank organized a big team to investigate and study the Chinese economy and submitted an economic survey report named "Issues and Options for Long-term Development" to China's government in 1985. This report used modern economic analysis and demonstrated the feasibility of quadrupling in respect to theory and experience. This report spread far and wide among Chinese economists and policy researchers.[5]

Based on the thorough survey, the demonstration and the economic development practices, the strategic concept of "three-step" was elaborated when Deng Xiaoping met the foreign guests before the 13th National Congress of the Communist Party of China. The 13th CPC National Congress systematically defined the strategic plan of "three-step": the first step was to double the GDP of 1980 from

1981 to 1990 and solve the problem of food and clothing for our people; the second step was to double it again from 1991 to the end of the 20th century, thus enabling our people to lead a fairly comfortable life; the third step was by the middle of the 21st century to reach the per capita GDP level of moderately developed countries. This would mean that modernization had been basically accomplished and that our people had begun to enjoy a relatively affluent life. In 2050 when it's the 100th anniversary of the founding of the People's Republic of China, "making China a prosperous, strong, democratic, culturally advanced and harmonious modern socialist country" is one of The Two Centennial Goals set forth in the 18th CPC National Congress.

In 2002 the 16th CPC National Congress made a major decision relating to the reform and opening-up and overall modernization drive: based on the original "three-step" strategic plan for modernization drive, the first two decades (2001–2020) should be separated from the first 50 years of the 21st century when the third step is being carried out as a developing period when we need to "concentrate on building a well-off society of higher standard in an all-round way to benefit over one billion people," and the two decades development will "serve as an inevitable connecting link for attaining the third-step strategic objectives for our moderniza-tion drive." "Building a well-off society in all respects" in 2020, the centenary of the Communist Party of China will be the other "centennial goal."

The "three-step" strategic plan and The Two Centennial Goals proposed by Deng Xiaoping are finally included into the general task to achieve socialist modernization and the great rejuvenation of the Chinese nation, proposed in the 18th CPC National Congress. On November 29, 2012, after the closing of the 18th CPC National Congress, the new General Secretary of the Communist Party of China Xi Jinping led the new central committee leaders to visit the exhibition of "the Road to Revival" in the National Museum of China and first proposed the philosophy of "Chinese Dream." He said the greatest dream in modern times for the Chinese nation was to achieve the great rejuvenation, and he was quite confident that this dream would "finally come true." We take "Chinese Dream" as the "colloquial version" of the general task proposed in the 18th CPC National Congress.

Since the 18th CPC National Congress, economic and social development in China have been changed greatly, and historical achievements have been obtained; socialism with Chinese characteristics has entered a new era. The two-step strat-egy was further defined at the 19th CPC National Congress, i.e., basically realize socialist modernization by 2035 based on the building of a moderately prosperous society in all respects in 2020, realize the strategic goal at the third step proposed by Deng Xiaoping in advance and then build China into a great modern socialist country that is prosperous, strong, democratic, culturally advanced, harmonious and beautiful by 2050.

Since ancient times, the ordinary people of each nation have expected to live a happy, well-off and safe material and spiritual life. Versions of "dreams" are developed in all countries, though the common people in all countries share similar dreams and expectations. However, the "Chinese Dream" has many differences from the dreams of other countries. The fundamental difference is the path and the means to realize the dream.

As a dreamer emigrating from Europe to the United States, Arnold Schwarzenegger expected one day everyone would be able to spell out his complicated name before he was a Hollywood action celebrity. Finally he succeeded. No matter whether in the entertainment circle or political circle, he is such a real world celebrity that most English speakers can spell out his name now. This is a typically individualistic "American Dream." However, the United States and other Western countries have not enabled each group to get equal benefits in the process of economic globalization; instead, the middle class disappears, income and wealth gaps tend to be widened, which leads to fragmentation of society and political polarization; the American Dream also drifts away from the expectations of the American people.

The "Chinese Dream" is also based on the efforts of millions upon millions of Chinese. The most attractive for the Chinese is the collectivism and the common prosperity contained in this dream. China's economic strength, scientific and technological strength, national defense strength and overall national strength become leading in the world and promote China's international status to be unprecedentedly high, people-centered development thinking enables China's development process to be more and more inclusive and sharing, and the Chinese Dream increasingly comes true. Facing the present challenges for China, adhering to the development is an unyielding principle; making more development achievements to benefit all people more fairly is the necessary and sufficient condition for the Chinese Dream.

10.3   China's objectives of building a moderately well-off society

The National Congress of the Communist Party of China is convened every five years, therefore, the period between the 19th National Congress in 2017 and the 20th National Congress in 2022 is the period in which the timeframes of The Two Centennial Goals converge. In this period, not only must we finish building a moderately prosperous society in all respects and achieve the first centennial goal, we must also build on this achievement to embark on a new journey toward the second centenary goal of fully building a modern socialist country. Therefore, establishing and achieving the objectives of building a Moderately Well-off Society is a critical connecting link to realize the Chinese Dream of national rejuvenation.

Requirements were raised for completing the building of a moderately prosperous society in all respects in 2020 at the 18th CPC National Congress in aspects of sustained and sound economic development, continuously expanded people's democracy, significantly improved cultural soft power, fully raised living standards, major progress in building a resource-conserving and environmentally friendly society etc. in which doubling the 2010 GDP and per capita personal income is a real restrictive index.

China's total GDP was 41.3 trillion Yuan in 2010. Double by 2020 means that China's economic aggregate should be up to 82.6 trillion Yuan then according to constant price. This was determined to meet the expectations of people of national income doubling at that time. Many people will associate it with the famous "Income Doubling Programme" of Japan, i.e., the economic development program formulated by Ikeda Hayato Cabinet, which was implemented in the period from 1961–1970.

In 1955, the Japanese economy completed the post-war recovery and returned to the prewar normal growth rate. In such background, policymakers are expected to formulate an inspiring plan to maintain the high growth rate during the recovery and surpass European and American economies in a faster way. This plan aimed at fueling investment, accelerating technological advancement and promoting high industrialization by stimulating demands so as to attain the goals of accelerating income growth and improving employment and resident income. During that period, Japan had an over 10% annual economic growth rate. When the plan was accomplished, Japanese economic aggregate surpassed Germany and France; Japan became the second largest economy after the United States, and its per capita income was substantially increased.

Although China's economic growth slowed down obviously after 2012, at medium-to-high speed of growth the GDP calculated according to the constant price in 2010 reached nearly 69 trillion Yuan by 2017; average annual growth rate only 6.3% or so is required to attain the goal of 82.6 trillion Yuan in 2020. At that time, China's level of GDP per capita will be significantly close to the threshold from middle-income countries to high-income countries.

It is noteworthy that, although doubling of GDP was mentioned in the 18th CPC National Congress Report, special attention was not given to economic growth rate; instead, it was emphasized that the goal should be achieved based on significantly improved development equilibrium, compatibility and sustainability. This goal was not mentioned in the 19th CPC National Congress; of course it is practically certain to achieve this goal; what's more important, an essential judgment was made at the 19th CPC National Congress: China's economy has changed from the high speed growth stage to the high quality development stage. The Amendment to the Constitution of the Communist Party of China passed at the 19th CPC National Congress also changed the expression "sound and rapid development" to " better quality, more efficient, fairer, and more sustainable development," fully indicating that "rapid" and "good" cannot be achieved simultaneously, only trade-off is possible.

Interestingly, when Japan made the "income doubling programme," its original intention was not to gain a faster economic growth rate. In fact, some of the plan-makers intended to plan a more stable growth rate according to the circumstances after the rapid growth in post-war recovery, but the decision-makers were finally inclined to promote a faster rate.[6] What the superior favors will receive excessively enthusiastic responses from his subordinates. Japan eventually achieved rapid economic growth from 1961 to 1970. Whether it's a fortune or misfortune, it's not conclusive at this time. Such reliance on incentives to promote growth rate pushed Japan's economy into a bubble era in the 1980s, finally stuck in "Lost Decades."

To synchronize resident income growth with economic growth, the income doubling goal was established at the 18th Party Congress for urban and rural residents. Since then, resident income growth has outperformed GDP, while income growth of rural residents is faster than that of urban residents. In the period of 2013–2017, actual mean annual growth rate of disposable income of urban residents was 6.5%, while actual mean annual growth rate of disposable income of rural residents was 8.4%. Based on this trend, even at a slightly slower income growth rate, the doubling of actual disposable income of urban and rural residents in 2020 compared with 2010 may be fully realized.

The Fifth Plenary Session of the Eighteenth Central Committee of the CPC held in 2015 established new objectives for completing the building of a moderately prosperous society in all respects by 2020; we need to help lift out of poverty all rural residents falling below the current poverty line, and achieve poverty alleviation in all poor counties and areas. The "current poverty line" mentioned here refers to 2,300 Yuan determined in 2011, which was adjusted to 2,885 Yuan according to the prevailing price in 2015, and will be 4,000 Yuan according to the prevailing price in 2020. This solemn promise fully embodies the decision to let the Chinese people of all ethnic groups enter a moderately prosperous society together, not one less.

In the 19th CPC National Congress Report, another new requirement was raised for 2020, i.e., build a modern economic system. The following was pointed out in the report: building a modern economic system is both an urgent requirement for getting us smoothly through this critical transition and a strategic goal for China's development. However, a time node for completing this task was not defined in the report itself.

The author thinks the time node for completing the core task and goal should be 2020, mainly based on three reasons. First related to the stage of new normality. Since General Secretary Xi Jinping made the significant judgment of economic development in China entering new normality, leading economic cadres at all levels experienced concept transition from recognizing new normality to adapting to new normality and should enter the new stance of leading new normality as soon as possible. Next, logically related to securing a decisive victory in building a moderately prosperous society in all respects and embarking on a journey to fully build a modern socialist China, building a modern country requires a modern economic system. Third, consistent with the time schedule of comprehensively deepening reform proposed at the Third Plenary Session of the 18th Central Committee of the CPC, it was required at the Plenary Session to achieve decisive results in the reform of key areas and crucial links by 2020.

10.4 Connotations of modernization

If the "great rejuvenation of the Chinese nation" is interpreted as Chinese people basing themselves on the history and expecting to realize the "Chinese Dream" by the middle of this century, modernization is a definition of Chinese tasks based on the more universal context. It's generally believed that the deep-going reform process that every country has experienced or strived to explore since the Industrial Revolution and that involves all circles of social life is so-called modernization. This process takes some existing features as the symbols of the end or the periodic end after all, indicating that a society has completed the transformation from traditional to modern. Thus, modernization is a process and an objective as well.

"Making China a prosperous, strong, democratic, culturally advanced and harmonious modern socialist country by 2050," stated at the 18th CPC National Congress, concludes modernization as a mission and an objective simultaneously. Based on completing the building of a moderately prosperous society in all respects by 2020, it was further divided into two stages at the 19th CPC National Congress: at the first stage, basically realize modernization by 2035 and complete the great mission established by Deng Xiaoping in advance, at the second stage, build China into a great modern socialist country that is prosperous, strong, democratic, culturally advanced, harmonious and beautiful by 2050.

No matter whether as an expression of goal or as a strategic deployment, comprehensive understanding of the connotations of Chinese modernization has both inspirational ideological meaning and pragmatic meaning to guide the direction and normalize the process. From an academic viewpoint, revealing the elements required for modernization – especially the modernization of a big country – and the challenges that China has to face toward the goal of modernization, is helpful to promote the construction process of a modern socialist country with Chinese characteristics and to achieve the goal in the prescheduled time.

It is worth highlighting that the attributes of "prosperous, strong, democratic, culturally advanced, harmonious and beautiful" in the 19th National Congress Report of CPC reveal modernization in the goals, including all contents of material, political, cultural and ethical, social and ecological advancement; China's system and capacity for governance; common prosperity for everyone; overall understanding, comprehensive policy implementation and taking moves across the board are required in the process of realization.

One of the connotations of modernization is that building a "prosperous and strong country" is symbolized by hard power or comprehensive national power. By far, people still take GDP as the most general index to measure the wealth and the production capacity of one country. If consulting the economic growth and income growth in the past years since the reform and opening-up, in 40 years so far, the prosperity level of China has been enhanced unprecedentedly and will be further improved after 2020. Since the United States has been the largest economy in the world for a long time with world leading science and technology strengths and is one of the richest countries, we use the data of International Monetary Found (IMF)[7] for historical comparison between China and the United States to address the issues.

In terms of total GDP calculated according to current rate of USD, China was less than 10% of the United States until the mid 1990s. After entering the 21st Century, catch-up speed was quickened obviously, total GDP of China reached 60.3% of United States in 2016, and will reach 78.2% in 2022. In terms of total GDP calculated according to the purchasing power parity, China reached the level of the United States in 2013 and overtook the United States by 14% in 2016. This means that China will surely surpass the United States in term of economic aggregate before 2035.

Meanwhile, in terms of GDP per capita calculated at current prices, China was among $309 low-income countries in 1980 and entered the upper middle-income countries after it became the second largest economy in 2010, $8,123 in 2016. According to the predictions of IMF staff, China's GDP per capita will reach $12,835 by 2022. And according to the classification standard of World Bank in 2016, Gross National Income (GNI) per capita at the current price $12,235 is the threshold level to enter high-income countries; this means that China will become a high-income country as a whole when it has completed the building of a moderately prosperous society in all respects.

International experience and lessons show that, once a country is in the transition from medium income to high income, the series of measures is that used to help break the poverty trap and enter into middle-income level is not effective any more. Reforming the institutional factors impeding productivity improvement, transforming the economic development mode and eliminating the institutional defects weakening the cohesiveness are unavoidable tasks for China to accomplish modernization.

It was mentioned in the 19th National Congress of CPC Report that China's economy has been transitioning from a phase of rapid growth to a stage of high-quality development; this is clearly targeted. That is to say, the achievements of China so far mainly come from growth speed and expansion of aggregate. Speed and aggregate are vital for an economy to step from low income to middle income, and then strategy of success through quality is required to step from middle income to high income, i.e., better quality, more efficient, fairer and more sustainable development.

When demographic dividend disappears rapidly, with labor shortage, especially subsequent increase in unit labor cost and decrease in rate of return on investment, a conclusion may be drawn very easily that it's difficult to sustain traditional investment-driven economic growth, which should be changed to the total factor productivity-driven growth model urgently so as to get the new driving force increasingly needed for economic growth. However, many people haven't fully recognized that, similarly due to demographic factors, increase in total factor productivity also faces the challenges of declined traditional sources, that is to say, the increase model of total factor productivity also faces transition; the transformation of economic growth drivers is still an arduous task.

The Human Development Index (HDI) advocated by the United Nations integrates per capita income level, resident health level and educational attainment into one index to reflect economic development level as well as being inclusive and sharing degree more thoroughly. In 2010, China's HDI was 0.663, ranked 89th in the world and belonged to moderate human development level. This index increased to 0.738 and ranked the 90th in 2015. In component factors of this index the increase in China's GNI per capita may exceed most countries obviously, and undoubtedly the increase in life expectancy is also barely satisfactory, therefore, stagnant ranking of this index of China in the world is held back by the educational level.

Both economic growth and globalization are undoubtedly helpful to social progress processes, but these processes will not generate a trickle-down effect automatically and cannot ensure each group will get equal benefits naturally and automatically. It was pointed out in the 19th National Congress of CPC Report that the principal contradiction facing Chinese society has evolved. What we now face is the contradiction between unbalanced and inadequate development and the people's ever-growing needs for a better life. To solve unbalanced and inadequate development problems, we should insist on development, make the pie bigger and solve development equilibrium, dividing the cake properly. A series of problems such as unequal distribution of income; impeded social mobility, especially the longitudinal mobility channel; low level of equal access to basic public services; low social security level and coverage rate are still conspicuous and must be solved for more equitable development.

Traditional concepts consider the relationship between growth and pollution similar to an inverted U-shaped curve, so control after pollution is an alternative or inevitable method. China has mainly relied on material input-driven economic growth for a long time, which is undoubtedly related to such cognitive deviation and already owes a debt to resources, environment and ecosystem. Once resources are exhausted, and environment and ecosystem are destroyed, they will be irreparable, or an extremely high cost must be paid. Especially for the damages caused by environmental deterioration to human living environment and human health, the cost is particularly expensive. The attribute "beautiful" in the goal of modernization construction highlights that the people's sense of happiness from development should never be at the cost of resources, environment and ecosystem.

Another symbol of hard power is the science and technology and the innovation capability. When China becomes an economic giant, it also takes more efforts to ascend to a scientific and technological giant and has already gained tremendous achievements. For a long time, our press has kept reporting some technological breakthroughs to inspire our national pride, but as a middle-income country the fact that we do take the lead in some technological fields doesn't represent our comprehensive position in the world's technology. On the other hand, it's more like news when it's assessed by more comprehensive indices, some of which reflect the true side of efforts, achievements and deficiencies when China implements the strategies for making it strong by developing science and education.

In the period of 1997–2016, average annual growth rate of China's total R&D expenditure calculated at variable price was 20%; its ratio to nominal GDP increased from 0.64% to 2.11%. Considering its unique total GDP growth rate in the world during the same period, it's understood how much China has input into the science and technology in these years. The input has many tangible consequences, for example, average annual growth rate of the nominal amount of high-tech product export and technology market transactions was about 20% in the same period; growth rate of applications and authorizations of patents for inventions were up to 28.4%. In the period of 2005–2016, the number of scientific papers published by research and development institutions increased by 60%, of which the number of papers published abroad increased from 14.2% to 28.5%. China was ranked among the best in the world on such indices.

Aggregate indices are quite persuasive but also limited; pursuit of aggregate growth is necessary, but caution should be taken. The inertia of striving for public resource investment between regions and between sectors according to importance and achievements has existed for a long time, and this is especially pertinent for China. Excessive pursuit of aggregate growth also caused flooding of low quality and banality and even a lot of fakes. Further analysis shows China is far behind developed countries and even many developing countries in the aspect of quotation of its published papers and applied patents.[8]

After massive increases in scientific and technological input, we should reflect what the goal of scientific and technological input is, what the law of scientific and technological innovation is and who the innovator is. Philip Campbell, the chief editor of *Nature*, a British magazine, has a targeted saying – "science is not a contest." Scientific and technological development is to lay a foundation for sustainable economic development. The solidness of this foundation is not just piled up by money but by innovations of thousands of individuals, enterprises and institutions.

Innovation, since it was invented by Economist Joseph A. Schumpeter, has been correlated with creative destruction. Innovation may succeed or fail, and destruction is bound to follow creation. The Fourth Scientific and Technological Revolution or Tide people delightedly talk about has a distinguishing feature that computers, artificial intelligence, information technology and the Internet have changed the mode of how people organize innovation activities and commercialize products and services. But this new tide doesn't change the creative destruction nature of scientific and technological innovation; it somehow enhances this nature. Therefore, science and technology represent the overall national power; innovations to improve the national power need initiative exploration and the consequent undertaking of many individuals.

Soft national power is one of indispensable connotations of modernization. Soft power was first proposed by an American scholar and applied into the international relations circle. Some scholars suggest a country should rely more on soft power such as culture and ideology than hard power such as military forces and economic means to gain international influence. Hard power emphasizes who wins the economic war or the military war while soft power focuses on who wins the voice. Some other scholars believe hard power and soft power should be combined together as smart power. The latter is accepted by American officials. As mentioned above, no matter whether hard power, soft power or the combination of the two powers is the means to play the game of international relation for Western scholars.

With China increasingly close to the center of the world stage, Western scholars conjectured the international orientation of China in many ways, which reflected the standpoint, anxiety and intention of Western scholars and politicians. The first statement was the so-called Thucydides Trap proposed by an American scholar, Graham Allison, resembling the historical war between the status quo state (Sparta) and challenger state (Athens) to compete for dominance; it expressed concerns about the relationship between China and the United States. The second statement was the so-called Kindleberger Trap proposed by an American scholar, Joseph Nye, resembling no supply of global public goods in the hegemony transition period between Britain and the United States in the early 20th century; it expressed the concerns about China being unwilling or unable to supply global public goods.

An important aspect in Xi Jinping's thought on socialism with Chinese characteristics for a new era and basic strategy is to build a community with a shared future for mankind. This thought and its practice abandon the cold war mentality and power politics uncompromisingly but adheres to correct righteousness and profit, highlights the building of new state relations, settles disputes through dialogue, and resolves differences through discussion. The successful development and sharing practices of China's reform and opening-up, through theoretical summary and sublimation, not only guide it to secure a decisive victory in building a moderately prosperous society in all respects and embark on a journey to fully build a modern socialist China but also contribute Chinese wisdom and Chinese solutions to solve a series of global issues, especially economic and social development issues, with theoretical innovation achievements on the understanding of the law of human society development, which is the largest soft power of China.

Actually, even if the international relations circle is not involved, a country also faces the task to enhance soft national power during its modernization. Charisma and popularity of national culture is indeed a part of soft power, but the stronger social cohesiveness, the widely resonated values and the universally accepted voice are more material symbols of the soft power of a country. Soft power is a benchmark of modernization and also creates more favorable internal and external environments for the rise of a nation.

10.5   Climbing growth and difficulty overcoming

For the European and American countries, which were the first to achieve modernization, technological advancement is made step by step, with no predecessors to learn from, while their per capita income is increased by slow and time-consuming economic growth. On the contrary, thanks to the theory of Advantage of Backwardness, the later mover is able to surpass the first movers at a faster speed. For example, we use the data summarized by the Economic historian Maddison to compare China with the "rapid developing" giants (Britain, USA and Japan) in different periods in their growth rates.

From 1880 to 1930, Britain had only 0.9% annual growth rate of per capita GDP. Assuming that the British born in 1880 were expected to live to 50 years old, a British individual was estimated to improve his livelihood by 56% throughout his life. This growth result obtained by Britain as the hometown of industrial revolution is not amazing from today's perspective, yet the increase in Britain was the first and also the most revolutionary breakthrough for the Malthusian poverty trap in thousands of years.

The USA became another modern power after Britain and other Western European countries. During the period from 1920 to 1975 when it was surpassing Britain, the USA had only a 2% growth rate of per capita GDP. Assuming that the Americans born in 1920 were expected to live to 55 years old, an American would improve his livelihood by almost 100% throughout his life. Unusually the USA maintained a similar growth rate in its following economic development and is by far the most powerful nation in economy, science and technology and is among the countries with the highest standard of living.

Japan is the next country to successfully surpass its predecessors and the first Asian country to realize modernization. From 1950 to 2010, Japan had over 4% annual growth rate of per capita GDP. Assuming that the Japanese born in 1950 were expected to live to 60 years old, a Japanese individual would improve his livelihood by almost 1000% throughout his life. However, Japanese economic performance after 1990 had nothing good to show, and thought its income increase was staggering, international ranking of its innovation capacity and competitiveness dropped.

Since the early 1980s, the reform and opening-up has driven China to the track of rapid economic growth. In the period of 1981–2016, annual average growth rate of China's GDP per capita was 8.8%, which means the Chinese living standard increased over 200% since the reform and opening-up. Assuming that the Chinese born in 1981 are expected to live to 68 years old in 2049, the centenary of founding of the People's Republic of China, if the previous growth rate is maintained, a typical post-80's Chinese will improve his livelihood by up to hundreds of times throughout his life.

No matter whether in horizontal or vertical comparison, the Chinese has by far experienced the unparalleled speed of income improvement. This already happened. However, it's not realistic to maintain such growth rate in the following decades. The 2010 population census estimates China's total population will reach the peak value of 1.38 billion in 2022 and start to experience absolute reduction thereafter. It contributes to the increase of per capita income but also has such negative effects on the future economic growth that the demographic dividend represented by the changes of the working-age population and dependency ratio disappeared in 2010, so the economic growth is consequently going to slow down.

We are proud that the high level the Chinese economy has reached is a surprising achievement and also vigilant as it's an unprecedented challenge. From now on, the Chinese economy will experience the climbing economic growth and have to overcome all difficulties in the institutional reform.

In a higher-level development stage and on a larger base, the economic growth of a country will definitely experience increasing marginal difficulty and decreasing marginal efforts. With the improvement of overall national power, the dramatic gap between China and the cutting-edge developed countries has been narrowed in terms of science, technology, management, market maturity and industrial structure, although it has not been completely removed. It means the advantage of backwardness available for Chinese economic growth is not as useful as it was in the previous development stage.

This change has double meanings. One is since then Chinese economic growth relies more on technological and institutional innovations, updated industrial structure and TFP improvement. Only then will the growth quality, especially the tolerance of development, be much better, though the growth rate will slow down in the future. The other is, as discovered by Gerschenkron, the initiator of the theory of Advantage of Backwardness, the later movers are inclined to excessive intervention of governments and rely more on big enterprises and unbalanced industrial structure during the surpassing process, and their corresponding institutional patterns are thus established.[9] Therefore, when the advantage of backwardness weakens, the tough institutional transformation will be the premise of the transformation of the mode of economic development.

The innovation process has potential failure risks; industrial restructuring won't be that all enterprises keep up the pace of updating. On the contrary, it's the period when innovation and restructure reform are accelerated that survival of the fittest is more likely to happen. It means those conservative and stubborn investors and enterprises and those who make mistakes in decision-making will be expelled from the market by competitors, but, in the period when innovation-driven TFP improvement becomes the only source of economic growth, such development consequences are unavoidable. Governments need to build a social security network to protect the uncompetitive laborers but shouldn't protect backward economic activities, otherwise the creative destruction mechanism will be injured.

The difficulty of competition and the risk of failure may prompt some enterprises and departments to seek protection or even try to hinder the necessary institutional reform. The institutional barriers to maintaining the pattern of vested interests will inevitably further hinder the sustainable growth of the economy, resulting in a more serious slowdown or even stagnation of economic growth. Therefore, in order to achieve the long-term sustainable development of China's economy and the great rejuvenation of China, we must break through the obstruction of dominant and recessive vested interest groups and promote reform in important fields with greater political courage and wisdom in order to obtain the necessary institutional dividends after the disappearance of the demographic dividend.

Notes

1 See Kenneth Pomeranz. (2003). *The Great Divergence: China, Europe, and the Making of the Modern World Economy*. Nanjing: Jiangsu People's Publishing House.
2 The proposer of "high-level equilibrium trap" is Mark Elvin. The Most Simple and Concise Summary of This Theory Is Referred to in Daniel Little. (1998). Chapter 8: The High-Level Equilibrium Trap. In *Microfoundations, Method and Causation: On the Philosophy of the Social Sciences* (pp. 151–169). New Brunswick: Transaction Publishers.
3 Michael Kremer. (1993). Population Growth and Technological Change: One Million B.C. to 1990. *The Quarterly Journal of Economics, 108*(3), 681–716.
4 Angus Maddison. (2009). *The World Economy: Historical Statistics* (pp. 270–271). Beijing: Peking University Press.

5 Lin Chonggeng. (2008). Opened Thoughts during China's Reform and Opening-up. *Comparative Studies, 38.*

6 Miyazaki Isamu. (2009). *Memoir of Witnesses of Japanese Economic Policies* (Chapter 5). Beijing: China CITIC Press.

7 IMF Website. (2018, January 20). Retrieved from www.imf.org/en/data

8 For example, observing the ratio of international proportion of referenced scientific papers to the international proportion of published papers, China is merely 25% of the most cutting-edge technically innovative country, Switzerland, even behind South Africa, Mexico and Brazil. Sachi Hatakenaka. (2010) The Role of Higher Education in High-Technology Industrial Development: What Can International Experience Tell Us? In Justin Yifu Lin and Boris Pleskovic (Eds.), *People, Politics, and Globalization* (p. 240). Washington, DC: The World Bank.

9 Alexander Gerschenkron. (2012). *Economic Backwardness in Historical Perspective.* Beijing: The Commercial Press.

Index

Note: Page numbers in italic indicate a figure and page numbers in bold indicate a table on the corresponding page.

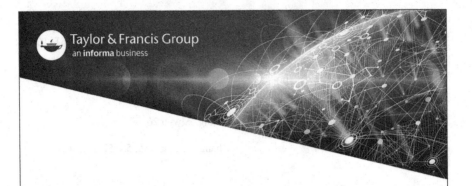